D1560172

In this book Keith Graham examines the philosophical assumptions behind the ideas of group membership and loyalty. Drawing out the significance of social context, he challenges individualist views by placing collectivities such as committees, classes or nations within the moral realm. He offers a new understanding of the multiplicity of sources which vie for the attention of human beings as they decide how to act, and challenges the conventional division between self-interest and altruism. He also offers a systematic account of the different ways in which individuals can identify with or distance themselves from the groups to which they belong. His study will be of interest to readers in a range of disciplines including philosophy, politics, sociology, law and economics.

KEITH GRAHAM is Professor of Social and Political Philosophy at the University of Bristol. His publications include *J.L. Austin: A Critique of Ordinary Language Philosophy* (1977), *Contemporary Political Philosophy: Radical Studies* (edited, 1982), *The Battle of Democracy* (1986), *Karl Marx: Our Contemporary* (1992), and many journal articles.

PRACTICAL REASONING
IN A SOCIAL WORLD

How we act together

KEITH GRAHAM

University of Bristol

CAMBRIDGE
UNIVERSITY PRESS

PUBLISHED BY THE PRESS SYNDICATE OF THE UNIVERSITY OF CAMBRIDGE
The Pitt Building, Trumpington Street, Cambridge, United Kingdom

CAMBRIDGE UNIVERSITY PRESS
The Edinburgh Building, Cambridge CB2 2RU, UK
40 West 20th Street, New York, NY 10011-4211, USA
477 Williamstown Road, Port Melbourne, VIC 3207, Australia
Ruiz de Alarcón 13, 28014 Madrid, Spain
Dock House, The Waterfront, Cape Town 8001, South Africa

http://www.cambridge.org

First published 2002

Printed in the United Kingdom at the University Press, Cambridge

Typeface Baskerville Monotype 11 /12.5 pt.   *System* LaTeX 2ε [TB]

A catalogue record for this book is available from the British Library.

Library of Congress Cataloguing in Publication data
Graham, Keith, 1945–
Practical reasoning in a social world: how we act together / Keith Graham.
p.   cm.
Includes bibliographical references and index.
ISBN 0 521 80378 0
1. Social sciences – Philosophy.   2. Reasoning.   3. Social groups – Moral and ethical
aspects.   4. Individualism – Moral and ethical aspects.   I. Title.
H61.15 .G72   2002
302.3 – dc21   2001043122

ISBN 0 521 80378 0 hardback

To the memory of Deborah Fitzmaurice

'To see what is in front of one's nose needs a constant struggle.'
George Orwell

'Understanding the world is a way of changing it, perhaps the most potent one ...'
Ernest Gellner

Contents

Preface

I have accumulated large debts in writing this book. Thoughts for it began to form when I was a Simon Senior Research Fellow in the Department of Government at the University of Manchester, and developed further when I was Visiting Research Fellow at the Centre for Philosophy and Public Affairs in the Department of Moral Philosophy at the University of St Andrews. I am deeply grateful to both departments for providing such a congenial and intellectually stimulating atmosphere. My luck continued with a brief Visiting Research Fellowship at the Institute of Advanced Study of the University of London. I am grateful to Jo Wolff and the University for finding me a peaceful room buried deep in the bowels of the University Senate House (the building which provided the model for George Orwell's Ministry of Truth in *1984*). My past and present colleagues in the Department of Philosophy at the University of Bristol agreed to my having study leave on more than one occasion, and I am greatly indebted to them for their generosity. Finally, I am also happy to acknowledge the award of a research fellowship from the Arts and Humanities Research Board of the British Academy, which enabled me to complete final drafting.

I owe an impersonal debt to the handful of analytical philosophers who have written works which swim against the individualist tide in various ways. I have learnt much from the work of Peter French, Margaret Gilbert, Susan Hurley, Larry May, John Searle and Raimo Tuomela. In addition, I am indebted to a large number of people for conversations, comments on papers, and the like. I know that this includes the following, and I hope that anyone whose name is omitted will forgive me: David Archard, Richard J. Arneson, Alison Assiter, Ted Benton, Chris Bertram, Ed Brandon, John Broome, Jessica Brown, Malcolm Budd, Will Cartwright, Dario Castiglione, Andrew Chitty, Maurizio D'Entrèves, Cécile Fabre, Colin Farrelly, John Featherstone, Katrin Flikschuh, Bob Frazier, Miranda Fricker, Norman Geras, John Haldane, the late

Martin Hollis, John Horton, Charles Jones, James Ladyman, Sheldon Leader, Adam Morton, Ken O'Day, Onora O'Neill, Ross Poole, Andrew Pyle, Joseph Raz, John Skorupski, Bill Valinas Jr, R. Jay Wallace, John White, Patricia White, Robert Wokler, Jo Wolff, and Andrew Woodfield.

I am especially grateful to G. A. Cohen and Hillel Steiner for generously finding the time to give me written comments on draft chapters and for giving me encouragement at a crucial stage in the project. The customary absolution from responsibility for the end-product applies both to them and to everyone else mentioned here, especially since some of the people on my list are probably unaware that they have helped to shape it.

Two notes on the text: first, italics are in the original quotations unless otherwise specified; second, I should mention my strategy for dealing with the problem of pronouns and how to avoid offending one half of the human race. The generic 'she' seems to me as excluding as the generic 'he' and I have opted instead for the inclusive singular 'they'. As an extension I have also used the relative neologism 'themself'. If 'ourself' was good enough for Shakespeare and Dickens, 'themself' should be good enough for the rest of us.

Finally, the book is dedicated to the memory of Debbie Fitzmaurice. I had the privilege of working with her on a summer school in Krakow shortly before her tragically premature death. She was a fine philosopher, and a warm and compassionate human being.

Acknowledgements

An earlier version of some of the material in chapter 1 appeared in 'Being Some Body: Choice and Identity in a Liberal Pluralist World', published in B. Brecher, J. Halliday and K. Kolinská (eds.), *Nationalism and Racism in the Liberal Order*, Aldershot, Ashgate, 1998, pp. 176–92. An earlier version of some of the material in chapter 2 originally appeared in 'Are All Preferences Nosy?', *Res Publica* 6, 2000, pp. 133–54. An earlier version of some of the material in chapter 3 appeared in 'Collective Responsibility', in T. van den Beld (ed.), *Moral Responsibility and Ontology*, Dordrecht, Kluwer Academic Publishers, 2000, pp. 49–62 and in 'The Moral Significance of Collective Entities', *Inquiry* 44, 2001, pp. 21–42. Earlier versions of fragments of chapter 5 appeared in 'Coping with the Many-Coloured Dome: Pluralism and Practical Reason', in D. Archard (ed.), *Philosophy and Pluralism*, Cambridge, Cambridge University Press, 1996, pp. 135–46; in 'Being Some Body: Choice and Identity in a Liberal Pluralist World' (cited above); and in 'Normative Argumentation in a Pluralist World', *Proceedings of Fourth International Conference on Argumentation*, International Society for the Study of Argumentation, Amsterdam, Sic Sat, 1998, pp. 266–70. In all cases I am grateful to editors and publishers for kind permission to reprint revised versions of material previously published.

Introduction

This book has the immodest aim of saying something significant about how human beings should behave. Or, to speak more cautiously, the aim is to say something about how a proper understanding of ourselves and our circumstances should make a difference to our practical reasoning. (I use the latter phrase throughout the book in a wholly non-technical sense.) In particular, I want to explore how the reasons we have for acting are affected by the simple thought that we are *social* creatures. Whenever we act, either singly or in collaboration, we act together. My aim is to introduce some philosophical precision into that thought and to increase our understanding of why it is true and why it matters.

When I speak here of the reasons we have for acting, I refer to *normative* rather than explanatory reasons: that is, reasons which constitute considerations in favour of particular courses of action, reasons why agents *ought* to act in particular ways, reasons which are good or bad, rather than reasons which account for why agents *do* act or *have* acted in particular ways. My concern is with the general category of normative reasons for acting rather than with any sub-category. I am not concerned in any special way with moral reasons. These are one but only one kind of normative reason; there are also, for example, prudential and legal normative reasons, and no doubt many other kinds which are not so easily categorised. I take for granted the idea of a reason for acting and ignore any problematic features it might be thought to possess from a metaphysical point of view. For my purposes, a (normative) reason for acting is a consideration either about agents or about their circumstances which ought to incline them in the direction of acting in a particular way.[1] A distinction is sometimes drawn between rationality

---

[1] Cf. 'Every reason can be formulated as a predicate. If the predicate applies to some act, event, or circumstance (possible or actual), then there is reason for that act, event, or circumstance to occur' (Nagel 1970: 47). For a similar view of the category of reasons, see Scanlon 1998: 56, 62–3. For enlightening discussions which do not take for granted the category of reasons for acting,

and reasonableness (cf. Rawls 1993: 48–54), but for the purposes of my argument they can be treated as equivalent. What is rational or reasonable is what there is good reason for. That is as minimal and non-question-begging as possible; as for what makes something a good reason, that must be argued on substantive grounds rather than by means of arbitrary definition.[2]

The position which arises from my account of the social nature of human beings was once described[3] as moderate anti-individualism. It is anti-individualist to the extent that I believe that some of the recognisably individualist received views in our culture underestimate the implications which follow from our social nature. Even if we begin from wholly uncontentious facts about our sociality, then I believe these received views eventually come under threat and must be replaced by views which allow for the important consequences resulting from the existence of irreducibly collective agency in the world we inhabit. The position is moderate to the extent that it is no part of my programme to 'eliminate' the individual in the way that some contemporary challenges to the received views do. We are individual centres of consciousness as well as individual material bodies. Part (though not the whole) of our lives as human beings should be understood by reference to that fact, and it seems to me that nothing is gained by constructing theories which deny it.

What seems to me most important, however, is to get beyond blanket labels like 'individualism' and 'collectivism', to distinguish the separate thoughts which may lie behind the labels and to acknowledge that we should feel free to endorse some of those thoughts and reject others. Consider two examples which illustrate the importance of doing this. In *A Theory of Justice* Rawls embraced an avowedly individualist theory. He said that

we want to account for the social values, for the intrinsic good of institutional, community, and associative activities, by a conception of justice that in its theoretical basis is individualistic. For reasons of clarity among others, we do not want to rely on an undefined concept of community, or to suppose that society is an organic whole with a life of its own distinct from and superior to that of all its members in their relations with one another. (Rawls 1972: 264; cf. 520)

see Hampton 1998: 44–82; Korsgaard 1996: 90–1, 131–42; and the papers in Cullity and Gaut (eds.) 1997. For helpful discussion of the connections between normative and explanatory reasons, see Smith 1994: 94–101, 131–7.
[2] Cf. Graham 1988: 5. For further argument see Scanlon 1998: 191–3.
[3] By Jonathan Dancy, and I am grateful to him for the label.

A number of features are ascribed here to the implied alternative to individualism, but these features need to be separated out from one another. There is, first, the idea of relying on an undefined notion of community. This may be undesirable, but there is no reason to suppose that non-individualists are more likely to do so than individualists: probably the reverse, since commitment to the centrality of a notion is likely to lead to an articulated account of it. Then two ideas are linked together: that of society's being *distinct* from individuals and that of its being *superior* to them. But it would be perfectly possible to hold that a society was distinct from individuals while holding that it was not superior, or that its superiority was at best problematic, or that it was superior in certain ways which needed to be specified but inferior in other ways which also needed to be specified. Rawls's individualism cannot be thought to gain in plausibility by an implicit contrast with an alternative which possesses just this mixture of features, since there are alternatives which possess a different, preferable and more defensible mixture of features.

In contrast to Rawls, Larry May rejects individualism and makes many claims about the nature of collective entities to which I am sympathetic. Nevertheless, he also rejects collectivism, which he characterises as follows:

[C]ollectivism is the view that groups are themselves entities that act in the world and that groups act in more fundamental ways than individuals. Individuals are really only parts of groups. There are no truly personal values that are uniquely chosen by discrete individuals; all of our ideas and values are imposed on us by the social groups to which we belong. I am as suspicious of this view as of individualism. (May 1992: 74)

But notice again how many different claims are run together here in the characterisation of collectivism. It would be possible (and in my view sensible) to hold that groups are entities that act in the world but that they are not necessarily more fundamental than individuals, much less that there is nothing more to individuals than their membership of groups. It is also a separate matter whether *all* our values are *imposed* on us by groups, and it would be highly implausible to hold that they are, as though individuals could never transcend the groups to which they belong. Here, too, therefore, it is necessary to distinguish a number of theses which might go under the label of 'collectivism' and assess each in its own right.

It might be thought that a term like 'collectivism' is beyond redemption since so many awful things have been done in its name. But then awful things have been done in the name of almost *anything* at some time or another. I shall continue to use the term in the hope that its stipulative use is still defensible. It goes without saying, I hope, that the idea of collectivism which I explore – the idea that there are irreducibly collective actions and agencies – is entirely distinct from the idea of collectivism associated with regimes based on authoritarian, centralised state planning.

I attempt to bring philosophical precision to the thought that we are social creatures by generating arguments from two truths about the social nature of our existence which I take to be so obvious that no one could deny them. The first is that *everything a person does carries causal implications for the lives of other human beings*. The second is that *some of the things a person does gain their significance from being part of some collective action*, carried out by a number of human beings rather than just one. I refer to these respective facts subsequently as *the fact of causal interconnection* and *the fact of collective agency*. I select these truisms for exploration because I believe that philosophically interesting and surprising consequences can be generated from them and because their implications are largely ignored in a predominantly individualist culture.

Misgivings might be felt about the wisdom of starting a philosophical argument in this way. After all, it has been a truism at least since Aristotle that we are social creatures. Why suppose there is any point in repeating these truisms, and why suppose that we can use them to arrive at anything more interesting than more truisms? Such misgivings run counter to Bertrand Russell's dictum that 'the point of philosophy is to start with something so simple as not to seem worth stating, and to end with something so paradoxical that no one will believe it' (Russell 1956: 193). A similar view of philosophy has recently been expressed by G. A. Cohen:

One way of doing philosophy well is to assemble premises which even opponents will not want to deny, and by dint of skill at inference, to derive results which opponents will indeed want to deny but which, having granted the premises, they will be hard pressed to deny. The trick is to go from widely accepted premises to controversial conclusions. (Cohen 1995: 112)

Cohen adds (wisely): 'It is, of course, no trick at all to go from premises which are themselves controversial to controversial conclusions' (112).[4]

---

[4] Compare also Charles Larmore's suggestion that 'a justification is a proof directed at those who disagree with us to show them that they should join us in believing what we do. It can fulfil this pragmatic role only by appealing to what they already believe, thus to what is common ground between us' (Larmore 1990: 347).

This last point indicates why there are grounds for starting as I do. One obvious alternative procedure to that of beginning from truisms would be to test philosophical claims against our considered judgements. The problem with that is that, where the judgements in question are about what sorts of things we have reason to do, there is no consensus which can be used as a touchstone (unless we rig the referent of 'we' so as to embrace only those in broad agreement with us). Moreover (as I shall argue in chapter 1), the circumstances of contemporary pluralism make the fact of likely disagreement in such judgements all the more apparent and all the more pressing. Because people hold such varying and clashing views on what they have reason to do, it is therefore preferable to start at a point where the temperature is lower. We may be got to agree more readily on what constitute irresistible premises about ourselves and our circumstances, and then a sensible discussion about what we have reason to do can at least begin. We must then follow the argument where it leads, and, however deeply attached we may be to our initial beliefs about what we have reason to do, we may end up having to change our minds.

There is a procedure, rejected by Rawls, in which an attempt is made 'to find self-evident principles from which a sufficient body of standards and precepts can be derived to account for our considered judgments' (Rawls 1972: 577–8). Amongst other reasons he rejects that procedure because 'while some moral principles may seem natural and even obvious, there are great obstacles to maintaining that they are necessarily true, or even to explaining what is meant by this' (578). My own procedure may bear a superficial resemblance to the rejected one but is in a number of respects quite different. It begins from the fact of causal interconnection and the fact of collective agency, but although these are *obvious* truths they are certainly not moral in character, and their status is contingent rather than necessary; my concern is to arrive at conclusions which are equally about reasons for acting in general, rather than specifically moral reasons; and my aim is to *test*, as much as to underscore, even considered judgements. I believe it is vital to test them if we are to avoid an illegitimately conservative cast of mind.[5]

Other considerations reinforce the idea that there may be a point in focusing on truisms. It is easy to assent to a truism when asked for an opinion, less easy to allow that truism its appropriate force in all the rest of our thinking: we may simply forget it when our mind is on other things, and in that case we may unwittingly come to hold beliefs that

---

[5] Cf. 'A philosophic justification is not to be confused with popular acceptance, rough consensus, or even probable acceptance by all reasonable parties' (Gaus 1996: 9).

clash with it.[6] It is also not easy to be sure what all the implications of
a truism are, or what follows from it in conjunction with other truths.
The danger of ending up with beliefs which clash with the belief in some
truism is especially great if, as seems likely, we are liable to compartmen-
talise our beliefs into subsets; for then we may simply fail to recognise
inconsistencies between beliefs in different subsets (cf. Gaus 1996: 107).

Consider an illustration. Charles Taylor has enunciated the 'social
thesis', which holds that the capacity for self-determination can only be
exercised in a certain kind of society with a certain kind of social environment, and has complained that some liberal theories ignore this thesis
(Taylor 1985: 190–1). Will Kymlicka's response is that liberals like Rawls
and Dworkin do not deny the social thesis, and he cites passages from
their work where they acknowledge the kind of requirement mentioned
by Taylor (Kymlicka 1990: 216). But the critical intent of Taylor's claim
cannot be met in this way. What is crucial is not whether these thinkers
affirm the social thesis but whether they go on to affirm anything else
which clashes with it. I do not say that Rawls and Dworkin do embrace other theses which clash with the social thesis: that may or may
not be true. What I do say is that the question of whether they ignore the
social thesis cannot be entirely settled just by citing some place where
they explicitly allow that the social thesis is true.

There are some grounds for believing, therefore, both that the enun-
ciation of truisms is an appropriate starting point and that, if we trace
the consequences which follow them and compare this with other beliefs we hold, we may eventually arrive at a more interesting destination.
The only final test of whether there is mileage in attempting to generate
interesting conclusions along this route is to see whether something of
interest does actually emerge. I must leave the reader to make their own
judgement on that question, but certainly some of my conclusions (that
some collective entities, and not just the individuals who compose them,
may be held morally responsible, that some collective entities have intrinsic moral importance, that considerations of our materiality play a
special role in practical reasoning and provide a culture-neutral means of
judging different cultures) are, to put it no more strongly, philosophically
contentious.

Philosophical discussion takes place in a context which is in certain
respects perennial and in certain respects historically specific (and it is

[6] In Austin's immortal words, 'There's the bit where you say it and the bit where you take it back'
(Austin 1962: 2).

not always easy to know or to remember which respects are which). In chapter 1 I locate the issues I am concerned with in their current historical context. I suggest that contemporary pluralism gives a particular urgency to them, though it does not actually give rise to them. I also review different responses available to the problem of disagreement in practical judgements, and I sponsor the adoption of a universalist strategy for dealing with such disagreement. I then begin the analysis of a doctrine (or as it turns out a cluster of doctrines) which constitutes one expression of our individualist culture and is often referred to as *the distinctness of persons*. I attempt to unravel the different thoughts lying behind that slogan and begin the process of casting doubt on them.

In chapter 2 I begin the process of arguing for a contrasting cluster of claims – what I shall call the *indistinctness* of persons – by addressing the fact of causal interconnection. All human action, no matter how private or trivial or self-regarding, involves interconnection with other human beings. But I attempt to take this unexceptionable platitude in an unexpected direction by suggesting that it follows that causal *preconditions* of our actions should concern us as much as causal consequences. The suggestion is bound to seem outrageous, and I attempt to defend it against a series of obvious objections.

Chapters 3 and 4 constitute the core of the book. I have assumed in my arguments that we have a sufficient understanding of the *nature* of human agency – how the role of deliberation and consciousness distinguishes it from the agency of inanimate things, the action of acid on metal or of rain falling on rocks, for example. But in chapter 3 I address the more difficult question of what implications follow for the *scope* of human agency. I focus on a form of collective agency which is a familiar part of our experience and suggest that it shares important characteristics with individual human agency.

It will be as well to give an indication at this point of how my arguments relate to questions of moral philosophy. For reasons which I cannot fully address in the present work, I am sceptical about the extent to which moral thought is intellectually or motivationally compelling. I believe it should occupy a less central role than it does both in philosophical deliberation and in practical life. That is partly why I address the broader question of what reasons for acting in general (rather than what specifically *moral* reasons) can be inferred from our social nature and circumstances. But moral thinking is pervasive both in philosophy and in practical life, and I have therefore attempted to relate my argument to moral thinking at various points. I believe that some of the claims I make for collective agency have implications for specifically moral thinking, and in chapter 3 I suggest that there are good grounds for treating certain collective agents as moral entities if we treat anything as a moral entity at all.

Membership of collectivities of the kind described in chapter 3 raises a series of questions for the individuals who compose them. Precisely because we *are* individuals, whose existence is not exhausted in the social relations we participate in and the groups to which we belong, questions can arise about whether to *identify with* or *dissociate from* collective agencies of which we are members. In chapter 4 I emphasise the importance of the option of dissociation from collectivities, as an instance of a much more general option of dissociation which exists for rational agents; and I develop an account of the different forms which identification with a collectivity can take, arguing that some forms are not readily understood if they are viewed from the assumptions of rational choice theory and related simply to the efficient realisation of individually chosen goals.

In chapter 5 I review the reasons for acting which are available to us, in the light of the social aspects of our existence which have been described in preceding chapters. The burden of choice imposed on us by possibilities of dissociation has to be recognised, and the extent to which choice itself can provide a reason has to be assessed in the light of the very heavy premium placed on autonomy in many theories. But it is also necessary to recognise the *constraints* on practical reasoning, and I attempt to categorise some of these. I also suggest that our materiality occupies a special (though not necessarily unique) position in our practical reasoning.

In chapter 6 I consider the objection that my claims about practical reasoning must remain provisional precisely because morality has not been central in my discussion. I assess the challenge which morality lays down and point out that the connection between morality and action is more complex than it is often taken to be. I reinforce my claim that the category of the moral must in consistency be extended to certain kinds of collective entity, and I argue that some of the forms of collective identification described earlier in the book compel us to abandon a simple, exclusive or exhaustive contrast between the interests of self and the interests of others.

This book has been written against the background of two bodies of philosophical literature: the literature of rational choice theory and the debate between liberals and communitarians. But it is not a book *about* that literature. I reach conclusions about what sorts of agents there are and what sorts of appeal they should be susceptible to which I believe are deeply at odds with any instrumental theory of rationality, but rational choice theory is a moving target and for all I know there may be some thinkers who would describe themselves as rational choice theorists but who would be prepared to accept more of my conclusions than I imagine. In any event, it would not do much to increase the plausibility of my own claims simply to list what I see as the deficiencies of theories of that kind.[7] So far as the liberal/communitarian debate is concerned, I have attempted to move beyond it and address questions which it seemed difficult to address within the terms of that debate. The stark choice between the stripped-down ego of the Original Position and the embedded self situated in a community with pre-existing values did not encourage a recognition of the useful thoughts contained in *each* of these images, nor did it encourage further thought on the immensely difficult question of the extent to which, and the grounds on which, embedded agents could and should distance themselves from their surrounding values. I have attempted at least to begin an answer to that question.

Any philosophical book, even the most abstract, is written in a particular political climate. The political climate which surrounds this book is one in which sociability has been downgraded in favour of individual enterprise and individual selfishness has received strengthened cultural endorsement. That is a climate which I find repugnant. But there is more than one way of subjecting it to a critique. One way is to criticise head-on the beliefs of those who subscribe to it. An alternative way of encouraging them to have second thoughts about their current beliefs is to proceed along the indirect route of questioning the security of the grounds on which those beliefs rest in the first place. This indirect route has something to recommend it, given that human beings like to think that their beliefs are well grounded, and it is the one which I have tried to follow.

The doctrine of the distinctness of persons is often appealed to in support of the ideology of licensed selfishness. I have attempted to show that the doctrine contains confusions and implausibilities which *pari passu* reduce the plausibility of the beliefs the doctrine is meant to support. Moreover, the soundness or otherwise of the doctrine is of some importance since it is appealed to, and indeed taken as obvious, in support of other less local and less unappealing ideologies. The appeal to the doctrine is standard, for example, in a much wider band of liberal theories of

---

[7] But for pertinent discussion see Hampton 1998; Hurley 1989; Hollis 1998; and Parfit 1984.

other types. If it is unsound, therefore, it is not merely the local ideology of licensed selfishness which loses its support.

But the more I considered this doctrine, the more complicated it seemed to be and the more examination it seemed to me to require. The consequence is that, in one respect, this book has turned out to be less political than I expected it to be. I believe that if the doctrine of the distinctness of persons is replaced with a more adequate doctrine, reflecting the implications of the fact of causal interconnection and the fact of collective agency, this has consequences for a whole range of current political issues such as nationalism, identity politics and the recession of class as a central category in current debates. I have axes to grind on all these questions, but they do not get ground here. (Well, hardly ever.) Instead, I have tried to build up a general, systematic account of the ways in which our social nature should influence the exercise of our powers of practical reasoning, and it is at this level of establishing general philosophical principle that I hope the book will be judged. Not everything can be done in one book, and the question of the more concrete political implications which follow if this account is correct must wait for another occasion.

Practical reasoning in context

Human beings, we can be sure, have always disagreed about what there is reason to do. But the nature of the disagreements, and the views that we can form about how to deal with them, will vary with context. In this chapter I outline the broad modern context of practical disagreement, survey some of the strategies available for dealing with it, and locate my own project in relation to them. This is necessary for establishing what I shall *assume* as much as what I shall argue for. It also enables me to begin the examination of the doctrine of the distinctness of persons and to indicate the problems connected with it.

1.1 THE MODERN CONTEXT

It is commonly observed that the *disenchantment* of the modern world has rendered it a place of hard realities, investigable by the methods of modern science, and at the same time divested it of values.[1] Many people no longer believe that we can simply infer our values from some set of premises about the natural order and our place in it, because they no longer believe that brute nature has the teleological character which would be necessary for that process of inference even to be possible. That problem is exacerbated because the loss of belief in a purposive *natural* order is often accompanied by the lack of belief in a purposive *social* order. Indeed, even talk of a social *order* may seem anachronistic in a world which is now so fluid and mobile that social identities are no longer fixed. Perhaps there were earlier times when a clear understanding of your social position allowed you to make inferences about what to do, but those times have gone. In the circumstances of social flux and mobility, any reference to 'my station and its duties' as the source of values would

---

[1] For recent discussion, see for example Benhabib 1992: 41, 152–4; Hollis 1998: 83, 88–9; Korsgaard 1996: 1–5, 18–19; Sandel 1982: 175–6; and Scheffler 1992: 14–15.

for many people simply raise the prior question of how one is to decide what one's station is.[2] If meaning and purpose are excluded from the natural world and it is also impossible to infer conclusions about values from our position in the social world, then it seems we must somehow construct our own values.

I speak with deliberate ambiguity of *values*, by which I mean the thoughts which inform practical reasoners' decisions about how to act, about what states of affairs are worth realising, about what objectives are worth achieving, and I shall continue to speak of values in this sense. The problem of disenchantment is often couched in terms of specifically *moral* values. Morality and practical reasoning are not the same thing, as I shall be at pains to point out in chapter 6, but there is an overlap, and the same set of difficulties can be raised for the whole process of practical decision, whether it involves decisions from a narrowly moral point of view or not. An investigation of an inert world, it may be felt, can tell us how things are, but it cannot tell us what to do – not even when we are concerned in some general way with decisions about how to act rather than with specific decisions about the moral thing to do. It is the problem of finding reasons for acting in this broader sense, not the sense tied specifically to morality, which is the main focus in this chapter, and more generally in this book.

It is of course possible to exaggerate the extent to which the need to construct values is a product of specifically modern conditions. A certain kind of individuality, as well as a certain social identity, is an ingredient in a human life in all contexts. And it was, after all, in a world long before disenchantment that Spartacus departed from the script and challenged his place as a slave. What is true, however, is that the scope for individuality is probably much greater in modern conditions. At least in many parts of the world we are less bound by traditional roles and expectations, as well as being more mobile in literal and metaphorical senses. It is less predictable at birth where we shall live, what kind of work we shall do and who our circle of acquaintances will be. In modern conditions too the idea of leisure pursuits as a distinct part of life is more entrenched, and with that comes a greater need for choices and decisions.

[2] F. H. Bradley said that 'collisions of duties are avoided mostly by each man keeping to his own immediate duties, and not trying to see from the point of view of other stations than his own' (Bradley 1876: 198 n. 5). The limitations in this strategy are perhaps evident in P. F. Strawson's report: 'A certain professor once said: "For me to be moral is to behave like a professor"' (Strawson 1961: 33). Critical reflection on one's station is something I am keen to encourage, and in chapter 4, section 3 I argue that mere occupation of a station or membership of a group gives no reason whatever for active identification with it.

I now turn to a separate feature of the present historical context of practical reasoning, namely the fact of *pluralism*. In order to see the bearing of pluralism on practical reasoning, it is useful to conduct the following thought experiment.[3] Imagine that the world contains only two human communities. Community A is deeply religious, and its members observe a strict sabbatarianism. They also believe that it is natural for women to be the subordinates of men, so that obedience is regarded as an appropriate relation between a woman and her husband, and women are barred from the same kind of participation in public life as men. They regard abortion as one form of murder, and treat it as such. So far as property is concerned, they believe that it is morally indefensible to deprive anyone of legitimately acquired property except in so far as that might be necessary for purposes of common defence. Community B, by contrast, is wholly secular. Its members believe that they have a right to conduct their leisure time as they see fit as long as they do not infringe the right of others to act similarly. They believe that women and men are equal and strive to ensure that women are represented in public office in just the same way as men. They believe that a woman has a right to control over her own body, and regard the choice of abortion at will as one manifestation of that right. So far as property is concerned, they believe that transfer of property from the better off to the worse off, if necessary by coercion, according to certain defined principles is morally defensible.

Imagine now three different possibilities.

(1) Communities A and B are geographically separated and their members never come into contact or even know of one another's existence.

(2) A persons and B persons do come into contact, but in a peripheral way. Perhaps they have occasion to trade and in that way they come to learn about their differing views about the world, but otherwise they continue to live their lives separately from one another.

(3) There continue to be A persons and B persons but there are no longer two separated communities. There is just one geographical area, in which A persons and B persons live in close proximity.

In example (1) there is, in one clear sense, disagreement between communities A and B. Their respective members hold beliefs which are the contradictories of one another. This is to assume, of course, that beliefs about values express coherent propositional thoughts which can enter into logical relations with one another, and that there are no problems of

---

[3] For the use of similar thought experiments for other purposes, see Nozick 1974: 185 and Gauthier 1986: 219–21.

reference or identification as between the two communities, when they
mention, say, an act of abortion. These are philosophically contentious
assumptions, but I am prepared to make them. In any event, in another
clear sense there is no disagreement between communities A and B.
Since they do not even know of one another's existence, there is no
occasion when an A person makes a claim which a B person then goes
on to dispute.

In example (2) there is liable to be disagreement in the second sense
as well as the first. A persons and B persons may well take issue with one
another where they differ, so that one will deny what the other asserts.
But if we imagine that contact between the communities is minimal, the
disagreement may not issue in conflict of any further kind.

In example (3) there will not merely be disagreement in the two senses
distinguished. There will be practical difficulties directly connected with
the beliefs of A persons and B persons. In acting on the respective beliefs
they hold, A persons and B persons will come into conflict. They will
be respectively committed to realising states of their world which cannot
jointly be realised, and those commitments will arise directly from their
beliefs. (Notice, however, that as well as conflict there must also be a level
of agreement between A people and B people if they are really to live in
the same geographical area on any continuing basis.)

It is the forms of conflict outlined in (3) which most closely mirror
the circumstances of much of the contemporary world. There is not just
the abstract fact of unwitting attachment to contradictory propositions,
nor just the further fact of witting denial of the propositions asserted
by someone else. There is, in addition, the fact that manifest doxastic
dissension issues in practical dissension. The content of the beliefs in
imagined communities A and B was chosen to reflect the content of
some of the beliefs which, in the actual world, result in practical conflict
between people. We live in a *de facto* pluralist world, that is, a world in
which incompatible systems of value as a matter of fact coexist, systems of
value whose adherents are led to conflicting commitments and conflicting
courses of action in virtue of their espousal of those systems.[4]

No doubt, as with disenchantment, it is possible to exaggerate the
novelty of *de facto* pluralism: perhaps earlier societies have been less uniform and homogeneous than we sometimes think. But for all that, our
current historical circumstances are distinctive in at least two respects.

---

[4] The claim of *de facto* pluralism carries no implication about the status of conflicting values or
the possibility of resolving such conflicts. For discussion of those distinct questions, see Berlin
1991: 80, Raz 1986: 395 and Larmore 1994: 61–79.

First, we have an unprecedented accumulation of knowledge of other cultures and their differing values, we are much more aware of how differently people may reason about what is worth doing and what states of the world should be realised.[5] Secondly, cultures with widely different values have interpenetrated geographically to an unprecedented extent. Is it acceptable or unacceptable to publish pornography, to eat meat, to hang criminals, to wear make-up and a skirt in the street if you are a woman, to wear make-up and a skirt in the street if you are a man, to abort foetuses, to teach children about customs and values different from those they are growing up with? People hold conflicting views on such questions, but the people holding those views are now much more likely than previously to live, literally, next door to one another.

It is not my purpose here to provide developed theories of disenchantment and *de facto* pluralism, or to determine the exact degree of truth in the claim that they are distinctive features of the contemporary world. The strength of fundamentalist religions shows that the disenchantment of the world is less than complete, and the coexistence of many forms of religious belief with one another and with secular beliefs in the contemporary United States makes plain that *de facto* pluralism can thrive where disenchantment is absent. But I hope to have given sufficient characterisation of disenchantment and pluralism to make plain that they are a significant part of the circumstances in which the question 'What reasons do we have for acting?' currently arises. The question is not generated by these circumstances; indeed, it is hardly separable from human action at all, at least in the full-blown form in which it involves conscious choice and decision. Nevertheless, the urgency of the question, the way it is understood, and the range of answers thought acceptable to it are likely to be heavily influenced by these circumstances. Thus, although spatial proximity has not brought into being the question of how to handle widely varying views on acceptable behaviour, it has made that question a much more pressing one at a practical level.[6] Underlying

[5] 'Neo-Hegelian and other nostalgic writers typically exaggerate the extent to which any society has ever had a homogeneous outlook, and one may perhaps doubt whether contemporary societies are really more pluralistic in their composition than many societies of the past. But they are certainly more pluralistic in their outlook, and consciously accept that attitudes which are substantively different from one another in spirit and in history actually coexist. People realise, too, that this fact itself makes demands on ethical and political understanding and invention. Meeting those demands provides one dimension of ethical thought that is now particularly important' (Williams 1995a: 139–40).

[6] '[I]n our world an inability to account for cross-cultural reasoning ultimately has fierce practical consequences. Many contemporary societies are culturally plural; nearly all have significant and varied relations with other, differing societies. A particularist account of ethical relations

the practical question is a theoretical one about how to evaluate reasons for acting, which I do want to address. There is, after all, more than just a practical problem here. People with differing values in a pluralist society are not like two stubborn and aggressive individuals who meet on a narrow bridge and attempt to barge past each other. The practical conflicts of a pluralist society are freighted with *beliefs* about the (not necessarily moral) rightness and wrongness of different courses of action. The question, therefore, is how we arrive at decent beliefs of that kind.

1.2 AUTONOMY AND DISAGREEMENT

We must make decisions about what constitute good reasons for acting. One possible response to this fact is to make a virtue of necessity, to argue that the need to create one's own values is not a predicament to be endured but a state which is itself of enormous value. That response is reflected in our culture in the form of bestowing high importance on *autonomy*, in one sense of that ambiguous term.[7] Choosing our own forms of behaviour is seen not as something we are stuck with but as something which gives us our dignity, something to be prized. After all, it might be said, endorsing certain values in the light of critical reflection and consideration of alternatives is far more worthy than merely reading them off from a description of the world or finding oneself attached to them by accident of birth or whatever other circumstance. Charles Taylor identifies Herder as one of the early articulators of the idea and paraphrases his thought:

There is a certain way of being human that is *my* way. I am called upon to live my life in this way, and not in imitation of anyone else's life. But this notion gives

and reasoning that might have been practically adequate in a world of homogeneous, closed societies will almost certainly prove practically inadequate in a world marked by cultural pluralism within states, vastly intricate interregional, international and transnational relationships, and constantly shifting patterns of integration and connection between different spheres of life and different social groups' (O'Neill 1996: 20). 'But typically in our day and age pluralism exists within every society, indeed within every culture. That generates conflict between competing and incompatible activities and ways of life. When valuable alternatives we do not pursue are remote and unavailable, they do not threaten our commitment to and confidence in the values manifested in our own life. But when they are available to us and pursued by others in our vicinity they tend to be felt as a threat' (Raz 1995: 180).

[7] One ambiguity lies in the fact that the term may be used either to describe a state where individuals choose their values, rather than simply inferring them from data amassed about the world without any original input of their own, or to describe a state where individuals choose their values rather than having them imposed by some other individual(s) or by their social environment. For discussion of the range of uses of the term, and of what can reasonably be expected by way of definition, see Dworkin 1988: 5–20.

a new importance to being true to myself. If I am not, I miss the point of my life; I miss what being human is for *me*. (Taylor 1992: 30)

In the same vein Joseph Raz articulates the ideal of personal autonomy:[8]

The ruling idea behind the ideal of personal autonomy is that people should make their own lives. The autonomous person is a (part) author of his own life. The ideal of personal autonomy is the vision of people controlling, to some degree, their own destiny, fashioning it through their own decisions throughout their lives. (Raz 1986: 369)

The preconditions for enjoying such autonomy are 'appropriate mental abilities, an adequate range of options, and independence' (372).

The sponsorship of autonomy as specified so far is not something I wish to challenge. It should be noted, however, that, familiar though it may be to me and my likely readers, its sponsorship is not uncontentious. What was described above as 'endorsing certain values in the light of critical reflection and consideration of alternatives' might be described by someone less enamoured of autonomy as allowing the rot to set in by being exposed to wicked ways, the very exposure to which will lead people away from virtue. Such a thought might underlie, for example, a resistance to a certain range of curriculum subjects being taught to girls, which it is feared will implant in them the idea that they ought not necessarily to be in a position of unquestioning obedience to their fathers. Or it might underlie the fears on the part of members of the Amish sect that exposure to other ideas and other forms of life will seduce people away from the simple, non-invasive and technologically undemanding life which their sect leads. I find the second example less offensive than the first, but in any case I set aside any difficulties there might be thought to be in defending the importance of autonomy in general.[9] Instead, I call attention to a number of specific problems which have a bearing on practical reason and will be taken up later in the argument.

Notice, first, a certain elasticity in the ideal: the aspiration is to be *part* author of one's life and to control *to some degree* one's own destiny.

---

[8] Raz distinguishes between *personal* autonomy and *moral* autonomy. Whereas moral autonomy is a doctrine about the whole of morality, to the effect that it consists in self-enacted principles, personal autonomy is one specific moral ideal (Raz 1986: 370 n. 2).

[9] One possible defence is developed by Joseph Raz: 'For those who live in an autonomy-supporting environment there is no choice but to be autonomous: there is no other way to prosper in such a society' (Raz 1986: 391). See also Kymlicka 1989: ch. 9. This defence will not convince someone who raises doubts about the value of having an autonomy-supporting environment in the first place. For further scepticism see Gray 1996: 150–5.

This is not the accident of one author's formulation; it is, rather, an essential qualification. One aspect of the fact of causal interconnection ensures that anything more than this would be a vain hope. There is, literally, nothing one human being can do without the prior causal input of other human beings, from which it follows that others must always in that straightforward sense be part authors of a person's life. The reasons for making this claim, and the consequences which follow from it, will concern me in chapter 2 (The indistinctness of persons: causal interconnection).

Notice also that, whatever the scope of control over one's own life turns out to be, there is an incompleteness in the ideal of autonomy as articulated. Does the *mere* fact that someone is shaping their life have value independently of the shape which results, or does its having value depend on the nature of the choices that they make in doing so? In other words, does the fact of my choosing a particular course of action carry any weight, on its own, as a reason for so acting, or does it not? If it does, we need to explain why choice as such should have this power (and to make sure that this answer does not yield results we find difficult to live with). If choice does not of itself carry weight, then we still have to ask what are the sources of sound choices. I pursue the question of the independent value of choice in chapter 3, section 7 and chapter 5, section 3.

Notice, next, that the ideal is one of *personal* autonomy. The fact of collective agency creates complications here. It is the autonomy of individuals which is most usually prized in liberal thought, but the idea of *collective* autonomy is not absent: the idea, for instance, that there is a right to national self-determination is fairly strongly entrenched. If collective autonomy were just a kind of shorthand for an accumulation of individual autonomy, then well and good. But if, as I shall suggest in chapter 3, collectivities possess independent importance, then it may follow that their autonomy is also of independent importance. Individual and collective autonomy may then end up fighting for the same space, as it were: it will be necessary to decide how the two kinds of autonomy relate to each other, and whether it is acceptable to say that individual autonomy must always take precedence over any collective autonomy. The tensions between personal and collective demands in general are further discussed in chapter 6, section 2.

Notice, finally, that the exercise of autonomy in the circumstances of *de facto* pluralism exacerbates the problem of practical disagreements among people, because it is more likely to lead to a divergence of views about what to do than a convergence.[10] The practical problem is not easily remedied. In some circumstances, if people's exercise of their autonomy in deciding how to act results in conflicting aspirations, a natural option for dealing with the practical problem is to arrange to have differing sets of expectations and laws in accordance with differing local loyalties and values, rather than assuming that the same norms of behaviour must prevail for everyone, everywhere. In that spirit, Nozick tells us that 'there will not be *one* kind of community existing and one kind of life led in utopia. Utopia will consist of utopias, of many different and divergent communities in which people lead different kinds of lives under different institutions' (Nozick 1974: 311–12; see also Graham 1984). But this is a solution only for examples (1) and (2) as described in section 1. In example (3), where local loyalties are not *geographically* local and people with conflicting aspirations intermingle in close proximity, it is simply unavailable as a solution.

What attitude should we take towards the diversity exhibited by *de facto* pluralism? Rawls suggests, plausibly, that it is the 'inevitable outcome of free human reason' (Rawls 1993: 37). It is, he argues, 'not a mere historical condition that may soon pass away; it is a permanent feature of the public culture of democracy . . . a diversity of conflicting and irreconcilable – and what's more, reasonable – comprehensive doctrines will come about and persist if such diversity does not already obtain' (36). The explanation for this is that the burdens of judgement in a modern society, including the fact that people's total experiences are very diverse, allow them to reach different views even when exercising their reason (58). Rawls's overarching question is: 'How is it possible that deeply opposed though reasonable comprehensive doctrines may live together and all affirm the political conception of a constitutional regime?' (xviii) As for *un*reasonable doctrines, 'the problem is to contain them so that they do not undermine the unity and justice of society' (xvii). They must be contained, as he puts it, 'like war and disease' (64 n. 19).

Recall the distinction made at the end of section 1 between the practical matter of conflicting decisions about how to act and the theoretical matter of evaluating the reasons for acting which underlie such decisions. A similar distinction is apposite now between *intervention* and *criticism*. Whether someone's views are open to criticism is one thing; whether the criticism licenses some particular form of intervention (or indeed any

---

[10] For some reasons why sponsors of autonomy should not make light of the problem of divergence, see Graham 1998: 178–80.

intervention at all) is another thing. It is consistent to believe both that some doctrine about how to act is unreasonable and that it would not be justifiable to contain it. I might believe that someone held views about what they should do which were morally undesirable or seriously self-harming, but also believe that it would be wrong to prevent them from acting on those views. For instance, perhaps I regard their personal autonomy as so important that my interfering would compound the moral undesirability, or believe that interference would serve ill their need to learn the effects of self-harm at first hand.

Rawls's talk of containing unreasonable doctrines makes it plain that he is concerned with intervention. The question 'What makes a doctrine reasonable?' obviously then assumes great importance, since on it turns the further question of whether the doctrine suffers containment or receives, as it were, a ticket to join the overlapping consensus. He avoids excluding doctrines as unreasonable without strong grounds (Rawls 1993: 59), and gives 'rather minimal necessary conditions' for passing the test of reasonableness, stating: 'It is not suggested that all reasonable doctrines so defined are equally reasonable for other purposes or from other points of view' (37 n. 38).[11]

It is entirely appropriate to make rather minimal requirements for a doctrine to qualify as reasonable when the question of intervention is at stake, since drastic consequences will follow from any judgement to the contrary. My own purpose is rather different from Rawls's. I am concerned with criticism rather than intervention, and with doctrines about how to act, which are considerably narrower than comprehensive doctrines. The result of this separation of criticism from intervention should be a removal of inhibition on appraising views as unreasonable. Obviously it will still be necessary to give good grounds for such an appraisal, but it will be clearer that negative appraisal does not in itself amount to intervention or bespeak intolerance. (Equally, it should be clear that tolerance does not imply an absence of criticism. I might believe it important not to intervene in the expression of racist views even if I believe that the views expressed are not merely obnoxious but also erroneous.)

---

[11] A reasonable comprehensive doctrine has three main features. It involves 'an exercise of theoretical reason: it covers the major . . . aspects of human life in a more or less consistent and coherent manner. It organizes . . . values so that they are compatible with one another and express an intelligible view of the world.' It involves, secondly, the exercise of practical reason in determining priorities. And thirdly, such a doctrine 'normally belongs to, or draws upon, a tradition of thought and doctrine' (Rawls 1993: 59–60).

The distinction between criticism and intervention should not be taken to imply an absence of connection between appraisal and action, however. A negative appraisal can feed into the nexus of decision that agents themselves engage in, for example. In simpler and more concrete terms, there is still a point in telling someone if we think their reasons for acting are lousy: *they* may then change what they do even if we feel that we should not be justified in making them do so. And of course the exercise of critical assessment is important for the agent themself. If you are going to be autonomous there must be something for you to be autonomous about: you must select some considerations over others as providing you with reasons for acting. The question is what facts about us and our circumstances should have a bearing on this selection.

1.3 RELATIVISM AND UNIVERSALISM

I have so far described, in very broad terms, the modern context faced by human agents and the response to it in the form of placing a premium on autonomy. I shall not discuss that context any further or subject alternative theories of disenchantment, pluralism and autonomy to detailed analysis. Rather, from now on I take that context for granted and ask how, given the context, agents should conduct their practical reasoning. The question is an implicitly *universal* one about all human agents, regardless of their particular circumstances. As such, it may evoke suspicion from two different relativist sources. The first source is the belief that any attempt to answer it must involve an illegitimate generalisation from the position of *individual agents*. The second source is the belief that any attempt to answer it must involve an illegitimate generalisation from the position of a *particular culture*. I describe and briefly comment on these relativist positions now, in order to distinguish them from the universalist position which will inform subsequent discussion.

From the first source it might be objected that, since the practical reasons which any given agent has will depend entirely on the nature of their circumstances and themself, what applies to one agent will not necessarily apply to another. Since one agent will differ from another in terms of the characteristics they possess, the objectives they happen to have, and so on, it will not be possible to generalise across cases. Loren Lomasky suggests:

An individual's projects provide him with a *personal* – an intimately personal – standard of value to choose his actions by. His central and enduring ends provide reasons for action that are recognized as his own in the sense that no one who is uncommitted to those specific ends will share the reasons for action that he possesses. Practical reason is *essentially differentiated* among project pursuers . . . (Lomasky 1987: 28, cited in Gaus 1996: 142. A similar view is put forward in Gaus 1990, Part 1)

In a similar spirit, Jon Elster comments: 'There is no alternative to rational-choice theory as a set of normative prescriptions. It just tells us to do what will best promote our aims, whatever they are' (Elster 1986a: 22).

The idea that practical reasons are specific to particular agents is ambiguous. It may mean, first, that all reasons for acting are *internal* rather than *external*. That is, it may mean that the reasons which are available for a given agent depend crucially on that agent's own particular aims, that a consideration cannot figure as a reason for acting for a particular agent unless it meshes in with some aim that they have.[12] Secondly, it may mean that all reasons are *agent-relative* rather than *agent-neutral*. That is, it may mean that a consideration can figure as a reason only when it is primarily (or only) a reason for some particular person to do something. What is excluded here is the idea that there might be a reason, objectively speaking, for bringing about some state of affairs which was only derivatively a reason for someone (or anyone or everyone) to bring it about.[13] That these distinctions cut across each other can be brought out in the following way. It might be held that all persons have a reason for looking after their immediate dependants and that their having this reason does not depend on whether doing so meshes in with their aims or not; hence, this reason is external rather than internal. At the same time it might be held that whereas *you* have a reason for looking after your dependants *I* do not have a reason for looking after *your* dependants; hence this reason is agent-relative rather than agent-neutral. The properties of internality and agent-relativity are therefore logically distinct. There are certain reasons for acting here which are operative for me but not operative for others, but this has nothing to do with my choices in the matter.

So far as the substantive issues are concerned, I do not believe that all reasons for acting must be internal or that they must be agent-relative.[14]

---

[12] For the distinction between internal and external reasons, see for example Williams 1980 and Williams 1995a: 35–45.

[13] For the distinction between agent-neutral and agent-relative reasons, see for example Parfit 1984: 143, and Nagel 1986: 158–9.

[14] For a systematic outline of the ways in which reasons for acting need not be merely relative to an agent's aims, see Nozick 1993: 139–51.

But suppose that they must. This would then itself be a significant truth about the circumstances of practical reasoning which human beings found themselves in – *all* human beings – and this illustrates how difficult it is actually to avoid universal claims. (Does the claim that each individual human being has unique features infringe the admonition against making universal claims or not?[15]) It is consistent with acknowledging important differences between agents to acknowledge that there are also invariant features of all human agents and their circumstances, which hold good across all particular contexts and ought to influence the values and courses of action which those agents adopt if they are to act reasonably. It is such invariant features which provide the focus of the present enquiry.

Consider now the second source of suspicion about basing practical reasoning on universal considerations. Michael Walzer puts forward a 'radically particularist' argument in opposition to what he takes to be the universalising tendency of current theories of distributive justice. He says:

Even if they are committed to impartiality, the question most likely to arise in the minds of the members of a political community is not, What would rational individuals choose under universalizing conditions of such-and-such a sort? But rather, What would individuals like us choose, who are situated as we are, who share a culture and are determined to go on sharing it? And this is a question that is readily transformed into, What choices have we already made in the course of our common life? What understandings do we (really) share? (Walzer 1983: 5)

This position at least allows that it would be intelligent for agents to raise questions which began from a consideration of universally shared characteristics, though it is clear that Walzer believes they do not and should not. But consider Richard Rorty's pragmatist attempt to distinguish between fanaticism and a conscience worthy of respect, a distinction which will be germane to any attempt to make a critical assessment

---

[15] Nagel argues that the ordinary process of practical deliberation presupposes objectivity and that objectivity in its turn draws us to generalisation (Nagel 1986: 149–50). Christine Korsgaard makes a similar point in connection with communitarianism. It is a standard communitarian criticism of the liberal conception of the self that it makes the self empty and abstract when in fact human beings need to conceive of themselves as members of particular communities, with particular ties and values. She comments: 'This is an argument about how we human beings need to constitute our practical identities, and if it is successful what it establishes is a *universal* fact, namely that our practical identities must be constituted in part by particular ties and commitments' (Korsgaard 1996: 118–19).

of reasons which agents have for acting. The criterion for the distinction, according to him,

> can only be something relatively local and ethnocentric – the tradition of a particular community, the consensus of a particular culture. According to this view, what counts as rational or as fanatical is relative to the group to which we think it necessary to justify ourselves – to the body of shared belief that determines the reference of the word 'we'. (Rorty 1991: 176–7)

On this view, there would be little point in beginning from universally shared characteristics if the only intelligible form of justification is relative to a particular group.[16]

As the thought experiment of section 1 has indicated, one of the difficulties with relativist doctrines is that it is precisely the reference of the word 'we' which has become problematic. A number of human beings may share a common life and common beliefs in all sorts of ways, and to that extent share a common culture, but yet disagree about a range of matters which issue in practical decisions. Living in the same street, working in the same factory or office, shopping in the same mall and sharing many beliefs on other matters, these do not rule out disagreements in practical reasoning. In other words, 'we' can be defined in terms of sharing a life and even in terms of sharing beliefs without this necessarily producing shared understandings or consensus on practical values. On the other hand, if 'we' are defined precisely in terms of such shared practical values, how much testing do those values receive on Rortyan assumptions? If we assume that we need to justify our views only to those who already share them, the reinforcement we receive in our convictions will be comforting but specious. We shall simply be in the position of Wittgenstein's man who buys several copies of the

---

[16] In contemporary debate there is a familiar extension of arguments of this kind in the name of a 'politics of identity and recognition'. It is suggested that any attempt at universality is bound implicitly to privilege one culture over others and ignore important differences between agents in the name of some abstraction. In that spirit, for example, it is claimed that theories based on the apparently neutral conception of the rational autonomous agent in fact privilege a particular kind of human being, namely propertied, white males. For discussion of such suggestions, see Benhabib 1992: 152–68 and Taylor 1992. Whilst I do not directly address issues of a politics of identity and recognition, some of my discussion is relevant to them. In chapter 4, section 3 I argue for the importance of agents' achieving a critical distance from themselves and the characteristics they possess. In chapter 5, section 4 and chapter 5, section 6 I draw distinctions between the different ways in which a person's characteristics can acquire significance for practical reasoning, depending on whether an agent themself chooses to endow them with significance, or whether they are caused to endow them with significance as a result of the actions or attitudes of others, or whether they carry significance independently of *anyone's* actions or attitudes. On that basis, I argue for endowing our materiality with primary significance, as against such characteristics as gender and ethnicity which would normally be emphasised in a politics of identity and recognition.

same morning newspaper to assure himself that what it said is true (Wittgenstein 1953: para. 265).[17]

An alternative to relativism at this point is to attempt to begin where the temperature is fairly low, with considerations about human agents and their circumstances which are minimally contentious as between different cultures, and to describe those considerations in terms which are themselves minimally contentious. In other words, we must avoid parochialism both in *content* and in *form*.[18] So far as content is concerned, we need to ensure that any features we take to be universal features of the situation of human agents really are such, rather than being historically or geographically local ones. We need, in other words, to show a decent regard for the range of evidence which can be turned up by historical and anthropological studies, rather than assuming that human beings and their circumstances are everywhere more or less just like us.[19] So far as form is concerned, we should express any relevant putatively universal truths in terms which are themselves not parochial. They should not, at least at the outset, be described in a way which is itself prejudicial from the standpoint of particular cultures. Debates on these matters are often conducted in the currency of *moral* conceptions, and that is not necessarily an advantage because moral conceptions often are local to particular cultures.[20]

Suppose we attempt to avoid these pitfalls by beginning only from the most general facts about human agents, facts whose existence would be acknowledged in any culture, and by describing them in as neutral a vocabulary as possible. This can be no more than a starting point. One person can be wrong, one culture can be wrong, *all* cultures can be wrong, when they begin to reason even from quite obvious and familiar general facts which hold good of all agents. Facts can be perfectly familiar and obvious while it is far from obvious what further conclusions they license or proscribe. Accordingly, although the general facts should not be described in a way prejudicial to any particular culture at the outset, there can be no commitment to saying nothing which might offend a

[17] For criticism of Rorty see Calder 1998 and Geras 1995.
[18] For further discussion of form and content in this connection, see Graham 1999b.
[19] For further argument on that point, see the discussion of constraints of precondition in chapter 5, section 5.
[20] For example, some theorists have argued from universal facts about the nature of human agency to conclusions about individual rights. They may or may not be right to do so, but when the language of individual rights represents one (contentious) option in the stock of concepts of one (relatively local) culture it will require further argument to justify any conclusions couched in that particular way. For such attempts see Gewirth 1994 and Steiner 1977. For scepticism about taking rights as a starting point, see O'Neill 1996: 141–6.

given culture in the inferences which we then go on to make. It may be that there is an unbridgeable gulf between the A people and the B people of section 1, that diversity in practical attitudes is the inevitable outcome of the use of human reason in a modern, free society. For all that, the *status quo* with regard to practical reason, in terms of the reasons for acting which people take themselves to have, should not itself be taken as an unalterable given, somehow beyond the reach of critical assessment. Nothing alterable by human decision and action should have that status.

We must, in other words, reserve the right to criticise the beliefs of any individual or culture, including our own. No doubt a certain humility is appropriate when faced with a set of values which have held the allegiance of a large number of people over a significant period of time, but the possibility cannot be ruled out that some values, even if deeply and widely held, may be in some way deficient or wrong-headed.[21] It goes without saying that if we countenance that possibility, then we must countenance it in relation to our own values as well as other people's.

As the argument proceeds, I shall attempt to show that this is indeed the case with some of the individualist values of our own culture: in various ways the thoughts informing reasons for acting inadequately reflect the social nature of human life. It is important to stress that the argument is pitched at the level of an examination of general (and quite possibly only implicit) philosophical assumptions. It would mislead the reader grossly to give the impression that a theory will be found between the covers of this book which will enable us to deliver verdicts on conflicting views of the kind expressed by the A people and the B people of the thought experiment in section 1. But I hope to be able to say something significant about the soundness of the assumptions underlying them.

There are many different forms of universalism relevant to the question of practical reasoning. As such forms go, the approach being adopted at this stage is a very modest one. It does not imply that there are any reasons for acting which are universal in the sense of being applicable to all human beings or that the soundness of reasons for acting is to be assessed by reference to universal criteria (though it will emerge later that there is much truth in both claims). It certainly does not amount to the idea that universally experienced circumstances imply that all human beings should be treated in the same way. It amounts only to the thought that it is useful to begin a theory of practical reason from universal

---

[21] Charles Taylor has argued persuasively that to assume without argument that all cultures are equally valuable is not to pay respect but to condescend. Assessment of a culture as valuable must follow, not precede, a critical examination of its values (Taylor 1992: 70).

considerations, considerations about what it is like to be a human agent in any circumstances. It then remains to be seen whether anything of substance follows from this.[22]

1.4 THE DISTINCTNESS OF PERSONS

Suppose, then, we wish to begin from a doctrine which possesses the universality just described, a doctrine which captures some of the unalterable features of the context of practical reasoning by specifying salient features of *all* human agents, without regard to any agent's particular characteristics or their particular circumstances. We do not have to look far for such a doctrine. Frequent appeal is made in philosophical discussion to the *distinctness of persons*, a doctrine which meets just that requirement. In this section I ask how exactly the doctrine is to be understood, and I distinguish a number of possible interpretations and a direction of dependency among them. I also raise questions about the conclusions which are thought to follow from them. The distinctness of persons seems to me the right *sort* of theory, but not the right theory. This preliminary discussion of it therefore prepares the ground for my arguments in favour of the rival idea of the *indistinctness* of persons, developed in chapters 2 and 3, which is similarly universalist but consists of a contrasting set of claims.

The doctrine of the distinctness of persons was brought into focus by Rawls, Nozick and Nagel, all around the same time, though it has longer historical roots than that.[23] In an apposite passage for our enquiry Sidgwick declared:

It would be contrary to Common Sense to deny that the distinction between any one individual and any other is real and fundamental, and that consequently 'I' am concerned with the quality of my existence as an individual in a sense, fundamentally important, in which I am not concerned with the quality of the existence of other individuals: and this being so, I do not see how it can be proved that this distinction is not to be taken as fundamental in determining the ultimate end of rational action for an individual. (Sidgwick 1907: 498, cited in Brink 1997: 103)

---

[22] For argument against the idea that uniformity of treatment follows from universalist claims, and other helpful points about the different kinds of universalism, see O'Neill 1996: 74–6. For Enlightenment-inspired defences of certain forms of universalism against current criticisms, see Assiter 1996 and Benhabib 1992. For a defence of specifically *moral* universalism, see Caney 1999. For the view that we should not use completely general arguments if our concern is to combat a scepticism which is local to our own intellectual and cultural situation, see Williams 1998.

[23] This corrects the inaccurate historical claim made in Graham 1998: 183.

Rawls argued in *A Theory of Justice* the need to give priority to individual liberty over aggregate increase in social welfare, and he criticised classical utilitarianism for supposing that all the desires of different people could be summed into one system and their satisfaction then measured. To do that 'fails to take seriously the distinction between persons' (Rawls 1972: 187) and 'the plurality of distinct persons with separate systems of ends is an essential feature of human societies' (29).

Nozick in *Anarchy, State, and Utopia* in a similar vein resisted any analogy between (i) an individual sacrificing something for the sake of an overall greater good in their own life and (ii) the sacrificing of some individual for a greater social good. For, he said, 'there is no *social entity* with a good that undergoes some sacrifice for its own good. There are only individual people, different individual people, with their own individual lives. Using one of these people for the benefit of others, uses him and benefits the others. Nothing more' (Nozick 1974: 32–3). Using someone in that way 'does not sufficiently respect and take account of the fact that he is a separate person, that his is the only life he has' (33).

Nagel similarly objected to treating the interpersonal case in the same way as the intrapersonal case, on the grounds that 'it fails to take seriously the distinction between persons'.

> It treats the desires, needs, satisfactions, and dissatisfactions of distinct persons as if they were the desires, etc., of a mass person. But this is to ignore the *significance* of the fact (when it is a fact) that the members of a set of conflicting desires and interests all fall within the boundaries of a single life, and can be dealt with as the claims of a single individual. Conflicts between the interests of distinct individuals, on the other hand, must be regarded in part as conflicts between *lives*; and that is a very different matter. (Nagel 1970: 134)

He adds: 'To sacrifice one individual life for another, or one individual's happiness for another's is very different from sacrificing one gratification for another within a *single* life' (138).

There is a level of agreement amongst these commentators. Most obviously, they all subscribe to some general form of individualism, though that form is in need of more precise articulation.[24] What all

---

[24] In characterising the different forms of individualism to which Rawls and Nozick are committed, Norman Care says that they 'centrally value individual lives, and they give great moral weight to individually defined self-realizationist aspirations and projects. These are views that speak in the vocabulary of the "inviolability", the "irreducible significance", and the "irreplaceable worth" of individual human lives' (Care 1987: 35). The problem is that individualism defined in these terms is critically ambiguous. Anyone would agree to giving individual lives central value: inviolability is a different matter, and the difficult question is whether there are any circumstances in which something may be more important than some individual's life or plans.

are agreed on is that the desires, interests, etc., which cluster within an individual (say, the desires of individual I, no matter what they are desires *for*) have a special status as compared with the clustering of such things on some other basis (say, the desires for outcome O, no matter *whose* desires they happen to be). In consequence, it is thought inappropriate to treat desires, interests, etc., clustered on some other basis in the same way as if they attached to an individual. There is also agreement that utilitarianism suffers from the defect of treating desires and interests in just that inappropriate way.

However, there are also some disagreements about what follows from the distinctness of persons among its proponents. For example, although Rawls and Nozick formulate the doctrine in a similar way and agree in invoking it to dismiss utilitarianism, Nozick also invokes it to dismiss just the kind of redistributive welfarism favoured by Rawls.[25] In the light of this, we must conclude either that at least one of them is wrong in some of the inferences they make from the doctrine, which is perfectly possible, or else that the distinctness of persons is itself an ambiguous doctrine (or, of course, both). I shall persevere with the thought that the doctrine itself is ambiguous, that it may express several different ideas which need to be distinguished and evaluated and from which different conclusions may follow.[26]

The doctrine might plausibly be construed in at least the following four different ways, D1 to D4.

(D1) QUALITATIVE DISTINCTNESS: Persons considered as a species of entity are distinct from <u>other entities</u>. It might plausibly be held that persons are distinct both from other animate entities and from inanimate entities in certain relevant respects. They exhibit a range of properties which are specific to them, such as intentions, desires, wishes and feelings, and perhaps most centrally of all (and connected with some of these other properties) they have the capacity for deliberative action. Other entities, it might be said, either do not exhibit these properties at all or exhibit them in a form quite different from that of individual persons.

From the thoughts expressed in D1 it might be held to follow, for example, that only individual persons are fully qualified members of

---

[25] Nozick objects in the following terms to Rawls's regarding natural talents as a common asset, such that those who by accident possess them should benefit from them only on terms that improve the situation of those who do not possess them: 'Some will complain, echoing Rawls against utilitarianism, that this "does not take seriously the distinction between persons"; and they will wonder whether any reconstruction of Kant that treats people's abilities and talents as resources for others can be adequate' (Nozick 1974: 228).

[26] For a similar enterprise, see Raz 1986: 271–87.

the moral realm; and that this makes it appropriate to have certain expectations about how they could reasonably be treated and to have a certain view of the responsibilities they can be expected to carry (cf. Kymlicka 1989: 241–2). The thoughts expressed in D1 are not the most dominant in appeals to the distinctness of persons, but they are likely to underlie Nozick's avowal that there is no social entity which undergoes a sacrifice for its own good, and I believe that they have an important role in justifying some of the individualist conclusions which appeals to the doctrine are thought to support.

(D2) DISTINCTNESS AS SEPARATENESS: Persons considered individually, rather than as a species, are distinct from <u>one another</u>. We share certain properties as members of a species, such as the capacity for thoughts, memories, experiences, actions and aspirations. But the instantiation of these properties occurs within separate individuals. My thoughts and actions and aspirations are not yours, any more than I am you. We each live a separate life, with our own separate experiences and behaviour, and our own separate views as to how that life should go. As Samuel Scheffler expresses the point: 'Different persons, each one with his own projects and plans, are distinct, though to say this is obviously not to deny the reality or importance of empathy, identification, sharing, co-operation, joint activity, and other related aspects of human experience. Indeed, as a moment's thought will show, these phenomena all presuppose the distinctness of persons' (Scheffler 1982: 77).

From the thoughts expressed in D2 about the peculiarly intimate relation between individual human beings and their own separate experiences, actions and aspirations, a number of things might be held to follow. Experiences, actions and aspirations are closely connected with interests. (For example, if I am experiencing pain I have an interest in my experience coming to an end; if I am walking along I have an interest in the ground not giving way beneath me; if I aspire to write a detective novel I have an interest in forming some ideas about a suitable plot.) If experiences, actions and aspirations are predicated of separate individuals, then it might be claimed that a similar separateness must be involved in dealing with those individuals' interests. William Galston suggests: 'I may share everything with others. But it is *I* that shares them – an independent consciousness, a separate locus of pleasure and pain, a demarcated being with interests to be advanced or suppressed' (Galston 1986: 91).

In the light of that claim, it might then further be thought in the interests of separate individuals that they be 'free to regulate their own personal lives', as Nagel puts it, 'according to their full personal conceptions of how they should be lived' (Nagel 1987: 238–9). That thought is extended and expressed more strongly by Scheffler as '*the intuitive idea that the best state of affairs is one in which as many distinct people as possible are carrying out their plans as successfully as possible and are hence achieving their good*' (Scheffler 1982: 77–8; italics added). This idea is immensely important, and clearly articulates a view which is widely held. I shall have occasion to discuss it at a number of points later in this book and I shall refer to it subsequently as *the intuitive idea*.

(D3) DISTINCTNESS AS INTEGRITY: Persons are distinct in <u>forming a unity</u>.[27] Bernard Williams observes: 'In general it can be said that one very natural correlate of being impressed by the separateness of several persons' lives is being impressed by the peculiar unity of one person's life' (Williams 1976: 6 n. 11). The idea of distinctness as separateness in D2 suggested that, just as there is a literal, bodily discontinuity between one person and another, so there is also a metaphorical hiatus between one person's life and another's. The idea of distinctness as unity suggests that there is no similar hiatus within persons. Rather, we can expect an internal psychological integrity, a coherence among the desires, actions and aspirations of a single person, and this supports the individuation we make into distinct human lives.

The thoughts expressed in D3 would provide part of the explanation of why it is considered appropriate to treat the cluster of desires within an individual differently from clusters formed on some other basis. If there is unity and coherence within an individual, it may seem reasonable correspondingly to treat them as possessing a bundle of interests which it would be inappropriate to untie in the way that utilitarianism demands. More generally, those thoughts might be held to support 'our everyday conception of persons as the basic units of thought, deliberation and responsibility' (Rawls 1993: 18 n. 20) and the idea that 'familiar bodily-individuated persons remain the normal units of rational agency' (Hurley 1989: 157). Finally, if individual human beings are taken as the basic units for moral purposes too then it may also be held that 'any moral duties to larger units (e.g. the community) must be derived from our obligations to individuals' (Kymlicka 1990: 235).

(D4) DISTINCTNESS AS UNIQUENESS: Persons are distinct in the sense of <u>being distinctive</u> and not being interchangeable. The accumulated

---

[27] Integrity as unity is a quite different matter from the sort of integrity which Raz associates with an interpretation of the distinctness of persons (Raz 1986: 284–7). Integrity in his sense concerns the relation of individuals to their own projects as discussed under my D2.

thoughts expressed in D1 to D3 still leave out something important about what it is to live a human life. It would be compatible with the qualitative distinctness of persons as a species, with their separateness and with their internal unity for the same individual human life to be reproduced over and over again on different occasions. But this does not happen. The concatenation of one person's memories, actions and aspirations is always in many respects different from any other person's, each individual biography is different from every other one, each life takes a different course. As Hannah Arendt puts it, 'each man is unique, so that with each birth something uniquely new comes into the world. With respect to this somebody who is unique it can be truly said that nobody was there before' (Arendt 1959: 158). (And, we might add, nobody is there afterwards, or at least not *that* person.) Bernard Williams expresses the 'optimistic belief . . . in the continuing possibility of a meaningful individual life, one that . . . is enough unlike others, in its opacities and disorder as well as in its reasoned intentions, to make it *somebody's*' (Williams 1985: 201–2).

The thoughts expressed in D4 might be held to explain why any person's death is a tragedy. As Williams observes elsewhere, 'Differences of character give substance to the idea that individuals are not inter-substitutable' (Williams 1976: 15). People are not just replaceable one by another and when someone dies a unique point of view and set of experiences and actions disappears with them. The point is eloquently put by George Orwell in his essay 'A hanging':

It is curious, but till that moment I had never realised what it means to destroy a healthy, conscious man . . . He and we were a party of men walking together, seeing, hearing, feeling, understanding the same world; and in two minutes, with a sudden snap, one of us would be gone – one mind less, one world less. (Orwell 1931: 45–6)

Consider now the links among D1–D4, and the difficulties in drawing inferences from them. The claim about the uniqueness of individual human lives expressed in D4 is surely correct; but the *mere* fact of uniqueness suggests nothing about why a person's death might matter to us. It is as true that every bicycle pedal is unique as it is that every person is unique, yet nothing of any importance follows in the case of a bicycle pedal. It is clearly the *nature* of the entity as much as their uniqueness that matters to us: it depends on what it is uniqueness *of*, and the claim must be that human beings are unique entities *of a particular kind*. In that way, any significance attaching to D4 is parasitic on the significance attaching to D1.

The claims embodied in D3 are more contentious than those in D4, and they are open to the challenge that within each separate person there is only the appearance of unity. Just as received thinking approves of the reduction of collective entities to individuals, so it may be argued that the process of reduction needs to be carried further, down to the deeper level of sub-personal states. The challenge to unity can be posed from a number of positions. For example, it may be argued that although an individual has a unified ego they will also possess an unconscious which is unruly and unintegrated into the personality, and that this fact should temper the picture of unity claimed in D3. Derek Parfit's work is another obvious source of doubts about the unity of a person over time and the importance which we attach to it.[28]

Now it might be replied to this that, whatever surprising truths might come to light about the internal structure of a human life as a result of abstract theorising, no theory could be stronger than the plain fact that there is, in Rawls's words, a plurality of distinct persons with separate systems of ends and that this is an essential feature of all human societies. Whatever the explanation for how we come to live our lives as we do, it must remain a fact that it is *we*, individual human beings, who live them, distinct from one another. No theory could be better founded than that fact, so no theory could dislodge it.

I have some sympathy with this rejoinder. I noted in the Introduction that it was no part of my purpose to 'eliminate' the individual: there *are* distinct individual lives, people with their own autobiography, their own set of memories, their own achievements and their own hopes for the future. The difficult question, however, is what precise significance we are entitled to invest this undeniable fact with. If the doctrine of distinctness as unity comes under challenge this is a serious matter, because it looked as though it was this version of the doctrine which would give a justification for treating an individual's desires or aspirations as a bundle, as against the alternative of untying the bundle and adopting the kind of person-indifferent aggregation thought typical of utilitarian calculation. A justification must certainly be given if such alternative ways of aggregating desires and aspirations are to be ruled out. In some circumstances it might make more sense to align myself with others who share

[28] As well as Parfit 1984, see for example Parfit 1973 and Parfit 1976. See also Dancy (ed.) 1997.

a particular desire with me and to take note of that cluster of desires rather than looking at all my own personal desires as a package; and we still need a clear explanation of what is wrong with that, either when I take that view or when it is taken by a spectator.[29]

The challenge to the thoughts expressed in D3 is a challenge to the idea that individual human beings must be taken as the basic units, or at least it forces us to consider more carefully exactly what kind of basicness can be claimed for them. (I argue in chapter 3, section 4 that there is no one kind of basicness or priority here: although individual human beings may be taken as basic in some senses, collective entities must be taken as basic in other senses.) But notice also that the rejoinder to the challenge in effect abandons the claim of *unity*, since this might turn out to be illusory on the basis of theoretical findings, and withdraws to the claim of *separateness*. In other words, just as the significance attaching to D4 turned out to be parasitic on the significance attaching to D1, so the claims of D3 come to be replaced by the claims of D2. In this way, D1 and D2 become crucial for articulating the doctrine of the distinctness of persons.

Consider D1. There can be little doubt that the fundamental thought expressed in it is correct. That is to say, we can sustain the claim that persons are qualitatively distinct from other types of entities by drawing up a compendious list of the relevant properties (intentions, wishes, sentience, deliberative action) and arguing that no other entities possess that list in its entirety. Once again, the problem is not with the truth of D1 but with the inferences to be drawn from it; and part of the reason for that is that there are other entities which certainly share *some*, even if not all, of the relevant properties on the list. In chapter 3 I shall argue that certain kinds of collectivities possess sufficient of the relevant properties to license their membership of the moral realm. If it is true not just that such entities are part of the moral realm but also specifically that they can be objects of moral *concern*, that their well-being can matter to us (as I shall argue in chapter 3, sections 6 and 7), then this is bound to have an effect on inferences from the qualitative distinctness of persons to conclusions about how they are to be treated. For it will then be

---

[29] Susan Hurley points out that there are horizontal divisions within agents as well as vertical divisions between agents, and this brings with it the possibility of binding different agents together (Hurley 1989: 317; see also Morton 1991: 186, Sandel 1982: 167 and the discussion of mediated collective identification in chapter 4, section 4 below). For recent scepticism about the defeat of utilitarianism by appeal to the distinctness of persons, see Brink 1993 and Brink 1997.

possible to assert, *pace* Nozick, that there *are* social entities with their own distinctive good, and questions can then be raised about how to settle conflicting claims on our consideration arising from the combination of individual and non-individual sources with which we are confronted.[30]

A similar problem attends D2. It is no doubt true in *some* sense that individual human beings live separate lives. My life is not your life, and my thoughts and actions are not your thoughts and actions. But here too the problem is in what inferences can be drawn from this, because individuals' lives are not *wholly* separate. This follows immediately from the fact that parts of our lives are collective: there are shared projects and actions, some of them indeed necessarily shared, as I shall argue in chapter 3. But as well as collective existence and the collective interests which arise from it, there is the further complication for the idea of distinctness as separateness which will form the basis of my argument in chapter 2: the ubiquity of causal connection in human action.

We should note, finally, that in drawing inferences from the separateness of persons great care must be taken in the use of the analogy between the interpersonal and the intrapersonal case, and we must ensure that we compare like with like. When Nagel says that sacrificing one individual's life or happiness for another's is very different from sacrificing one gratification within a single life (Nagel 1970: 138, quoted above) what he says is literally true. But that is because sacrificing a life or happiness is very different from sacrificing *one gratification*. If, instead, we compare like with like, it is not at all obvious that the case of sacrificing *one gratification of one person* for *one gratification of another* is very different from one person's sacrificing one gratification of theirs for another gratification of theirs. Much depends on the circumstances and on whether there are independent good reasons for thinking that the satisfaction of one gratification should take precedence over the satisfaction of another. The separateness of human beings' lives (to the extent that they really are separate) will

---

[30] Nozick's remarks purport to rule out two distinct possibilities: (i) that anything other than an individual might have a good and (ii) that there can be an *overall* social good, in the sense of a good of the whole society. We might want to agree in ruling out the latter for contingent reasons, for example because we live in a fragmented or class-divided society. The non-existence of an overall social good might well provide some support for the proponents of the distinctness of persons in their rejection of utilitarianism and its habit of making global aggregations. But that is a different matter from ruling out the existence of supra-individual goods in the various partial associations and collectivities within a society. It is just such a possibility which I shall attempt to rule in.

not of itself settle such questions. As Brink puts it, 'Properly interpreted, the separateness of persons is a conversation *starter*, not the conversation stopper opponents of utilitarianism have taken it to be' (Brink 1993: 258–9; for similar thoughts, see Scheffler 1982: 99–100).

1.5 CONCLUSION

In this chapter I have tried to prepare the ground for the discussion which is to come. I have called attention to the circumstances of the modern world which make it especially pressing to ask on what basis agents should make decisions about how to act, though that is a question which faces all agents in all historical circumstances, at least implicitly, just in virtue of their having to make decisions at all. I have also called attention to arguments against the attempt to found an answer to this question on universal considerations about the nature of human agents. I believe that those arguments license caution in the formulation of universal theses rather than the abandonment of the attempt to formulate them at all. All human agents will exhibit important similarities as well as important differences, as will all cultures, and it is important to give due recognition to these facts. So far as whole cultures are concerned, it is appropriate that we should show a decent sensitivity to the possibility that we may cloak a culturally parochial view in apparent universality. We need to be especially careful to ensure that we remain alive to the whole range of possible views on how to act and to ensure that any criticism of those views does not rest on some challengeable assumption which happens to be favoured by our own culture.

On the substantive issue of the universal circumstances of human agents, we have begun the examination of the idea that these circumstances are characterised by the distinctness of persons. My discussion so far is provisional, but I have sought to bring out some of the complexity of the doctrine of the distinctness of persons. The two main strands of the doctrine express: (D1) the qualitative distinctness of persons, as a type, from other types of entity; and (D2) the separateness of individual persons from one another. In whatever way we elaborate on these strands, and whatever conclusions we draw from them, they must remain compatible with *the fact of causal interconnection* and *the fact of collective agency* described in the Introduction. First, any human agent stands in relations to an indefinite number of other individuals in a complicated causal network stretching through space and time, and their actions reflect this fact. Secondly, part of the existence of human beings consists in their being

constituents in numerous collective agencies such as families, neighbour-
hoods, churches, committees and social classes, and the significance of
some of their actions is captured only by reference to the collective
agency within which they are acting. We need to appreciate the implications of these two facts when we frame theses about the distinctness of
persons.

CHAPTER 2

The indistinctness of persons: causal interconnection

We have noted already that we live in a culture which endows individual human beings with certain kinds of primacy or basicness. In accordance with that culture I begin in this chapter from a consideration of the individual human being, and I trace some of the consequences which follow once we surround that individual with other individual human beings. In chapter 1, section 4 the idea of distinctness as separateness (D2) was introduced. Any inferences from that idea must be consistent with the fact of causal interconnection, the truism that everything a person does carries causal implications for the lives of other human beings. My aim is to bring some precision to that truism and then consider what follows from it. I indicate the importance and the trickiness of the truism for Mill's discussion of self-regarding acts; argue for including causal *precondition* as well as causal *consequence* in the idea of interconnection; and suggest that both consequences and preconditions are relevant to practical reasoning and the moral assessment of actions. I then extend my argument from actions to preferences and suggest that interconnection carries implications for received views about the distinction between nosy and more acceptable preferences.

2.1 INDIVIDUALS AND CAUSAL CONSEQUENCE

Recall the intuitive idea referred to in chapter 1, section 4: that the best state of affairs is one in which as many distinct people as possible are carrying out their plans as successfully as possible and are hence achieving their good. That idea must coexist with the truism that any agent stands in a causal relation to other agents. For the moment, let us understand the truism to state that when any individual acts, (some) other human beings are causally implicated in their action. This is standardly taken to mean that any action has causal consequences for someone besides the agent. Understood in this way, the truism suggests that there is one universally recognised way in which individual human beings' lives fail to be separate, and it also suggests a difficulty for the position apparently adopted by John Stuart Mill in his attempt to distinguish the area where coercive interference in someone's life is justified from the area where it is not justified.

Mill said: 'The only part of the conduct of any one, for which he is amenable to society, is that which concerns others. In the part which merely concerns himself, his independence is, of right, absolute' (Mill 1859: 73). There is never unanimity in philosophy, but there must be near-unanimity that this attempt to distinguish between self-regarding and other-regarding acts requires reconstruction, at the very least. If 'concerns' here means 'affects', then Mill is open to the objection that every act we perform either does or may affect others as well as ourselves, so that there is no part of an individual's conduct which concerns merely that individual. His contemporary Fitzjames Stephen was merely first off the blocks with that complaint.[1] On the other hand, if 'concerns' means 'is the subject of justified control by' then the normative claim here is circular, and no *reason* has been given to suppose, once again, that there is any part of an individual's conduct which concerns merely that individual.

Indeed, the near-unanimity includes Mill, who puts to himself the objection: 'No person is an entirely isolated being; it is impossible for a person to do anything seriously or permanently hurtful to himself, without mischief reaching at least to his near connections, and often far beyond them' (Mill 1859: 136). It is significant that he does not rebut the objection but rather absorbs it: 'I fully admit that the mischief which a person does to himself may seriously affect . . . those nearly connected with him, and in a minor degree, society at large' (137).

Mill's position is not that there is a class of acts which have no connection with others' lives – that is only his apparent position. Rather, he holds that there is a class of acts where the nature of any adverse effects is not sufficient to justify interference. What does justify interference depends on which dominant interpretation of Mill's thought we then follow: an act's *directly* or *chiefly* affecting others rather than only myself, or its affecting others' *interests* rather than merely affecting them in some way or other, or its affecting others via the violation of some *distinct obligation*, for example.

---

[1] Stephen says that 'the attempt to distinguish between self-regarding acts and acts which regard others, is like an attempt to distinguish between acts which happen in time and acts which happen in space . . . every act that we do either does or may affect both ourselves and others . . . the distinction is altogether fallacious and unfounded' (Stephen 1874: x).

Consider an example of such an interpretation. It is sometimes stipu-
lated that self-regarding acts are those which *directly affect only the interests
of the agent* and therefore fall into Mill's protected sphere, while other-
regarding acts are those whose direct effects spread beyond that and
which are therefore not entitled to the same protection from interference.
Call this view *the stipulation*. It has been adopted by Joel Feinberg (1986)
and H. H. Malm (1995). Feinberg argues that at least in some times
and places a line can be drawn 'between other-regarding behaviour and
conduct that is primarily and directly self-regarding and only indirectly
and remotely, *therefore trivially*, other-regarding' (Feinberg 1986: 22;
italics added). The standard example of someone whose behaviour is
self-regarding in this sense is the hardworking bachelor who gets drunk
every night (56). Malm echoes the distinction, suggesting that, although
self-regarding acts as defined can have a 'ripple' effect on others, this
contrasts with acts which affect the interests of others directly and in
the first instance (Malm 1995: 7 n. 11). She argues, moreover, that the
distinction is one of kind. 'It focuses on the way in which an agent's conduct affects others (i.e., indirect vs. direct effect) and not on the degree
of the effect' (25), adding: 'Consider a son's decision to pursue a career
in rock music. It doesn't change from self-regarding to other-regarding
as his mother's reaction changes from mild disapproval to utter outrage.
Similarly, a sock in the jaw is not more other-regarding than a poke in
the shoulder' (25 n. 34).

There is a problem with the stipulation. Even if the most obvious and
direct effects of my action are on myself and my own interests, the most
severe or the most important may be on others (and this may not be
immediately apparent at all). An act can fall within the self-regarding
sphere in the defined sense and yet be far from only *trivially* other-
regarding. If that is so, the stipulation remains problematic because
it remains open to question whether such acts, though directly self-
regarding, are *eo ipso* exempt from legitimate interference.

Malm's example can be used to illustrate the point. Suppose the son's
decision produces not just outrage in the mother but the onset of a stroke
and then death. The reaction is produced along the same route and so
presumably the action remains a self-regarding one according to the
stipulation; but it becomes at least contentious to hold that from a moral
point of view no restraint on it would be justified. Now this possibility may
suggest that the distinction is not one of kind after all, and that a sufficient
degree of severity of effect can convert an act from self-regarding to other-
regarding. That appears to be Feinberg's view. He argues that in normal

times an individual's decision to withdraw from a town's garrison would be self-regarding, but if the individual is John Wayne and his withdrawal from the defence of the town will have a massive impact on others then '[t]here is no distinction in these circumstances between self-regarding and other-regarding, or between not helping and positively harming' (Feinberg 1986: 23). He allows, further, that a real society can approach the garrison model, and notes the important possibility that individual acts of withdrawal may seem to be self-regarding, but if carried out on a sufficiently massive scale they cease to be.

These concessions seem to me to express an appropriate recognition of the moral complexity of self-regarding actions but also to signify an abandonment of the claim in the original stipulation that self-regarding actions, as defined there, belong to a protected sphere. It is now plain that allocation of an act to a protected sphere will depend on further knowledge of the circumstances of the act, including knowledge about what other agents are doing. It will not be possible to pronounce on the question of the legitimacy or otherwise of interference *in advance* of acquiring such information, and so it will not be possible to pronounce on that question merely by looking at the direct and obvious effects of an action. It may be plain that an action is self-regarding in the sense that its direct and obvious effects are on the agent, but not plain that it has no more important effects on others, and therefore not plain that it should be protected from interference.

Of course we can pronounce on the question of interference once such further information is available. Lines of causation are complex and often indirect. They may run through the mediation of other agents' decisions and actions, and that may well make a difference to whether we regard the act in question as one which can be legitimately interfered with or not. If I am correct in surmising that that is the logic of the Feinberg/Malm position then it ends up where I believe it should. Feinberg asks rhetorically: 'What plausible alternative is there to using the distinction between self- and other-regarding decisions, such as it is, as a guide to mapping the boundaries of personal autonomy?' (Feinberg 1986: 57) The implicit answer which he provides himself is that there is the alternative of considering the whole complex of causal circumstances in which an act occurs. When that consideration has taken place and we have come to the conclusion that a given act should be exempt from outside interference, we may if we wish designate the act 'self-regarding'. But we cannot claim that any property designated in advance in that way is itself what justifies the conclusion about lack of interference.

We cannot assign acts to a self-regarding sphere merely by attending to their direct and obvious effects.

There is a familiar argument due to C. L. Ten (1980) according to which it is not necessary for Mill to claim that there is a self-regarding *sphere* of action; only that a certain kind of *reason* cannot be accepted for interference. Thus, even if all actions affect others beyond their merely finding them immoral or disliking them, the essential point is that interference must be justified by some other reason than mere dislike or disapproval. 'What is crucial for Mill's defence of liberty is therefore his belief that certain reasons for intervention – paternalistic, moralistic, and gut reactions – are irrelevant, whereas the prevention of harm to others is always relevant' (Ten 1980: 41).[2]

But there is something strange about this argument. Does anyone really believe that their disapproval literally gives a reason for intervention? Suppose I say

(1) 'A's performance of x should be prevented because I think it is wrong.'

Does this really mean

(2) 'My thinking that A's performance of x is wrong provides a reason for preventing A from performing x'?

Surely it is more plausibly interpreted as meaning

(3) 'A's performance of x should be prevented because it is wrong (in my judgement)'?

Compare the case where I say

(4) 'A's performance of x should be prevented because I think it causes harm.'

My thinking that it causes harm provides no more of a reason for prevention than in the first case. We should construe this claim too, therefore, not as the claim

(5) 'My thinking that A's performance of x causes harm provides a reason for preventing A from performing x'

but rather as the claim

(6) 'A's performance of x should be prevented because it causes harm (in my judgement).'

---

[2] For a recent re-statement of the argument see Gaus 1996: 172.

In both cases, symmetrically, the judgement does not give a reason, but it may be used as a clue to a state of affairs which might itself give a reason. Of course, it will be a matter for further argument whether x's being wrong does provide a reason for preventing A from performing it,[3] but that position looks a good deal less hopeless than the claim that someone's merely *thinking* that x is wrong provides such a reason.

To this it might be replied that people really do believe that disapproval can give a reason for intervention, and that this is most plainly seen where the disapproval is shared by a number of them: there is certainly a history of appeals to the outraging of public morals as grounds for intervention. But this reply is not wholly convincing. These appeals might best be understood not as implying that the mere disapproval is a ground for intervention but rather that widespread disapproval may be used as a criterion for whether there actually is something wrong about an action; and, as we have allowed, the wrongness of an action is not such a hopeless ground on which to argue for intervention. (I do not say that, understood in this way, such appeals are sound, only that they do not then rest on the hopeless case that they seem to.) Alternatively, it may be that we should construe the reference to outraging in a consequentialist way, so that the grounds for intervention are not the mere disapproval but the effects associated with the production of disapproval. (Once again, that does not make the appeals persuasive, but it does take them on to a different terrain.)

But suppose we allow that the reply is convincing. We have still then arrived at an important point. We cannot isolate particular *types* of act where impact on others is not possible. There are no forms of behaviour such that the only reason ever available for justifying intervention is the dislike or disapproval of others. It then follows that we cannot designate, say, sexual behaviour or the choice of a career in rock music as forms of behaviour where protection from interference is secured on the basis that the only reason available for interference would be an appeal to the dislike or disapproval of others. (Whether it can be secured on some other basis is a separate matter.) This difficulty does not itself cast doubt on the intuitive idea, the ideal of as many individuals as possible pursuing their good by carrying out their plans, but it does suggest that the idea must be developed with some care. Individuals pursue their plans in a world where there is the permanent possibility of their impacting on the plans of *other* individuals and *their* plans. We therefore have to qualify the intuitive

---

[3] As I indicated in chapter 1, section 2, the question of whether someone is acting for bad reasons is separate from the question of whether any steps to prevent them from acting in that way are justified.

idea with a convincing account of the grounds on which some individuals' plans are entitled to take priority over others' in circumstances where different individuals' plans clash.

2.2 INDIVIDUALS AND CAUSAL PRECONDITION

The difficulties noticed so far in the self/other-regarding distinction rest on interpreting the truism that everything a person does carries causal implications for the lives of other human beings as saying that any act is liable to have causal *consequences* for others besides the agent. On this interpretation (*the simple interpretation*) Mill's critics argue that even when an act appears to have consequences only for the agent, it is liable to have an impact on others: it may set a bad example, it may be difficult to conceal the fact of the act from others, and so on. But even these critics will standardly allow that although all actions are *liable* to affect others, many actions as a matter of fact have only trivial implications for anyone other than the agent, or even no implications at all. Hence we have familiar examples of agents deciding whether to start shaving on the left or the right in a well-lit room before a mirror that reflects the face with uniform clarity (Rees 1960: 188 n. 8), painting their kitchen a particular colour, choosing to lie a particular way up in bed (Barry 1986: 15), or doing a spot of yoga before retiring (Sen 1970: 79). In normal circumstances such actions have no significant effects on others. Hence it may be thought that we can isolate a category of acts in the spirit of Mill's original apparent position: they are self-regarding in the sense of having no effects on others *to all intents and purposes*. It may, further, be thought appropriate to conclude on those grounds that it is of no concern to others whether or not I perform them, in that sense of 'concerns' distinguished in section 1 in which it means 'is the subject of justified control by'.

However, there are alternative interpretations of the truism about causal implication which have, so to speak, a wider reach. For example, it might be argued (though I do not argue this myself) that since every act is also an omission, my act of doing a spot of yoga is also the omission to help the starving or to foster political consciousness, or that my sitting in a room and scratching my head is *eo ipso* taking up a space which someone else might have used for some purpose. Hence, it might be concluded, even in the case of the standard trivial acts what I am doing may have substantial consequences for others' lives and therefore the possibility that it should be subject to collective control cannot be excluded.

The interpretation of the truism about causal implication that I wish to pursue (*the complex interpretation*) differs both from the simple and from this alternative interpretation. It reminds us that there are both causal consequences and causal *preconditions* of human action. The significance of this lies in the fact that any human action has causal preconditions which carry implications for the life of some other human being(s) than just the agent. This is so both for *a priori* and for contingent reasons. It is, I take it, true *a priori* that a human being must have parents. If so, then my or any other human agent's doing anything will have causal preconditions in the shape of certain actions on the part of our parents.[4] That is less interesting for my purposes than the contingent truth supporting the same claim.

Take, for example, the act of shaving in a well-lit room. Now of course it is true that in the normal course there is no significance for the lives of others in the choice of *one or the other way* of performing actions of this kind. It would take the ingenuity of philosophers to think up circumstances where that would be otherwise. Nor does the act itself (however I choose to perform it) standardly make any *subsequent* difference to anyone else's life. Nevertheless, for contingent reasons, my performing even such an insignificant action does have implications for others' lives. Indeed, it has major implications for what others are able to do.

Think of the description of the action, with its reference to a room, lighting, a razor. The existence and availability of these objects is a precondition of my performing it, and it is a contingent truth that no individual human being could provide all of them for themself. The mining of minerals, the production of chemicals, the manufacture, transportation and sale of articles all require a massive cooperative effort on the part of at least tens of thousands of other people.

The point is made nowhere more eloquently or more forcefully than by Adam Smith when he discusses the division of labour.

The woollen coat, for example, which covers the day-labourer, as coarse and rough as it may appear, is the produce of the joint labour of a great multitude of workmen. The shepherd, the sorter of the wool, the wool-comber or carder,

---

[4] But what of the first truly human being, whose parents were merely humanoid? That being's actions will have causal preconditions, including actions performed by other beings, but no preconditions involving actions performed by other *human beings*. The shortest way with this objection is to allow that it provides a highly marginal, if not unique, exception to the truism about causal interconnection on the complex interpretation which I sponsor. It will be sufficient if my claims hold in all other cases. For a different kind of significance attaching to the prior actions of parents, see Charles Taylor's claims about the fundamentally dialogical character of human life in Taylor 1992: 32–3.

the dyer, the scribbler, the spinner, the weaver, the fuller, the dresser, with many others, must all join their different arts in order to complete even this homely production. How many merchants and carriers, besides, must have been employed in transporting the materials from some of those workmen to others who often live in a very distant part of the country! How many merchants and carriers, besides, must [*sic*] how many ship-builders, sailors, sail-makers, rope-makers, must have been employed in order to bring together the different drugs made use of by the dyer, which often come from the remotest corners of the world! What a variety of labour, too, is necessary in order to produce the tools of the meanest of those workmen! to say nothing of such complicated machines as the ship of the sailor, the mill of the fuller, or even the loom of the weaver . . . without the assistance and co-operation of many thousands, the very meanest person in a civilized country could not be provided, even according to what we very falsely imagine the easy and simple manner in which he is commonly accommodated. (Smith 1776: 116–17)

Locke makes a similar point in the *Second Treatise*:

For 'tis not barely the Plough-man's Pains, the Reaper's and Thresher's Toil, and the Bakers [*sic*] Sweat, is to be counted into the *Bread* we eat; the Labour of those who broke the Oxen, who digged and wrought the Iron and Stones, who felled and framed the Timber imployed [*sic*] about the Plough, Mill, Oven, or any other Utensil, which are a vast Number, requisite to this Corn, from its being seed to be sown to its being made Bread, must all be *charged on* the account of *Labour*, and received as an effect of that . . . 'Twould be a strange *Catalogue of things, that Industry provided and made use of, about every Loaf of Bread*, before it came to our use, if we could trace them; Iron, Wood, Leather, Bark, Timber, Stone Bricks, Coals, Lime, Cloth, Dying Drugs, Pitch, Tar, Masts, Ropes, and all the Materials made use of in the Ship, that brought any of the Commodities made use of by any of the Workmen, to any part of the Work . . . (Locke 1690: para. 43)

Moreover, the essential point, that the performance of any action has multiple causal preconditions, is not confined to actions using material *objects*. To be at the point of human agency at all presupposes, as a matter of contingent fact, an earlier provision of the material sustenance and nurturing which brings someone to that point. Even the standard examples of trivially self-regarding actions involve causal interconnection in that form. It arises just as surely in the case of, say, scratching my nose, and even in the limiting case of bringing all one's future agency to an end by committing suicide without the benefit of external means (for example by sticking one's tongue down one's throat).

Anything which I do has causal implications for others' lives, because as a matter of fact the causal preconditions of my doing anything carry such implications. The claim is not that my act produces some kind of weird backward causation, as if my shaving somehow caused someone to have made mirrors, rooms, razors, and so on. Rather, it is true that I could not now act as I choose to if it were not for the fact that others' lives had earlier taken a particular course. As a matter of fact, my now acting in this way requires that they should have done so. My act timelessly has implications for others' lives, for causal reasons.

I now suggest that the fact of human interconnection under the simple *and* the complex interpretations should be taken into account in practical reasoning and in such matters as the making judgements about the acceptability of actions, the limits to individual freedom and the area of justified collective intervention. The complex interpretation would not have the same relevance for judging *agents* as opposed to *acts*. For example, an agent does not have the same knowledge of and control over preconditions as they do over consequences, and this would affect judgements of responsibility. But judgements about actions and judgements about agents are clearly distinct. (At the limit, we are justified in intervening in certain forms of behaviour, say extreme aggression, whether or not the agents are responsible for them.) When it comes to judgements about actions, I suggest that it is morally arbitrary to give weight to the subsequent impact which an act has on others' lives and yet to ignore the facts about other people's lives which figure among the causal preconditions of the act.

Suppose that I am contemplating killing you and I am trying to decide whether to administer arsenic or strychnine. Suppose, further, that the administration of either will involve inflicting the same degree of pain on you and will result in your death in an equal amount of time. Then there is no *extra* moral significance in my choice of one or the other of these two actions. But there is much to be said against *either* of them because of quite separate considerations about their significance. So it is, I suggest, with standard trivial choices of the kind described earlier. That there is no significant difference between two possible courses of action does not establish that there is no significance to either of them for other reasons. In the arsenic/strychnine case the reasons come in the form of consequences; in the trivial cases, I am suggesting, they may come in the form of the significance of preconditions.

Many obvious objections can be raised against this suggestion. I address perhaps the most obvious one now. It might be objected that a consideration of causal preconditions of actions cannot possibly have any importance for practical reasoning or the moral and political questions

which Mill and his successors have been concerned with, precisely because preconditions lie in the *past* and cannot be altered. Indeed, many
preconditions may lie in the distant past and for that reason it may be
entirely indeterminate *whose* lives had to take a particular shape if I am
now to be able to act as I wish.[5] Hence, it might be concluded, the fact
of causal interconnection under the complex interpretation is of no consequence for a theory of practical reasoning or for a theory dealing with
the legitimate extent of personal freedom.

There are three points to be made in response to this objection.
First, although practical reasoning is future-directed, and although much
specifically moral judgement is driven by an interest in the future and an
interest in influencing the shape which that future takes, it is an exaggeration to suppose that what is past cannot play a role in that connection.
Moral thought, for example, has a multiplicity of functions besides that
of guiding future conduct, and one of them is that of expressing views
about and making moral evaluations of what has already occurred. Even
if it is true, therefore, that causal preconditions lie entirely in the past and
cannot be altered, this would not render them irrelevant from a moral
point of view. Not only that, but since moral considerations provide part
of the input for practical reasoning, the character of past actions and
events may have a bearing on whether I wish to become part of a causal
chain containing them. I may, for example, choose not to become the
beneficiary of other people's earlier misery.

Secondly, the indeterminacy of the identity of any people implicated in
the causal preconditions of a given act is not a good reason for withholding practical or moral significance from those preconditions either. It is
standardly the case with the act of leaving a bomb in a public place, or
planting a land mine, that the identity of people standing in a subsequent
causal relation to the act may be unknown. It is implausible to suppose
that moral assessment of the act is somehow inappropriate unless or until their identity becomes clear. Onora O'Neill observes: 'Activity that is
predicated on assumptions about others who cannot be *individuated* by
the agent often proceeds on the basis of adequately accurate assumptions
about others who can be *specified*' (O'Neill 1996: 115). She is speaking in
connection with the problem of future generations, but the point applies
symmetrically to causal preconditions. I can know that my wearing this

---

5 Locke comments that "twould be almost impossible, at least too long to reckon up' all the
  contributory acts involved in the production of a loaf of bread (Locke 1690: para. 43). Mill
  observes that contingent injury to society from an act which occasions 'no perceptible hurt to
  any assignable individual' is an inconvenience that society ought to bear (Mill 1859: 138).

shirt required workers in a third world country to endure oppressive and demeaning conditions of labour even if I do not know which particular people this is true of.

Thirdly, in connection with questions of individual freedom and coercive interference we should note that what Mill and his successors are often concerned with is the matter of legislation. This necessarily deals not with historically unique, datable acts but rather with recurrent *types* of act, which an agent may at some point in the future conceive the intention of performing. Not only may such acts themselves lie in the future, but so also may their causal preconditions. In that case it is not now too late to affect what happens, to have an impact in relation to those putative future actions, and to do so specifically by affecting the realisation or otherwise of the preconditions for their performance. Even on the strictest view, therefore, of the connection between morality and action, there is no reason to exclude from consideration as a category the preconditions of action. In some cases at least there will be the most straightforward reason possible for attending to them, namely that the question whether to realise them or not remains open. And what goes for morality will also go for practical reasoning more generally.

However, this rejoinder may raise a further suspicion which needs to be dealt with. When the causal preconditions still lie in the future they can still be affected, and that is intelligible in the ordinary way as a case of forward-looking causal implication. Contrast that with a case where the causal preconditions lie in the past. Suppose I have a carrot in front of me which was produced by slave labour. Whether I eat it or let it rot, no non-trivial effects on others' lives follow from my choice. Why, then, suppose that there is anything other-regarding about my act? (We assume that my act will not encourage others to benefit from slave labour. If it will, that is again an ordinary case of forward-looking implication.) The suspicion which the example raises is that causal preconditions do not have any significance *as* causal preconditions. It is just that we care anyway about certain states which people may suffer from, or certain actions which they may be coerced into performing, and this is not by virtue of any particular connection with later acts of mine.

The reply to the suspicion is this. There is nothing incompatible between caring about the causal preconditions anyway and also caring about them as preconditions for a later act of mine. On the contrary, it may be because I find them repugnant anyway that I also find it repugnant that they should connect with my own life in a particular way. Suppose that appalling infliction of suffering was among the preconditions of the production of lamp-shades with human skin. It is intelligible that I should choose not to buy such an object because of what *had been* involved in its production, even though those who suffered are now dead. It is equally intelligible that the trading of such objects should be banned, and in this way preconditions may become relevant to the issue of collective intervention. That the people were treated brutally is one objectionable thing; it is inflicting a further indignity on them that they should be part of a causal chain involving this kind of exploitation. What we have here is not a case of backward causation but a case where the significance of a past event changes by virtue of its place in a subsequent causal chain.

It might now be objected that this too is really just a straightforward case of ordinary forward-looking implication, on the grounds that my concern is in fact with the effect of past events on me in the present. This objection is erroneous, however, and it would involve an error analogous to that of claiming that Jim puts his own integrity into the scales in a utilitarian calculation, in Bernard Williams's example of Jim and the Indians.[6] In both examples the point is that a new category is being proposed for dealing with the circumstances involved. In Williams's example, it is being proposed that we view an agent's relation to their projects in a quite different way from that involved in utilitarian calculation. The analogous proposal in the present example is this. We are accustomed to distinguishing between *consequentialist* grounds for and against a putative action, which relate to the causal question of the effects which follow from its performance; and *deontological* grounds, which relate to the intrinsic nature of the action and have no connection with questions of causation.[7] What is being proposed is that we recognise a hybrid category of grounds: they are not consequentialist, since they do not relate to the effects which would follow from the action; but nor are they in the defined sense deontological, since they do indeed relate to questions of causation rather than to the intrinsic nature of the action. It is just that what they relate to is the role which the action would itself play

---

[6] In Williams's well-known example, the captor of twenty Indians puts Jim in the position of having to make a grisly choice between killing one of them himself, in which case the rest will be freed, or not killing one, in which case all will be killed by the captor (Smart and Williams 1973: 98–100).

[7] Cf. C. D. Broad's division of ethical theories into deontological ones which 'hold that there are ethical propositions of the form: "Such and such a kind of action would always be right (or wrong) in such and such circumstances, no matter what its consequences might be"' and teleological ones which 'hold that the rightness or wrongness of an action is always determined by its tendency to produce certain consequences . . .' (Broad 1930: 206–7). For a recent affirmation of the distinction see Blackburn 1996: 100.

as a causal consequence, rather than the consequences which it would itself generate.

I conclude that causal preconditions can have independent significance in judging the rightness or wrongness of an action or the morality of collective intervention, and that therefore the complex interpretation of causal interaction is appropriate in deciding such matters. It is common ground among commentators attempting to reformulate Mill's self/other-regarding distinction that any such reformulation must respect the fact that no action stands entirely outside causal chains, so that the self-regarding sphere must be redefined as the sphere where, notwithstanding the causal nexus in which an action stands, the action is entitled to protection from interference. Such commentators should take into account causal interconnection in the complex interpretation (as they standardly do not), and this interpretation calls attention to a whole dimension of the causal nexus whose significance may easily be missed. As a result, the range of actions generally thought to fall within or outside the protected sphere is liable to change markedly. I do not attempt to answer the practical question of what particular actions would change their status in this way once causal preconditions are taken into account, any more than I have attempted to determine which actions fall where in the light of their causal consequences. The point has been rather to establish the principle that a certain kind of consideration should figure in those practical calculations. (Notice also that the introduction of causal precondition as a relevant consideration stands independently of further contested questions about how to delineate the protected sphere. For example, there is the line of interpretation of Mill according to which what matters is not whether someone is affected by my action but whether their *interests* are affected (cf. Rees 1960). But there is every reason to think that causal preconditions will carry implications for others' interests as well as carrying implications for their states more generally.)

2.3 INDIVIDUALS AND NOSY PREFERENCES

Individuals pursue their own plans, but in circumstances where their doing so is inherently likely to impact on the plans of other individuals. Sometimes such impact will be adverse and unwelcome and unacceptable. Moreover, we know that we can expect no general agreement on which occasions do constitute adverse effects, which occasions do involve unacceptable impact on others, in the circumstances of *de facto* pluralism described in chapter 1, section 1. These will be hotly contested matters. This state of affairs produces dilemmas for agents trying to decide how to act and also for those whose lives will be impacted on by their decisions and who might, for that reason, wish to exercise constraint over those agents.

There is one deceptively and seductively *simple solution* to the dilemmas which arise in these circumstances, especially if we are attached to the intuitive idea of as many people as possible carrying out their plans. Why not give everyone an equal chance to express their preferences, aggregate the result and allow the result to determine what actually happens thereafter? This simple solution, however, is open to an equally *simple objection*. It is complained that moralities based on such a strategy 'are continually embarrassed by the fact that some preferences are so awfully perverse as to forfeit any right to our respect' (Goodin 1986: 75). The problem is that '[m]any people's . . . preference satisfaction, for example, [is] based on racist, sexist, envious, meddlesome, or malicious attitudes' (Vallentyne 1991: 295).

At this point the proponent of the simple solution might respond that such an objection can be made only by departing from neutrality on contested matters of the kind described in chapter 1, section 1: such matters as whether eating meat or aborting foetuses are unacceptable. Pronouncing on which preferences are objectionable, and deciding which are to be stigmatised in that way, will inevitably lead us into contention. In contrast, the proponent might claim, it is a virtue of the simple solution that it is neutral in its operation, it does not favour any particular preferences. If untoward results follow from its operation, they might argue, then the blame for this must lie with the preferences which are fed into the process rather than with the process itself.[8]

Now the strategy of taking preferences as given and aggregating them so as to maximise their satisfaction is, it is true, neutral with regard to the content of any particular preference; but the neutrality of this strategy is something less than thoroughgoing. The very idea that operating this strategy is valuable (or at the least that it is not unacceptable) is itself a contentious matter. It also needs to be made clear what is to count as a preference in this context. Does the mere opting for something count, or must there be some evidence of prior reflection? Connected to that, it is an important fact that we are creatures with meta-preferences as

---

[8] There is a connection here with economic theories of consumer demand which take consumers' wants as data and seek to maximise their satisfaction without attempting to reform them or indeed to pass any judgement on them. See Sandel 1996: 267–9.

well as preferences – we may prefer that we did not have a particular preference (I may want to smoke, but also want not to want to smoke). That will raise the issue of *which* preferences should be fed into any aggregation process. Given these complications, the point is well taken that 'to assign impersonal value to the satisfaction of all preferences is to accept a particular view of the good – a component of one form of utilitarianism – which many would find clearly unacceptable' (Nagel 1987: 227).[9]

Moreover, the simple objection to the simple solution can avoid at least the most obvious version of the counter-criticism that it involves a departure from neutrality over particular preferences. Some preferences can be stigmatised not by virtue of their content but by virtue of their form. There is a distinction between *preferences for oneself* and *preferences for other people*, and it can be argued that the latter, whatever their content, are *nosy* and do not carry the same entitlement to satisfaction as the former. Thus there is a crucial distinction between having a preference about what I should get and having a nosy preference about what Blacks should get; or between preferring subsidised opera because I want it and preferring it because I think other people should want it. But, so far as the content of these preferences is concerned, anyone can substitute anything they like by way of example here.

There is a widely shared view that it is inappropriate for such nosy preferences to have the same kind of influence as personal preferences. Kenneth Arrow, an early exponent of the view, is representative: 'Intuitively, of course, we feel that not all the possible preferences which an individual might have ought to count; his preferences for matters which are "none of his business" should be irrelevant. Without challenging this view . . .' (Arrow 1963: 18).[10] If the view is endorsed, then further questions may arise. Does the existence of nosy preferences constitute a particular problem for liberalism? Does their objectionable nature proceed entirely from the attitudes they evince? Are they always to be disregarded, or are there circumstances in which they may be allowed to carry weight?[11]

---

[9] For discussion of the problematic neutrality of unqualified preference-aggregation, see Sandel 1996: 49–53. For discussion of the complications arising from the existence of meta-preferences see Brennan and Lomasky 1993: ch. 9, and Goodin 1986.

[10] Sen suggests that figures as diverse as Mill, Hayek and Gramsci are united in subscribing to the idea of a protected sphere associated with the exclusion of nosy preferences (Sen 1976: 217–18).

[11] Opposing views on whether there is a threat to liberalism are returned by Sen 1970 and Barry 1986. Goodin 1986 argues that, regardless of outcome, counting nosy preferences is sanctioning lack of respect for people. Vallentyne 1991 agrees that nosy preferences incur stigma because

I touch on these questions in what follows, but my focus is rather different. It is fairly obvious that at least sometimes a nosy preference should not be allowed to determine what happens. But that will be true of *any* preference, simply because there will sometimes be countervailing preferences or countervailing considerations of some more general kind. Whether we wish to exclude nosy preferences altogether, or only in certain circumstances, or only to give them a lesser weight, we have to say *why* that should happen. I shall attempt to show that the account of why nosy preferences merit special treatment raises the question of whether they are really so special after all and whether we can assume without further ado that there is a clear category of non-nosy preferences.

I do so by examining some arguments put forward on the issue by Brian Barry and Ronald Dworkin. My strategy is to take the complex interpretation of causal interconnection outlined in section 2 and extend it from actions to preferences. Just as shaving before the mirror is doing something in which others' lives are causally implicated, so to *prefer* a razor, a room and good lighting and electricity, even if you want them only for yourself, is to *prefer* a state of affairs whose existence carries causal implications for a lot more people than just yourself. *What we aspire to* has an interpersonal aspect, just as *what we do* has. To conceive certain ends and to want to be able to pursue them is as a matter of fact to want the world, including other human agents, to be of a particular character; and that cannot possibly be a self-regarding aspiration in the original, rejected Millian sense that its realisation would not carry causal implications for others.

Barry's discussion occurs in the context of theories of voting. Two distinct questions can be raised in that connection. First, when people vote, are they expressing an *internal* or an *external* preference? That is, are they expressing a preference for something for themselves or for other people? This is a conceptual question, about the construction to be placed on voting in order to make best sense of it. That question may be followed by a second, normative question: under which of these constructions would it be defensible to aggregate votes and bring states of affairs into existence on the basis of what the majority has voted for?

Barry's answer to the normative question is that action on the basis of vote-aggregation is defensible only when votes are construed as expressions of internal wants (Barry 1986 and Barry 1990). In voting,

of their derivation from suspect attitudes, but suggests that we should adopt an intermediate position between disregarding them altogether and according them full weight.

people may express *privately oriented* evaluations, which Barry defines as 'evaluations with oneself or one's family as their object', or *publicly oriented* ones, defined as 'evaluations with everyone or some large group such as a country as their object' (Barry 1990: 12–13). He adds:

By 'privately-oriented' I mean having oneself (or at most one's family) as the reference group; or, more precisely, affecting oneself or one's family. When I speak of 'being affected' here I mean having one's life materially impinged upon by some change in opportunities or routine. I do not mean being made to feel, as in the phrase 'an affecting sight'. (63)

These distinctions can now be applied to voting issues in the following way. If we wish to pursue a policy of aggregating votes so as to maximise want-satisfaction, we immediately run into the problem of nosy preferences. It's all very well where people express what they want for themselves; but Barry suggests it would surely not be legitimate to add into the aggregate in the same way wishes that they have concerning other people.

Suppose that I am making up my mind whether it is fair for the *A*'s to get more of something than the *B*'s; and the *A*'s and the *B*'s are the only people directly affected by the division, in the sense of 'affected' which I have defined. Should I, in making up my mind, take account of the opinions of the *C*'s in the matter? I may, of course, let them weigh with me as having a certain authority, but surely it would be ridiculous to mix in the wants of the *C*'s for, say, the *A*'s to win, consequential on their belief that the *A*'s have the best case, on an equal footing with the privately-oriented wants of the *A*'s and the *B*'s. (Barry 1990: 63–4)

In the same way, 'Jones' want for some future state of Jones might well be thought to be worthy of a quite different sort of consideration from Jones' want for some future state of Brown' (72).

For Barry, this carries an implication concerning the acceptance of majority decisions. Counting only privately oriented wants avoids 'the most objectionable feature of the majoritarian principle, namely the way in which it commits one to handing over questions of right and wrong, justice and injustice, to the majority of a group in which one's own voice counts only as one' (Barry 1990: 63). At the same time it 'leaves one free to take account of desires which are put forward simply by people as wants in matters affecting themselves' (63).[12] 'Unlike a privately-oriented

---

[12] Barry argues further that confusion is liable to occur in computing the result of a vote where some people vote in a privately oriented way and others in a publicly oriented way (63). That argument can be questioned, however. See Graham 1996b: 184–90.

want, which carries a certain automatic claim to satisfaction with it, a publicly-oriented want carries a claim to satisfaction only as being a want for what ought to be done anyway' (65).

It is clearly essential to Barry's strategy in answering the normative question that there should be an unproblematic distinction between public and private orientation. Elsewhere he associates himself with the idea that 'when it comes to (say) what they read, people should have the power to take their own decisions because this is "self-regarding" or should be within the "protected sphere"' (Barry 1986: 14). He similarly quotes and endorses a remark of Sen's: 'There are certain personal matters in which a person should be free to decide what should happen . . . ' (33; cf. Sen 1976: 217).

But this strategy involves an unacceptable telescoping of the normative and conceptual questions which I distinguished earlier. It is no doubt true that there are matters in which a person should be free to decide what should happen, and it may be true specifically that people should be free to decide what they read. But, for reasons familiar from the previous section, I should argue that the reason cannot be that this particular activity or anything else concerns only oneself (except in the tautological sense of 'concerns' distinguished in section 1, in which it simply means 'is the subject of justified control by'). To decide to read a book is, as a matter of fact, to decide to act in a way which has as preconditions the activities of many other agents, including the author, publishers, manufacturers and transporters of the book in question. They are, from a timeless point of view, causally implicated in that decision. It is then always possible in principle to ask of such causally implicated agents, first, whether they would have any objection to the decision in question and, secondly, whether their objection would be something it was proper to take into account. There will be many situations where the answer to one or both questions will be no, but no situations in which such questions do not arise, no category of wants which preclude the questions. There is no domain of wants where the complication of possible counter-wants from causally implicated others is simply absent.

There is a very obvious rejoinder to my claims here. This is to argue that the other-regardingness in the book-reading example is of a quite different order from that involved in nosy preferences. After all, in this example it is mere *chance* that my aspirations are for states of affairs in which other people's lives are causally implicated, and this is quite different from cases where it precisely *is* my aspiration that others' lives should be affected. These latter cases, it may be urged, are the ones which involve really nosy preferences, since it is the *intention* of those who express them that others' lives be altered in certain ways. More briefly and more uncompromisingly, it may be said that aspirations, preferences and wants are referentially opaque, and that it is only by ignoring that fact that I can make the claims that I did in the preceding paragraph. If we bear it clearly in mind, we can distinguish between a particular kind of preference that should be excluded from any aggregation of preferences for the purposes of action, and a kind of preference which is by its nature harmless to others.

How far can my point be met by calling attention to the distinction between, as it were, accidentally and intentionally other-affecting judgements? I suggest that this distinction cannot bear the weight which it needs to carry in giving an answer to the normative question whether to allow certain kinds of votes into the aggregation, whether to allow them an influence over what happens. Even if we concede the technical claim that a preference is referentially opaque, so that in that way it can be insulated from effects on others, still there will be no such insulation in the case of *acting* on the preference. Accordingly, my central contention can be re-expressed in a way which is unaffected by the fact of referential opacity. Instead of saying that any given preference intended solely for oneself is, as a matter of fact, a preference in which others are causally implicated, I can say simply that *acting* on any given preference has causal implications for the lives of others.

Essentially, my claim is for the necessary relevance of *consequences and preconditions* to the normative question about aggregating votes, a subject on which the identification of referentially opaque preferences remains silent. Acting on intentionally other-affecting preferences will carry implications for others' lives, but so will acting on *any* preferences, including intentionally self-affecting ones. Undesirable effects may follow whether these are intended by the voter or not, and there is a case for saying that it is what does actually come out of the voting aggregation that is or is not acceptable.[13]

---

[13] No more than a case. Goodin argues that nosy preferences should not even figure as part of the *input* to the aggregation, separately from any question of how they might affect the output, on the grounds that even to count them is to allow the expression of a lack of respect for people, regardless of whether those preferences are acted upon (Goodin 1986: 79–80). The problem then, however, is to give an explanation of why evincing lack of respect in a nosy preference should have such drastic penalties for the person expressing the preference. What cannot be said is that they are unacceptably nosy by virtue of carrying implications for others' lives, for that will not be a distinguishing characteristic. Nor will it do to say that the implications are morally unacceptable. That may be true, but we are seeking an explanation of *why* it is true.

Similar conceptual distinctions to Barry's, and indeed similar arguments in their favour, are to be found in Ronald Dworkin's writings in terms of the contrast between *personal* preferences and *external* (or *political*) ones.[14] A *personal* preference is a preference for one's 'own enjoyment of some goods or opportunities'; an *external* preference is a 'preference for the assignment of goods and opportunities to others', a preference 'about how the goods, resources and opportunities of the community should be distributed to others' (Dworkin 1978: 234; Dworkin 1981: 192).

Dworkin then argues on egalitarian grounds that external preferences have no legitimate claim on our attentions in distributional matters. If someone's preferences (call her Sarah) were to count twice over, egalitarianism would be breached; and according to Dworkin the same kind of breach occurs if we take into account the consideration that some other people also prefer that Sarah's preferences count twice. That would simply be self-undermining for an egalitarian theory (Dworkin 1986: 361). The same goes for less fanciful and more malignant types of external preference. If a Nazi prefers that Aryans should get more of their preferences met and Jews fewer, just because of who they are, we cannot be neutral over that preference and egalitarianism requires that we reject it (362–3). Hence Dworkin concludes that if, for example, utilitarianism is to figure as part of an attractive working political theory it must abide by egalitarian requirements, and that means it must be 'qualified so as to restrict the preferences that count by excluding political preferences of both the formal and informal sort' (363–4). Dworkin is no utilitarian, but he *is* an egalitarian, he does endorse the egalitarian aspect of the utilitarian position and he does believe that external preferences are to be ignored.[15]

---

[14] In Dworkin 1978, Dworkin 1981, Dworkin 1986 and Dworkin 1990b. He uses the term *external* in Dworkin 1978 and the term *political* in Dworkin 1981 and Dworkin 1986. The definitions of external and political preferences are so similar, however, that I take it the difference is *merely* one of nomenclature: political and external preferences are the same thing. In what follows I normally use the term 'external'.

[15] Dworkin postulates the distinction between personal and external preferences in contexts where he is concerned to refute particular doctrines (utilitarianism and equality of welfare). It is clear from those contexts, however, that he does adopt this distinction *in propria persona* and not merely as part of an *ad hominem* argument. Barry comments: 'As far as I am aware, his [Dworkin's] only contribution to the assessment of public policies (say, protection of the environment) where individual rights are not at issue remains the proposal that the criterion should be a utilitarian one, with preferences "laundered" to eliminate from the calculus so-called "external" or "moralistic" preferences' (Barry 1995: 143–4). Note also Dworkin's comment concerning government intervention, that 'normally it is a sufficient justification, even for an act that limits liberty, that the act is calculated to increase what the philosophers call general utility – that it is calculated to produce more over-all benefit than harm' (Dworkin 1978: 191).

There is one initially puzzling aspect to Dworkin's theory. He introduces 'the associational preference of a white law student for white classmates' as an example of a *personal* preference, but then says that although this is a personal preference it is parasitic on external preferences, because usually someone holds it because 'he has racist social and political convictions, or because he has contempt for blacks as a group' (Dworkin 1978: 236). He also says that someone might have a *personal* preference for the consequences of segregation because it increases their own chance of success, or an *external* preference out of contempt for blacks (234). The reason why these remarks are initially puzzling is that association and segregation are relational. A preference for associating with or being segregated from certain other people is necessarily a preference about how things should be for others as well as oneself. It therefore seems surprising that Dworkin should countenance the possibility that they should qualify as personal preferences.

The explanation for this is that the focus in Dworkin's argument shifts (somewhat as it does in Barry's argument), and it seems that whether a preference is personal or not depends on the attitudes and reasons behind the holding of it rather than on its content. Moreover, it might be claimed that Dworkin's emphasis on attitudes and reasons is appropriate, since his concern is with something narrower and more specific than the impact of external preferences, namely the illegitimate impact on someone's life of the moral attitude that others take towards it. He is concerned that one's way of life should not depend on the respect or affection that others have for it (Dworkin 1978: 235), that no one should 'suffer disadvantage in the distribution of social goods and opportunities . . . just on the ground that their officials or fellow-citizens think that their opinions about the right way for them to lead their own lives are ignoble or wrong' (Dworkin 1986: 353). His target is really 'moral preferences about how others should behave' (364; cf. 367).

What is wrong with including moral preferences in aggregations of preferences made with a view to distributing some good? The standard liberal protection of certain actions from moral interference has to meet the *prima facie* objection that there is nothing wrong with moral interference in people's lives – interference on the grounds of the wrongness or ignobility of their behaviour – if that behaviour consists, for example, in murdering and maiming others. Hence the traditional attempt to isolate *merely moralistic* (and therefore unjustified) interference from genuinely moral (and therefore justified) interference. Presumably the idea is that moralistic interference is based solely on responses of approval or disapproval which have no acceptable grounding, whereas genuinely moral interference is based on acceptable substantive reasons. It is then important that any characterisation of moralistic preferences will be subject to the following, reasonable, 'like cases' principle: *if the objectionable characteristic of moralistic preferences is present in other, non-moralistic preferences, the presence of that characteristic gives the same (not necessarily non-defeasible) grounds for discounting the non-moralistic preferences as it does for discounting the moralistic preferences.*

The structure of Dworkin's argument is something like this. He wishes to claim that it is wrong to include moralistic preferences in aggregations, and moralistic preferences are identified by reference to the attitudes of those who hold them and the reasons they have for holding them. He insists on 'the right to moral independence', the right not to suffer distributional disadvantage because of what others think of my way of life (Dworkin 1986: 353). Moralistic preferences are therefore one species of external preference. (They are only one species because I may hold an external preference but not for moralising reasons: I may prefer that someone else receive a particular distribution because I like them, or because I feel it is their turn, or simply on a whim.) As a separate matter from *identifying* the sort of preferences in question, Dworkin has to give *grounds* for holding that they should be discounted. This structure of argument is more or less unavoidable. Moralistic preferences having been identified as preferences, held with particular attitudes and reasons, for a distribution which concerns other people, the question must then be raised of what is wrong with counting such preferences. It would be profoundly unimpressive to answer that it would be wrong to count them because they were preferences, borne of a particular kind of attitude, affecting others' receipt of some good. That simply reiterates the claim. So, once the *claim* has been made that people have a right that moralistic preferences be discounted, the *grounds* must be given for asserting that right.

Dworkin avoids giving the answer which would simply reiterate the claim. But what is striking and interesting about his answer is that it is thoroughly consequentialist. It consists in an appeal to the consequences of acting on such preferences for people's self-development and for their prospects of fulfilling their own preferences. Dworkin is concerned with the 'degree to which each person's preferences about his own life and circumstances are *fulfilled*' (Dworkin 1981: 204; italics added) and with the undesirable possibility that people might '*lose control* of a crucial aspect of their own self-development' (Dworkin 1986, p. 365; italics added) if others' moralistic preferences are counted. Thus, for example, my preference that orphans be looked after especially well must be discounted because then they will *gain* at the expense of other disadvantaged groups (Dworkin 1981: 200).

At this point the 'like cases' principle can be invoked. The objectionable characteristic of moralistic preferences is that acting on them produces a loss of control over self-development in the lives of people other than those whose preferences they are. But that will also be a characteristic of entirely non-moralistic preferences. I may have a preference about my own enjoyment of some good or opportunity which I do not intend to have such undesirable consequences for others' lives, or indeed any consequences at all, and I may be unaware that it does. But the causal facts of the world may be such that that is true of it. For example, my preference to own a cheap computer may be such that acting on it causally implicates many other people in conditions of life and of employment which deprive them of a large measure of control over self-development.[16] Indeed, if my arguments earlier in this chapter are correct, then the implementation of *any* preference carries implications for the lives of others besides the person holding the preference, either for reasons of causal consequence or for reasons of causal precondition. In that case, we have not been given any grounds for excluding a particular set of preferences from any aggregation.

One further point should be made clear about Dworkin's discussion. It takes place largely in connection with distributional questions, and there is some evidence that when it comes to questions of voting he might wish to take a different line. He observes that an actual vote will represent an overall preference, and that it will be impossible to devise a procedure which accurately distinguishes between personal and external preferences at the level of practice (Dworkin 1978: 276). He further implies that it may be acceptable for people's votes to reflect their external preferences, when he says: 'They will vote their external preferences; they will vote for legislators, for example, who share their own theories of political justice. How else should they decide for whom to vote?' (358; cf. Dworkin 1986: 365–6). His only qualification is that legislators cannot then justify particular legislation by appeal to the number of external preferences in favour of it.

---

[16] As Mill notes, 'trade is a social act' (Mill 1859: 150). On the complex interpretation of causal interconnection which I have sponsored, the implications of that remark for the self/other-regarding distinction will reach further than he anticipated. The same can be said of his remark that 'unfair or ungenerous use of advantages' over other people takes my action out of the self-regarding class (135).

It is not clear what justification there could be for taking up this differential position, with regard to the acceptability of external preferences, as between electoral and general distributional issues. Voting is usually at least in part a matter of opting for an increased likelihood of a particular programme of legislation, and certainly in the situation envisaged by Dworkin that seems to be the basis on which a vote is cast for a particular legislator. But if the influence of external preferences is outlawed when making decisions of distribution, why should it not also be outlawed when put forward in a slightly more indirect way? Dworkin gives no reason why we should take a different line with regard to the two notionally different kinds of preference in these two different circumstances.

It does not follow from any of this that all preferences are nosy. Clearly they are not, if it is part of the definition of such preferences that they are necessarily accompanied by a belief on the part of the preference-holder that other people should live their life in a particular way. However, what I hope to have established is that all preferences, as a matter of fact, exhibit some of the characteristics in virtue of which nosy preferences are looked at askance. Principally, it is true of all preferences that acting upon them carries causal implications for the lives of others besides the preference-holder.

2.4 CONCLUSION

The arguments of this chapter are not intended to dislodge the intuitive idea that the best state of affairs is one where distinct people carry out their plans successfully; but they should lead us to conceive that idea differently from the way in which we standardly view it. They are also intended to raise questions about how best to interpret D2, the idea of the distinctness of persons construed as separateness. It is a truism that persons are not causally separate, in the sense that the action of any given person will carry causal implications for some other person(s). My carrying out my plans, whatever they are, will carry implications for other agents and their ability to carry out *their* plans. In that way, any state of affairs which represents a fulfilment of some interest of mine will impact on the interests of some other person. The separateness of persons cannot therefore be taken to lie in the separateness of their respective interests.

I have suggested we adopt the complex interpretation of the truism, according to which not just causal consequences but also causal preconditions of an action are taken into account in determining the implications for others that a given agent's action carries. When causal preconditions as well as consequences are taken into account, the extent to which persons' lives are not separate but interconnected is much greater; and we shall face a test of correspondingly greater stringency in attempting to delineate the area in which an individual should be protected from interference in the pursuit of their plans. It is already plain on *any* interpretation of the truism that few acts will be 'purely my business' in the sense of carrying no causal implications for others. Even on the simple interpretation, therefore, it will be a matter of scrutinising whether the consequences of an act do or do not possess some further property, such as adversely affecting the interests of others. But if we adopt the complex interpretation such scrutiny must range over the past as well as the future. So, for example, if the causal preconditions for performing some act require that other people's lives should have taken a particular course, and if that course involves something demeaning or injurious to them, the act might well cease to be purely my business.

The arguments of this chapter, therefore, are intended to take us beyond the rather obvious truth that some individuals may choose, for example, to boycott a certain item because it was produced by slave labour or in the context of a repugnant political regime. They are intended, first, to show how a concern for preconditions of action may have a significance all of its own, which is not reducible to any story about subsequent, indirect consequences. They are intended, secondly, to show how the rationale for such a concern may be extended beyond mere personal choice into the arena of collective control of individual behaviour. If the link to other people via causal precondition is symmetrically important with the link via causal consequence, then the further tests which must be satisfied for an action to fall under the category of protection from interference must be satisfied in both temporal directions. A demonstration that a given action's causal *consequences* do not carry whatever further feature is thought necessary before interference can be justified will not be sufficient to place that action beyond the possibility of legitimate intervention.

It might now be tempting to conclude that if we follow the complex interpretation then *nothing* can be purely my business, and to conjure up the image of massive consultation with several tens of thousands of people before I can be sure that it is unobjectionable for me to do something as innocuous as shaving in front of the mirror.[17] Such a parody would not

---

[17] A related point is sometimes made in the context of democratic theory, in criticism of the principle that anyone affected by a democratic decision is entitled to a say in it. Anyone in the world might

be a fair reflection of my point, however. I have allowed throughout that any reasonable theory must recognise that there are cases where there is nothing objectionable in an agent's embarking on their own chosen course of action and therefore no justification for preventing them from doing so. There must be protected acts *in that sense*. It is another matter whether there is a protected *sphere*, and another matter again whether such a sphere could be specified in non-circular terms. That is to say, although we can *label* all those acts where interference would be un-justified 'personal' or 'self-regarding', it is not clear what substantive properties they must possess besides, trivially, the characteristic of being proof against legitimate interference. In other words, while no one can deny that a distinction must be drawn somewhere between public and private behaviour, the case still needs to be made for the claim that a distinction between self- and other-regarding behaviour can serve as a basis for drawing the former distinction, rather than merely providing us with a vocabulary for expressing the former distinction once it has been drawn. If the arguments of this chapter are correct, then drawing the dis-tinction between public and private behaviour will involve examination of two temporal dimensions rather than just one.

The matter is complicated, moreover, by the fact that this is not a situation where there is general agreement about what is right and we merely seek a philosophical theory which adequately explains why. People's intuitions about cases differ, as earlier debates about prostitu-tion and homosexuality and current debates about pornography testify. We cannot simply line up the range of uncontentious protected acts and then attempt to reach an account of what they have in common that gives them that status, because there is no such uncontentious list.[18]

be affected by foreign policy decisions of the US government, but surely, it is sometimes said, it would be crazy to allow them to participate in the making of those decisions? This criticism seems to me not so much to show that the principle is wrong as to remind us that it may need to be overridden by other considerations, including pragmatism or indeed stronger normative reasons. In this connection, Thomas Christiano usefully develops the idea of a *collective property*, defined as a property such that in order to change one individual's welfare with regard to it, it is necessary to change almost all others' welfare with regard to it, and he argues that there is an intrinsic argument for democratic control over collective properties (Christiano 1993). This is a stringent definition, and it must remain an open question how many actions possess collective properties as defined here. I have argued that *all* actions possess the weaker property of having significant causal implications for *some* people other than just the agent, and in ways we do not always take into account. For further discussion see Dahl 1970: 65–7, Graham 1986a: 12–14, McMahon 1994: 11–12 and Nozick 1974: 268–70.

[18] For some anti-pornography campaigners, Barry's example of reading a book would not neces-sarily figure on such a list. For a strikingly wide range of activities thought *not* necessarily entitled to protection, and in particular not entitled to protection from the state, see Sunnstein 1993.

I have tried to add to those complications by calling attention to causal precondition, a form of causal interconnection which needs to be taken into account in deciding questions of freedom and interference, a form which we often ignore. Since there is neither a formula for identifying protected acts nor an agreed range of protected acts, it is in principle necessary to take into account causal considerations of that form in reaching conclusions about particular cases; and in practice that may lead to different conclusions from those which would be reached if those considerations were not taken into account. If the complex interpretation of causal interconnection is adopted, then the range of implications associated with any act will be far wider than if only the simple interpretation is adopted. It will then be a far more complex matter to determine, concerning any particular act, whether or not it can legitimately be free of any intervention.

CHAPTER 3

The indistinctness of persons: the personhood of collectivities

In the previous chapter I called attention to some of the difficulties in embracing D2, the idea of the distinctness of persons construed as *separateness*. In the present chapter I do the same for D1, the distinctness of persons construed as *qualitative* distinctness: the distinctness of persons not from each other but from other kinds of entity. As in the previous chapter, I begin from premises which I hope are truistic and therefore the most likely premises to command general assent: in this case the fact of collective agency mentioned in the Introduction, the fact that some of the things a person does gain their significance from being part of some collective action. I then attempt to derive conclusions which are far from truistic and would certainly not command general assent.

I argue that collective entities of a certain kind are an irreducible part of the social world we inhabit; that membership of such entities is a significant part of the identity[1] of individual persons; and that such entities exhibit some important characteristics in common with individual persons. The title of this chapter therefore introduces a topic rather than enunciating a thesis. I do not claim that collectivities *are* persons; but I raise the question how far they share important characteristics in common with persons, and the answer I suggest is that they do so to a significantly high degree. In particular, they share enough characteristics to enter the moral realm in their own right. I indicate how individual human beings themselves enter the moral realm by virtue of a combination of active and passive characteristics, and I argue that (some) collective entities possess the same or analogous characteristics.

---

[1] 'Identity' is a freighted term to use in a philosophical context. When I speak of collective membership being a significant part of the identity of individuals, I mean simply that something important is missing from a description of any individual's life which does not include reference to the collectivities to which they belong. For a related but slightly different view, see Bell 1993: 94.

3.1 THE DEFINITION OF COLLECTIVITIES

The previous chapter dealt with *individual* human action and the present chapter deals with *collective* human action. There is an intermediate phenomenon, mentioned in passing in chapter 2, section 1, which might be called *coordinated* human action. For example, suppose I am a member of the town's garrison and leave it in circumstances where others do so too, so that the town's defence collapses in a way which would not be possible if I alone had left. Or I act with a number of others to lift some heavy object which I could not possibly lift on my own. Or I change my habits along with a number of others to achieve a threshold effect in saving a significant amount of water during a drought. In these cases I act as an individual in coordination with a number of other individuals, and the significance of what I do is thereby transformed. An important part of what I am doing cannot be brought out without reference to what others are doing: my action has to be seen as part of a larger action undertaken by a plurality of agents. In constructing a notion of collective agency I want to focus on a phenomenon which is similar to this but is also distinctive, in ways which I shall describe.

I begin with some examples to illustrate the truism that sometimes what an individual human being does gains its main significance only as part of a collective action, an action carried out by some corporate entity. The examples all have further special features, as I go on to explain.

When I cast a vote, I act *as a member of an electorate*. My action might be described in many different ways, such as marking a cross on a piece of paper; but in a fairly straightforward way its main significance is not captured without implicit or explicit reference to the fact that I act as a member of the collectivity, the electorate. In the same way, I may express certain views *as a member of a jury*, and *what I am doing* in that context is quite different from what I would be doing if I expressed the same views when not a member of it. Or my action may be a contribution to the performance of a symphony by an orchestra or the mounting of a movement by a battalion or a football team. In all of these cases, what I do I do *as* a member of a certain kind of collective entity, and this entity is itself an agent.

Let me take as the fixed point, then, the ineliminable reference to the collective entity in an adequate description of an individual's actions. It is characteristic of some of the actions we perform that that is involved. This feature of our relation to collectivities is logically separable from two other features which nevertheless are often present in contexts where we are acting as part of a collectivity. *One* further feature is that often the action-description applying to the individual is different from that applying to the collectivity. For example, it is only the collective entity the electorate which can *return a government to power*, whereas what I do is *cast a vote in an election*. Similarly, it is only the football team which can *win a game*, whereas I perform various actions which may contribute to the achievement of that end. This further feature is logically separable from the idea that my action can sometimes be adequately described only by reference to the collectivity's action. For example, I may be *applauding a performer* where an adequate description of my behaviour must make reference to the fact that I am doing this as part of a claque, a group of people who are paid to produce an ovation. The ineliminable reference to a collectivity is there, but both the individual and the collectivity are doing the same thing: the same action-description, applauding, applies to both kinds of entity.[2]

The *second* further feature is this. Often the persistence of the collectivity as an entity does not depend on the persistence of the particular individuals who compose it. For example, many football clubs have been in continuous existence since the 1880s, but none of the original members remain and the clubs will survive the departure of their present members. Similarly, the British electorate continues to exist despite the entry and exit of many of its members over a period of time. But once again this is not a logically necessary feature of all collective entities. An *ad hoc* group of individuals may constitute an informal collectivity which is pushing a car up a hill, and my act of pushing may be inadequately described except as part of the action of that collectivity. But the individuals may disperse simultaneously in a way which brings the life of *that* collective entity to an end. In one terminology, this *ad hoc* group is an aggregate collectivity whereas the British electorate is a conglomerate collectivity.

For my purposes, a collectivity[3] will be defined as existing if and only if all three of these features are present. That is, a number of individual human beings form a collectivity if and only if

(i) *they act in ways whose significance can be adequately captured only by an ineliminable reference to some corporate body as part of which they are acting, where*

---

[2] Claques are not the same thing as cliques, though they are connected by etymology. See Valinas (forthcoming) and my comments on cliques later in this section.

[3] With some hesitation I have opted to refer to collective entities of the kind which concern me as *collectivities*. To refer to them as *collectives*, as I have in the past, is to invite the unappetising and inapposite image of Stalinist collective farms. To refer to them instead as *corporate* entities is to conjure up the image of IBM. Collective farms and IBM are both examples of collectivities as I shall define them, but I develop the idea of collective agency of a much wider kind.

(ii) *what that corporate body does is distinct from anything which they as individuals do, and where*

(iii) *the corporate body is a persisting one whose survival is relatively indifferent to the persistence of the particular individuals which compose it at any particular moment.*[4]

Notice, first, that the individuals' actions referred to in (i) need only be episodic. For example, when the significance of my behaviour in running round a pitch can adequately be brought out only by reference to the fact that I am doing this as part of a football team, I remain a member of the team even if I spend a period off the pitch; or I may be absent from a committee on a particular occasion and, notwithstanding that, correctly regard its acts on that occasion as something which *we* have done. It is not necessary for all who would be recognised as belonging to a collectivity to be acting on a particular occasion when *it* is clearly acting. Raimo Tuomela puts the point by saying that a collectivity's actions may be carried out by its *operative* members, who may not be its total set of members (Tuomela 1989: 244). Indeed, at the limit it may be possible for *one* person to act on behalf of the collectivity, because they are authorised so to do. And at the limit it may be that some individual belongs to a collectivity but *never* acts in the way specified in (i), for example someone who is a member of a committee but never attends any of its meetings or carries out any of its tasks. But when collectivities are defined in terms of the actions of their members, such a case must necessarily be exceptional. Both the exceptional and the central case, where I do act as part of a collectivity, raise important questions about an individual's assuming of responsibility which I touch on in the following chapter.

Notice, secondly, that the difference between the individual's and the collectivity's actions specified in (ii) is contingent rather than necessary. Sometimes it will be *impossible* for an individual to do what a collectivity does. That was the case in the example of a collectivity returning a government to power, while an individual can only vote. But it will not be the case in the example of finding a defendant guilty. A member of

---

[4] It will be observed that this specification of collectivity fails in one obvious respect to meet the requirements of an analytical definition. It involves reference to the idea of a corporate body, and it might be objected that this idea is either synonymous with that of a collectivity or else so close that the specification suffers from circularity. My concern is less with meeting such requirements than with the substantive point that there are corporate bodies with the characteristics described and that a number of important consequences follow from that fact. If I can rely on the reader's assent to the existence of collectivities by appeal to the many examples of corporate bodies such as committees, clubs, families, electorates, firms and so on, then I am happy to forego the demands of analytical definition. The question of the ontological status of these corporate bodies is taken up in section 4 below.

a jury cannot do that, and only the jury can; but in another context a judge or magistrate can, as an individual, perform that action. What is essential in this definition is not that the action-description applying to the corporate entity *must be* but only that it *is* different from that applying to the individuals.

Notice, thirdly, that there is a Theseus problem, as it were, lurking in the specification of the relatively individual-indifferent persistence of a collectivity in (iii). Over a period, a football team, West Bromwich Albion, may lose all of its original players; yet it is *that* team, West Bromwich Albion, which is gradually transformed. Or is it? Suppose that someone collects up all the discarded players and forms them into a new team. Isn't there a case for saying that it is this new team which is West Bromwich Albion? Having mentioned this problem, I propose to leave it lurking. It is an entirely general one which arises in connection with any entity made up of constituents such that the composition of the entity may change over time while the original constituents survive (though no longer as constituents). It is not a problem which arises specifically in connection with this definition of collectivities.[5]

Notice, finally, one more general fact about the definition of collectivities. The idea has been introduced with the aid of a number of examples in which the participants are conscious of their membership of some corporate entity and intend that their actions should contribute to the corporate entity's activities. These features of participants' consciousness and intention are often made a central part of the account of collective activity,[6] but they do not form part of my definition. On this definition, therefore, it is possible for a number of individuals to constitute a collectivity without intending to and without being aware that they do. That suggestion may be thought to raise problems, which I address in the next section.

3.2 COLLECTIVITIES AND CONSCIOUSNESS

How should we respond to the idea of individuals constituting a collectivity without intending to and without being aware that they do? The most extreme response would be to object that such a possibility is ruled out. One reason which might be cited for ruling it out is that it would

---

[5] For discussion of the Theseus problem, see Wiggins 1967: 37–8.

[6] For accounts which make individuals' consciousness and intentions central in this way, see, for example, Bratman 1992: 327–41; Dworkin 1989: 479–504; French 1984: 40–5; Gilbert 1996: 6–7; Searle 1995: ch. 1.

infringe the Davidsonian principle that all action is intentional under some description (Davidson 1974: 41).[7] This is the first indication that the views we take of collective agency are liable to depend heavily on the views we take of individual agency, where many received wisdoms may themselves be open to question. That includes the Davidsonian principle itself.[8] People do things in a completely absent-minded way or while fast asleep, for example, and it is not clear that their actions are in those circumstances intentional under *any* description. Unintentional collective actions might indeed usefully be compared precisely to sleep-walking. But even if the Davidsonian principle is allowed to stand, it is not clear that it is infringed by the possibility of individuals engaging in collective action without intending to. After all, an individual's contributory acts to collective action may well be intentional under all sorts of other descriptions; my claim is just that they are not necessarily intentional under the description 'contribution to a collective action'.

This leaves a residual problem, however. If there is an irreducibly distinct action which is attributed to the collectivity itself, as opposed to the individuals who compose it, it might be objected that *that* action will not be intentional under any description. Indeed, how could it be, unless we swallow the implausibility of positing a super-entity with super-intentions? How, it might be said, could there be any analogue in the case of irreducibly collective acts to the intentions which are associated with individual acts?

There can be such an analogue, provided we are prepared to recognise that some intending has the form of we-intending rather than I-intending (cf. Searle 1995: 26, and Tuomela 1995: ch. 3). Individuals can *share* intentions, as members of a collectivity, to bring about some collective act. We can, for example, jointly intend that *we* perform a piece of music. This preserves the idea that all intending is done by individuals, but some of it is done by them *as* members of a collectivity. Thus, the actions of a collectivity can be, and frequently are, intentional in a completely unproblematic way, and its constituent members can be, and frequently are, conscious of their intentions as collective ones. But though this may be so, it *need* not be so. In that connection, Searle introduces an interesting example of non-human collective action (Searle 1995: 38; cf. 47). A pack of hyenas can coordinate in very subtle ways in collectively stalking and

---

[7] For recent subscription to the Davidsonian principle see Williams 1995a: 57, and for subscription to it in the course of constructing a theory of collective agency, see French 1984: 38–9, 205 n. 15.

[8] For material relevant to questioning the Davidsonian principle see for example Goldman 1970; Cornman 1971; Davidson 1971.

killing a lion. Though it may be presumed that they have intentions in doing so, they do not have the linguistic apparatus necessary for being aware of the intentions they have, and so *a fortiori* they are not aware of any such intentions being collective ones. A similar unawareness of collective intentions may be exhibited in human cases such as that of a mob, whose actions can be seen as directed towards some definite end and may involve a very complex division of labour, but without any apparent conscious coordination (cf. May 1987: 35–8, 58–9). To explain their individual actions by reference to individual intentions is not to explain what they achieve collectively. We might say that the collective action was entirely coincidental, but it can instead be explained by postulating a shared collective intention of which the members of the mob were nevertheless unaware.[9]

There are distinct grounds on which someone might want to rule out the possibility that individuals should constitute a collectivity without intending to and without being aware that they do. It might be objected that this alleged possibility falls foul of the fact that social phenomena are *transparent*. Such a response seems to be implied by Searle's view that 'social reality is created by us for our purposes and seems as readily intelligible to us as those purposes themselves' (Searle 1995: 4). It also seems implicit in Margaret Gilbert's claim that 'in order to form a social group, it is both logically necessary and logically sufficient that a set of human beings constitute a plural subject', where the existence of a plural subject itself depends on the relevant intentional states of the individuals who compose it (Gilbert 1996: 7–9, 187).

I believe that this response should be rejected. In order to see why, consider *the phenomenon of the clique*. Imagine a number of individuals who know one another well, have an easy rapport with one another, and are liable to engage in exchanges which presuppose a great deal of prior acquaintance with their interests, their sense of humour and their ways of relating to one another. Such a group of individuals may collectively exclude other people from their social exchanges, making it difficult or impossible for these other people to join in banter, contribute to the humour of the occasion, and so on. This group of individuals would constitute a collectivity: the significance of what each of them was doing would not be adequately captured without reference to the fact that they

---

9 For further discussion see Tuomela 1989. He posits a supervenience of intentional action such that a collectivity brings about X intentionally if and only if some of its members bring about X intentionally (248). This places a constraint on a collectivity's bringing something about intentionally; it does not itself state that for a collectivity to act at all its action must be intentional.

were doing it as part of the whole group; no individual would be doing what the group as a whole was doing, namely freezing a person out of a whole social atmosphere; and the clique would survive a change in its composition. But of course the members of the clique might act in this way quite unwittingly and unintentionally. They might be mortified to discover that this is what they had been doing. (Notice that there is more than one possibility here. They might not be aware that they form a collectivity at all; or they might not be aware that they form a collectivity of *this* kind; or they might be aware of all of this, but unaware that they had collectively performed some particular action on a particular occasion.)

The behaviour of a clique is a recognisable social phenomenon, which conforms to my definition of a collectivity but does not exhibit the transparency demanded of social phenomena here. It may not be of any great significance in itself, but it provides the model for social phenomena of more consequence. For example, the process it embodies may be reproduced in circumstances where a native population unwittingly visits certain kinds of psychological exclusion on strangers in their midst (immigrant workers, perhaps), or in circumstances where a police force practises institutional racism without its individual officers intending this to be the case.[10]

The existence of such phenomena is a reflection of the fact that it is an oversimplification to say that social reality is created by us for our purposes. Much of social reality evolves in the course of our pursuing our purposes, but it evolves in ways which we did not intend, could not foresee and may not understand. We may *discover* that we have been doing something collectively, and that new awareness may bring with it new descriptions: both for the collectivity and for the collective actions it performs. It will be a contentious question how widespread these phenomena are, and that will be a matter for detailed empirical investigation. But I assume that the existence of the phenomenon of the clique is not itself contentious, and if that is correct then we should construct our concepts in a way which does not ignore or rule out the possibility that its features may be reproduced elsewhere.[11]

---

[10] The general case of unwitting collectivities may also be important for understanding the history of feminism. See Assiter 1996: 82.

[11] In fairness, Searle appears to acknowledge the general possibility in his subsequent discussion of money. He observes that functions may come to be unconsciously imposed on it which are quite different from anything originally intended. Money may have the manifest function of being a medium of exchange but the hidden function of maintaining power relations, for example (Searle 1995: 21–2).

There is a less extreme response to the suggestion that individual agents may be unaware of actions which they perform collectively. It would consist in conceding this as a possibility, but arguing that it is such a different matter from the examples originally employed in introducing the idea of collective agency that it would be better to regard it as a distinct phenomenon, one which should therefore receive some distinct description. In that spirit, Gilbert argues that too wide a conception of social agency may cause us to lose sight of the 'delicate, consequential, highly social structures of plural subjecthood' in which individuals express willingness to constitute themselves into a plural subject in conditions of common knowledge. Too wide a conception of the social, she suggests, may have the effect of obscuring our understanding and even our conscious perception of the phenomena included under the description of plural subjects (Gilbert 1996: 273–4).

This response is far more eirenic in character, and it may seem that no more than a verbal difference remains if the possibility of unconscious collectivities is conceded in this way. All that remains, it might be said, is the question of how we decide to label this possibility. Something may still turn on how that possibility is conceptualised, however. Similarities as well as differences need to be observed, and this can be illustrated by means of a further example: the phenomenon of the *witting* clique. Imagine the same description of the original clique, except that this time we populate it with a group of people who know exactly what they are doing and do it intentionally. They are not merely socially insensitive but socially malicious. There are, then, both witting and unwitting cliques. If both the original example and this new variant example exhibit the *same* type of action being carried out by the *same* type of agency then it is important to have a concept that covers both cases. Moreover, one could claim on the same principle as Gilbert's argument that concentration on the familiar and straightforward case of witting and intentional collective agency is rather more likely to obscure our understanding and even our perception of the far more elusive case of unconscious collective agency.

Two opposite considerations need to be given due weight in an account of collectivities: on the one hand, the general characteristics genuinely shared in common by all cases where individuals come together and act collectively; on the other hand, the great diversity manifested by those cases, necessitating a recognition of many distinct species within the genus of collective action. It is a standard philosophical aspiration to capture generality, as indeed in the Davidson account of the nature of individual human action in general, and in that respect collective action is no different. The examples of the witting and the unwitting clique, as well as acting as the model for more important social phenomena, illustrate the importance of noticing similarity between otherwise diverse cases. An unwitting collectivity may come to be a witting collectivity, in the sense that its members may come to a realisation of what they are collectively doing which had not been apparent to them hitherto. This parallels the case where an individual agent comes to see a significance in their action which had previously eluded them. ('I thought I was engaging in banter when in fact I was being offensive.') In both the individual and the collective case questions may then arise about whether the agents involved, now that they know what they are doing, wish to acquiesce in their activity or not. But in neither case is there any doubt that both before and after such realisation it is one and the same agency which is performing one and the same action. Questions about decisions to identify with or dissociate from collectivities will be the topic of the next chapter.

For the remainder of the present chapter it is the diversity of different types of collectivity which will assume greater importance, and it is necessary to correct any mistaken impression which might arise from the introduction of the idea of a collectivity in section 1 via a particular set of examples and a particular definition. It should now be plain that the definition will allow a wider range of collectivities than might be suggested by the particular examples given there. Such collectivities as committees and teams, it is reasonable to suppose, are necessarily intentional. This will follow, however, not simply by virtue of their being collectivities but by virtue of their being a specific *kind* of collectivity. To invoke an apposite analogy: it follows from the nature of murder that an individual could not commit an act of murder without premeditation, but it is not true of *all* individual acts, of whatever kind, that they require premeditation. In the same way, it follows from the nature of committeehood or teamhood that intention and mutual recognition be present, but it is not true of all collectivities that they require these features. Hence, I have argued for a division between collectivities which are and collectivities which are not intentional.

In a similar way, the idea of a collectivity is not confined to conventionally constructed entities with formal decision-procedures such as business corporations or committees. It will also cover naturally occurring and evolving entities such as cultural groups. It will cover entities with informal decision-procedures and entities with no decision-procedures at all, such as crowds and mobs. On my account collectivities will range from very large to very small, from multinational companies to families. Whole nations and classes may be collectivities in the required sense. Perhaps the largest collectivity might be constituted by the whole human race and perhaps the smallest by a couple.[12] Many complications will arise from this enormous variety. To give just one example, there may be the formally constituted collectivity of a committee within an organisation which is charged with making certain decisions on the organisation's behalf, and an informal collectivity which is composed of identical constituents and which meets in the toilets prior to committee meetings. At that point it may be necessary to make a distinction between manifest and latent collectivities to make best sense of what people are doing in that context (cf. French 1984: 51). More generally, a great deal of further conceptual apparatus will be needed, beyond the skeletal definition of collectivities, for making sense of this variety.[13]

There is one further, and quite different, extension of the idea of collectivities which I wish to introduce. Individuals sometimes form *potential collectivities*. That is to say, sometimes we can designate groups of individuals who *could* meet the conditions for forming a collectivity when in fact they do not. Of course, it would be all too easy to overpopulate the world with any number of arbitrarily constructed potential collectivities, and Quine has long since warned us of the disorderly outcome

---

[12] It is contentious whether anything consisting only of two members can constitute a collectivity. Georg Simmel argues that 'the difference between the dyad [*Zweierverbindung*, 'union of two'] and larger groups consists in the fact that the dyad has a different relation to each of its two elements than have larger groups to *their* members. Although, for the outsider, the group consisting of two may function as an autonomous, super-individual unit, it usually does not do so for its participants. Rather, each of the two feels himself confronted only by the other, not by a collectivity above him. The social structure here rests immediately on the one and on the other of the two, and the secession of either would destroy the whole. The dyad, therefore, does not attain that super-personal life which the individual feels to be independent of himself. As soon, however, as there is a sociation of three, a group continues to exist even in case one of the members drops out' (Simmel 1908: 123). But is he right? Imagine the case of a tiny mediaeval painter's studio which consists of just the master M and an apprentice. There are grounds for saying that this constitutes the Studio of M and that when the apprentice is replaced it remains the Studio of M. I am happy to go either way on such a case. Either we can say that the persisting identity condition (iii), laid down in section 1 as a condition of the existence of a collectivity, is satisfied here, so that the studio counts as a collectivity; or we can say that it is not. But if it is not, what we should have to conclude is that a dyad could meet some but not all of the conditions laid down. In that case it would represent a distinct but related phenomenon. In either case the dyad can exhibit properties distinct from those of its individual constituents. See my further remarks on coupledom in section 7.

[13] For accounts which, while not following the same definition of collectivities as I have offered, envisage a comparably wide range of collectivities, see May 1987: 2 and Tuomela 1989: 244–5. For one attempt at a formal classification of different kinds of collectivity, see Tuomela 1995: 223–7.

of postulating unactualised possibles.[14] But there are sometimes good reasons for postulating quite specific potential collectivities with specific potential memberships.

Such postulation would be to the point in any of the following three circumstances: where reference to a potential collectivity singled out (i) some group of individuals sharing a common condition and common interests, and having the power to act collectively so as to further those common interests, even if in fact they do not; or (ii) a group of individuals who would have the power to act for the good if they chose to act collectively and who were thought to be collectively responsible for not so acting; or (iii) a group of individuals who, while not acting as a collectivity, are treated in some particular way by others who perceive and fear that the individuals might *come* to act as a collectivity. Respectively, these possibilities might be illustrated by (i) an appeal to a social class to recognise and act on its collective class interest; (ii) a theoretical position which held individuals responsible for their omissions as well as their acts, and by extension their collective omissions as well as their individual omissions; and (iii) the historically common practice of mixing very heterogeneous elements in a workforce so as to minimise the chances of workplace solidarity.[15] The significance of potential collectivities is taken up in chapter 4, section 1.

3.3 COLLECTIVITIES AS RESPONSIBLE AGENTS

In this and succeeding sections I lay out the case for regarding some collectivities as legitimate inhabitants of the moral realm and I defend that case against criticisms. At the same time I hope to enlarge our

---

[14] The outcome is 'a breeding ground for disorderly elements. Take, for instance, the possible fat man in that doorway; and, again, the possible bald man in that doorway. Are they the same possible man, or two possible men? How do we decide? How many possible men are there in that doorway? Are there more possible thin ones than fat ones? How many of them are alike? Or would their being alike make them one?' (Quine 1961: 4).

[15] For further argument on each of these three possibilities, see respectively Graham 1992: 26–7; May 1992: 105–6; Elster 1985: 372–3. In connection with the third, Hannah Arendt comments: 'An anecdote, reported by Seneca from imperial Rome, may illustrate how dangerous mere appearance in public was thought to be. At that time a proposition was laid before the senate to have slaves dress uniformly in public so that they could immediately be distinguished from free citizens. The proposition was turned down as too dangerous, since the slaves would now be able to recognize each other and become aware of their potential power. Modern interpreters were of course inclined to conclude from this incident that the number of slaves at the time must have been very great, yet this conclusion turned out to be quite erroneous. What the sound political instinct of the Romans judged to be dangerous was appearance as such, quite independent from the number of people involved' (Arendt 1959: 357 n. 53).

understanding of collectivities and the consequences which follow from acknowledging their existence. I expressed misgivings about the category of the moral in the Introduction. My claim in this section is best construed as the hypothetical one that *if* you employ the category of moral responsibility at all, you have no reason not to apply it to some collectivities. Similar considerations apply to the claim put forward in section 6 below that some collectivities can be objects of moral concern.

The metaphor of inhabiting the moral realm may be cashed in terms of the applicability of a characteristic vocabulary. A type of entity can be regarded as part of the moral realm if and only if a certain range of epithets can be applied to it. I take it for granted that there would be general agreement about which epithets count as moral, even if there might be disagreement around the margins and even though there would be strong disagreement about the logical status of such epithets. I take for granted, so to speak, an understanding of what counts as the moral realm and what counts as treating an entity as a member of it. If an entity can be described as wicked or virtuous, just, generous, malicious, dishonest, then it has been granted entry.

There are two quite different grounds on which we might treat an entity as part of the moral realm: either as a moral *agent* or as a moral *patient*. That is to say, we might treat it as inhabiting the moral realm either on account of what it *does* or on account of what *happens* to it. We might believe that it *engages in actions* for which it is not merely causally but also morally responsible, actions which can elicit specifically moral comment. In contrast, we might believe that it *undergoes states* which are an object of specifically moral concern. There is no guarantee that every moral agent is also a moral patient or that every moral patient is also a moral agent. The case of non-human animals illustrates the latter point at least: the standard view would be that what happens to them is a legitimate matter of moral concern but that what they do is not a legitimate occasion for moral praise or censure. In this section I argue that some collectivities enter the moral realm by virtue of being moral agents. In section 6 I argue that some enter it by virtue of being objects of moral concern.[16]

---

[16] Notice that it would be sufficient to regard collectivities as being part of the moral realm if they fell into only one of these categories. It would be equally true that all collectivities were part of the moral realm if some fell into one category and the rest fell into the other, even if none fell into both. In fact, I believe that some collectivities fall into *neither* category, so that it is not true that all collectivities are part of the moral realm. On the other hand, I believe that some collectivities fall into both categories. That is, there are some collectivities of which it is true both

Suppose that a number of individuals act as members of a university senate. The senate decides to close down a department and it does so: things which the individuals are not empowered to do. Now people are very likely to take up a critical or supportive attitude towards the senate's decision to close down a department. They will say either that it was a craven capitulation to market values or that it was a brave and unpopular decision in difficult circumstances. But notice that passing such judgement on that decision or action really is passing judgement on what the *senate* has done. It is distinct from passing judgement on what individual members have done, or the arguments they put forward, or the way they cast their votes, or even the contribution they made to what the senate did. Closing down a department is not something they can individually decide to do. They can do so only collectively and they can do so only *as* a senate. If, therefore, we wish to pass moral judgement on that action, we must pass judgement on the action of a collective entity. That entity is an ineliminable part of the moral realm.

The example is, of course, carefully selected. The senate has a deliberative structure and an explicit decision-making procedure, and it is arguably in virtue of these features that it is possible to ascribe responsibility to it. I have already emphasised that it is not a defining feature of collectivities to have such structures or procedures. Accordingly, if the presence of this structure and procedure is a necessary component in holding the collectivity morally responsible then it will not follow that *all* collectivities on my earlier definition are moral agents in this way. However, the deliberative structure is not the only vital feature. The presence of an irreducibly collective action is also vital: if that were not involved here, responsibility could be distributed unproblematically to individuals who happened to be acting together and all we would have is a case of collective responsibility in the colloquial sense where a number of individuals is *each and severally* held responsible for something. It is therefore the existence of irreducible collectivities (arguably with an appropriate deliberative structure and explicit decision-procedure) which makes the case for irreducibly collective responsibility in the sense of a collectivity itself being held responsible.[17]

Or rather: so far we have a *prima facie* case to that effect. It consists in pointing out the implications of the practice of passing moral comment

that their actions are the object of legitimate moral comment and that their states are the object of legitimate moral concern.

[17] I am concerned throughout this chapter with the *ascription* of responsibility to an agent by some other entity rather than with the *assumption* of responsibility by the agent themself.

on irreducibly collective actions. If that practice is acceptable then it must bring with it an acknowledgement that collectivities are part of the moral realm. But it might be objected that if that is the price to be paid it would be more defensible to abandon the practice instead. I now consider some reasons for thinking so.

3.4 ONTOLOGY

First, it might be objected that it is inappropriate to apply moral epithets to collectivities because they are, bluntly, fictions. In that spirit, Dworkin distinguishes between what he terms a practice view of collective entities, which he favours, and a metaphysical view, which accords ontological priority to them. He observes that, for example, an orchestra has a collective life not because it is ontologically prior to individuals but because of the attitudes and actions which those individuals take up (Dworkin 1989: 494). As he puts it more generally elsewhere, 'communal action depends not on the ontological priority of community over individual, but on a certain kind of shared attitudes among individuals' (Dworkin 1990a: 335). Dworkin's argument exhibits what might be called the *intentional strategy*. It is argued that reference to collective entities occurs within the scope of the thoughts and intentions, the 'shared attitudes', of those who compose them. But that is held to neutralise any commitment to the real existence of those entities. By way of analogy, it may be pointed out that if we explain certain forms of religious behaviour by ascribing irreducible beliefs about gods to those exhibiting the behaviour this does not commit us to the existence of gods (cf. McMahon 1994: 53 n. 2).

McMahon has furnished further material which might be used for the purpose of regarding collectivities as fictions. He draws a distinction between the use of terms for *explanatory* purposes and their use for *practical* purposes. He then argues that if reference to a certain entity is an indispensable part of our best explanation of some phenomenon then we can regard the entity as really existing, in accordance with inference to the best explanation. But '[t]o take talk about things that is best regarded as serving only practical purposes as genuinely referential is to make the mistake of reification' (McMahon 1994: 54–5; cf. Tuomela 1995: 356–66). McMahon does not himself conclude that collective entities are fictions: he leaves the question of their ontological status open, on the grounds that there is no clear consensus among social scientists over whether reference to them is necessary for explanatory purposes or not (McMahon 1994: 61). He adds the further thought that someone who wishes to be a realist about social objects can avoid metaphysical embarrassment by an appeal to *supervenience*:

> [A]ny group instantiating a social kind will have a set of nonsocial properties
> such that any other group of individuals possessing those properties will instantiate that social kind as well. For every riot, there is a description of the behavior
> of the individuals involved that does not employ social terms and which is such
> that any other set of individuals satisfying that description would be rioting
> too. (56–7)[18]

How should we assess these arguments? There are three connected but distinct issues here: *supervenience, priority* and *ontology*. So far as supervenience is concerned, it must be true at least in a broad and crude sense that the actions of collectivities are supervenient on the actions of their constituent individuals.[19] The individuals provide the fuel, as it were, for the collective action. There is simply nowhere else for it to come from, and if the individuals do not act then it does not occur. It is common ground on all sides that there is no super-entity which somehow acts all on its own initiative. But it does not follow, nor is it true, that the *collectivity's* behaviour can be described in a way which does not employ social terms, or that any similar description of individuals *qua* individuals would carry the same implication of collective action. Descriptions of individuals' behaviour in the voting booth which omits all mention of their participation as a member of an electorate will fail to capture the most central aspect of what they are doing. Where collective action occurs it is an ineliminable part of the description of individuals' behaviour that they are acting, precisely, *as* members of a collectivity.

These considerations suggest that it is misconceived to think in terms of priority *simpliciter*, either of the collectivity over the individual or vice versa. Already we can see that individuals have one kind of priority, in providing the raw material for collective action, while the collectivity has another kind, since reference to the collectivity itself is ineliminable for securing the most significant description of the individuals' behaviour. Sometimes, indeed, the existence of a collectivity may bring with it the possibility of individual actions which are literally inconceivable in its absence: scoring a goal is possible only where there are teams of which one is a member. But as well as this conceptual priority, collectivities

---

[18] Larry May similarly argues that it is a mistake to postulate any social entity, on the grounds that collective groups are simply individuals in relation (May 1987: 9, 23).

[19] Not that the concept of supervenience is an entirely unproblematic one. For exposition see Kim 1984, for a formal account see Tuomela 1989: 243–66, and for some doubts see Blackburn 1985.

sometimes have a *causal* priority over individuals. Individuals may come to possess powers and skills which as a matter of contingent fact they would not possess were it not for the role of some collectivity in developing them. Playing in an orchestra developed my music skills, say, or playing in the team developed my dribbling skills. There is already enough evidence here that both individuals and collectivities will exhibit priority in a number of different ways.

So far as the ontological issue is concerned, why should explanatory usefulness be thought to have a uniquely privileged status in determining ontological questions? Suppose that methodological individualism were true, for example, and that all social phenomena were explicable in ways which made reference only to individuals. Still, there is a separate question from the question of whether the only ultimate *explanans* in social matters is one involving reference exclusively to individuals and their states. There is an intermediate consideration between explanatory theory and mere practicality which is also of importance in determining ontological matters. Prior to explanation and prior to practical decision, there is the question of the vocabulary we need for *specifying the data* which either stand in need of explanation or furnish the basis on which we shall decide how to act.

On any tolerably comprehensive understanding of our social life, those data will include a certain range of irreducibly collective actions which have substantive consequences in the world, actions which we wish to notice and to which we wish to respond in certain ways. Accordingly, we require a vocabulary with which we can do this. That is the basis for postulating the existence of collective entities in the first place. Such postulation would be unnecessary if all social behaviour could be described in terms of the examples of *coordinated* action mentioned in section 1, as when a number of individuals cooperate in jointly lifting some heavy object. But individuals engage in collective behaviour which goes well beyond cases of contingent, temporary coordination of this kind. The existence of committees and clubs, and indeed of cliques, implies the need to recognise persisting structures whose conditions of existence are distinct from those of their constituents and whose actions are similarly distinct.

It is a reasonable principle that an action requires an agent, and it is a reasonable extension of that principle that an irreducibly collective action requires an irreducibly collective agent. Unless, therefore, we are prepared to excise a very wide range of action-descriptions from our account of the social world we inhabit, we must acknowledge the existence of the collective agents whose actions they are. Wars are declared

by states, policies are initiated by governments, cultural exclusion is prac-
tised by populations. Reference to collectivities, even if it could be avoided
in any *explanans*, would be unavoidable in many *explananda*: we cannot
avoid postulating them in a description of what is there.

It is not clear that the intentional strategy can make any impact on
this point. The aim of the strategy is to rule on the ontological status of
collectivities by putting them into the minds – and *only* the minds – of
their participants. In Dworkin's hands the strategy is pursued on the
assumption that collective action divides exhaustively into merely statistical action, which is a straightforward function of what individuals do on
their own 'with no sense of doing something *as* a group', and communal
action, which 'cannot be reduced just to some statistical function of individual action, because it is collective in the deeper sense that does
require individuals to assume the existence of the group as a separate
entity or phenomenon' (Dworkin 1990a: 329). But we have seen in the
phenomenon of the unwitting clique that *tertium datur*. There can be
collective action which is not merely statistical but which is also not
perceived as such by those who collectively produce it, collective action
which is not therefore merely in the minds of the agents since it is not in
the minds of the agents at all. There can be good reasons for postulating
collective action even where the protagonists themselves do not.[20]

I would not want to press the ontological claim any harder. I have used
the terminology of ontology in earlier publications[21] and continue to
do so here, but it may be that *descriptive* collectivism would be a more
appropriate term than ontological collectivism to express the point that
there are cases where there is an ineliminable reference to the collective entity in an adequately informative description of the behaviour of
the individual. In any event, the point being expressed is quite distinct
from any commitment to *explanatory* collectivism, which would urge that
collective terms are ineliminable from some specified range of explanations of social phenomena. Nothing I say implies a commitment on either
side of that question. My claim is that collective terms are ineliminable

---

[20] We should not be deflected from this thought by the fact that collectivities to which moral
responsibility is ascribed perhaps do have to be perceived as such by their constituents. That is a
condition on treating a collectivity in a particular way, not a condition on being a collectivity at all.
It cannot therefore be invoked in the service of a general claim about the nature of collectivities
as such.

[21] See for example Graham 1986a: 103–6 and Graham 2000. In Graham 1986a I erroneously con-
flated two claims which in the present work I have separated: the claim that there are irreducibly
collective actions and the claim that there are irreducibly collective actions which are appropriate
objects of moral appraisal.

from the data: they cannot be removed from a range of *explananda*, whether or not they must form part of any *explanans*. And if the criterion for an entity's existing is that ineliminable reference to it occurs in our best *descriptions* of the world, then collectivities exist.

3.5 COLLECTIVITIES AND INDIVIDUALS

There is a more limited objection to the idea of holding collectivities morally responsible. Even if the question of their ontological status is waived, it may be objected that they are so unlike individuals in the relevant respects that we should discontinue the practice of ascribing such responsibility to them. In dealing with this more limited objection, there is the complication that it is a matter of great philosophical contention just what the relevant respects are in virtue of which it is appropriate to ascribe moral responsibility to *individual* agents. I shall take it, however, that the possession of a range of mental predicates, including the capacity to deliberate, to form intentions and to make choices, is at least a necessary condition in the individual case. If that range of predicates is not applicable to collectivities then the grounds for ascribing moral responsibility to them are greatly if not fatally weakened.[22]

I shall consider this more limited objection in two versions, one put forward by Geoffrey Brennan and Loren Lomasky, who are in a more general way hostile to any degree of personification of collective entities, and one put forward by Larry May, who is far more sympathetic to such a project but still reaches a conclusion similar to theirs. I shall argue that the requisite range of predicates applies to some collectivities either in literal or in analogue form, but in any case in a form sufficient to ground ascriptions of responsibility. Even in the case of collectivities where the predicates do not apply I shall suggest that there are instructive parallels between collectivities and individuals, since individuals themselves do not always act in a deliberative and ratiocinative way. In attempting to fix the degree of personhood which is appropriately ascribed to collectivities, we need to bear in mind the full range of attributes possessed by persons themselves.

---

[22] In the individual case, the most plausible additional necessary condition for moral responsibility is the availability of alternative possibilities of action. Extension of this condition to collectivities is far less problematic, once the idea is accepted that collectivities are agents, capable of deliberating and deciding in the first place. Causal responsibility as a further necessary condition is far from uncontroversial in the individual case; but I shall assume that if it *is* taken as a necessary condition, its fulfilment in the case of collectivities is unproblematic given their causal role in the performance of actions.

Brennan and Lomasky enter a robust denial that the required range of predicates can be ascribed to collectivities in the course of a discussion of democracy. They applaud the eclipse of an organic conception of society and its associated 'picture of democratic action as individual choice writ large' (Brennan and Lomasky 1993: 169). Examples of the Prisoners' Dilemma illustrate that the translation of individual actions into social outcomes is complex and sometimes perverse. 'Any theory that treats social aggregates as choosing entities, much like individuals, sweeps away many of the most interesting intellectual questions in social analysis and many of the most pressing practical problems in social policy' (169). They offer two analogies. The first is that of a littered beach. 'Because the littered beach is not in any meaningful sense collectively *chosen* (or, for that matter, chosen by any one of the individual litterers), the sense in which the litter is by the people must be quite different from that involved in the individual case. Individual and collective choice are sharply disanalogous in this respect' (170). They offer, secondly, the even less flattering analogy of a situation where individuals pull levers which are causally efficacious in the selection of candidates and policies, but the levers themselves are unmarked. Here, they suggest, there is causal responsibility but no moral responsibility, since intent is absent. But, they object:

In elections where the numbers are even modestly large, the political outcome is, for each and every voter, essentially incidental to his action – and that is so whether or not the levers are identified . . . And when a large number of persons all engaged in doing something *else* produce as an incidental byproduct of their action a particular state of affairs, then the insinuation that this state of affairs is, in some meaningful sense, expressive of their *will* must be regarded as highly suspect. (171)

May's greater sympathy for the project of assimilating collectivities to individuals is evident in his view that a group which has a decision structure 'acts and even takes on attitudes as a unit by exercising its equivalent of a mind' (May 1992: 84). Yet he reaches a similar conclusion to Brennan and Lomasky. He argues that it is only in rare cases that it may be appropriate to speak of collective intentional guilt for harm, and even in a case where a university was alleged to discriminate against Blacks as a matter of policy, 'there is not the same kind of intentional guilt that is displayed by individual persons, since the university's "mind" was at best conflicted, with a sizable minority of the community opposing its racist policies' (84).

Although Brennan and Lomasky are concerned specifically with democracy, they couch their argument in terms of general claims about collectivities. Indeed, part of the problem is that their claims are *too* general and fail to take into account the varieties of collectivity described in section 2. The beach-littering collectivity is one such variety, but even this collectivity is analogous in some respects to an individual. It is analogous to a very irrational and uncoordinated individual whose responsibility is indeed itself only causal and not moral, an individual whose actions are not rational or of any use to themself. But neither all individuals nor all collectivities behave in that way all of the time. *Some* do all of the time: individuals who are incapable of normal processes of reasoning and (at the very least) collectivities whose members are totally unaware of the nature of their actions *qua* members of the collectivity. Indeed, it may be that *all* individuals and collectivities behave in this way some of the time: that every instance of either kind of entity falls away from standards of rationality on some occasion or other. But still the essential point is that the features of the beach-littering case and the unlabelled levers case do not generalise to all cases of collective action.

Specifically, they fail to apply where individuals recognise themselves as part of a collectivity and attempt to deliberate and decide *as* members of it, in accordance with explicit decision-procedures. Here there is the possibility of performative indications as to the will of the collectivity and its intention to act in a particular way. Thus, the procedures may lay down that for the meeting to say that it holds that p or resolves to Φ just *is* for it to hold that p or to resolve to Φ.[23] In these circumstances, the capacity to deliberate and to make choices is a capacity which can be unproblematically ascribed to a collective entity, and the link between action and outcome is not in the least accidental or attenuated. The original example of the senate's decision and subsequent actions can be interpreted as conforming to this specification. Its possession of formal and explicit decision-procedures is one respect in which, as I indicated in section 1, it belongs to a group of examples of collectivities which possess some special features over and above those features definitive of collective action as such.

These considerations apply to May's argument. Having a minority of a community opposed to a decision does not make it any less true that the community itself did make that decision. It may be explicitly

---

[23] The explicit performative is a common device for creating institutional facts (cf. Searle 1995: 34, 54–5).

laid down in its procedures, for instance, that a simple majority or a two-thirds majority in favour of a course of action constitutes a decision of the community in its favour. Nor does the fact of opposition preclude holding the community itself morally responsible for its decision or for its subsequent actions. Legal responsibility is no doubt a fallible guide to moral responsibility but it is a guide nonetheless, and it may be entirely appropriate to penalise the collectivity as such – for example, by seques-trating its assets – even if there are some within the collectivity who were opposed to what it did.

Once again, there is a useful analogy between the collectivity and the individual. What May refers to as a collectivity with a conflicted mind is analogous to an individual who makes a particular decision even though they see some reasons against it, and maybe even have to resist some of their own impulses in favour of their stronger impulse. The fact of these accompanying tensions does not affect the appropriateness of holding the entity responsible for what, in the end, it decides and does.

Collectivities, indeed, will vary in the relevant respects as much as individuals. At one extreme is the instance of the individual who goes through a self-conscious and explicit process of deliberation and deci-sion about how to act, while at the other extreme is the instance of the individual who blunders about with a total lack of self-knowledge and reason-guided behaviour. Both extremes can be paralleled by collecti-vities: respectively by those of a formal and explicit kind and by those unconscious collectivities modelled on the phenomenon of the unwitting clique. No doubt there is plenty of ground between these extremes in both collective and individual cases, too.

The parallels between individual and collectivity in these respects could be pursued further, but as regards the specific question of moral responsibility, my suggestion is that, in so far as the possession of powers of deliberation and decision is a necessary condition of its ascription, this does not constitute an obstacle to ascribing moral responsibility to some collectivities on some occasions. The claim I have tried to establish, as I stressed earlier, is that there are occasions when moral responsibility can be ascribed to a collectivity *itself*. This leaves open the question of how the responsibility of collectivities relates to the responsibility of the individuals who compose them. That question arises most obviously and most acutely where some members of a collectivity are individually opposed to what the collectivity as such decides to do.

A very wide range of positions is possible concerning the relation of the collectivity's and the individual's responsibility. It might be said that even in relation to one and the same event both kinds of entity can be held responsible; or that guilt accrues to any individual who is a member of a collectivity just by virtue of membership, even if the membership is not voluntary and even if the guilt is not deserved; or that there is a defeasible presumption that any individual who is a member of a collectivity shares responsibility for its wrongdoing; or that an individual's responsibility depends on the role which they played in the collective wrongdoing; or that their responsibility depends on the role they *could have* played in it, whether they chose to or not; or that each individual is responsible for all wrongdoing of the collectivity; or that individuals' responsibility remains just what it would be in the absence of any collectivity.[24] I do not attempt to pronounce on these alternative views about the distinct and further question of the devolution of responsibility to individual members of a collectivity. It is characteristic that pre-existing *moral* views are liable to be invoked to establish rival claims at this point, and that leaves the problem of how to convince someone whose pre-existing moral views are different from one's own.[25]

There may be a more general lesson for questions of responsibility here. Moral responsibility is sometimes treated as a precondition which must be fulfilled before moral comment becomes appropriate. That commonly held position gains expression in remarks like the following:

> Questions of 'moral responsibility' are most often questions about whether some action can be attributed to an agent in the way that is required in order for it to be a basis for moral appraisal ... To say that a person is responsible, in this sense, for a given action is only to say that it is appropriate to take it as a basis of moral appraisal of that person. Nothing is implied about what this appraisal should be – that is to say, about whether the action is praiseworthy, blameworthy, or morally indifferent. (Scanlon 1998: 248)

The danger is that a circle is involved here and that prior moral considerations are actually what ground ascriptions of moral responsibility in the first place. In other words, it is because we believe at the outset that an action is, say, morally reprehensible that we then argue that it is appropriate to hold its perpetrator to be morally responsible for it. An alternative position is not to claim that moral responsibility is a prior condition which must be satisfied before moral comment becomes appropriate, but rather to allow mutual interdependence between ascriptions

---

[24] For discussion and/or occupancy of these positions see French 1984: 113–14; Gilbert 1996: 281, 386; Lewis 1948: 17; May 1992: 106–7; McMahon 1994: 208–11; and Mellema 1997: 110.

[25] Hence we have an instance here of the need, described in the Introduction, to begin from premises which an opponent would themself accept if they are actually to be convinced of anything.

of moral responsibility and the making of moral comment, so that responsibility and susceptibility to blame or praise stand or fall together.[26] The problem I see with this alternative position is that it provides no resources against a sceptic who raises doubts about the reasonableness (as opposed to the moral acceptability) of the entire practice of blaming, for this position abandons the attempt to describe a precondition whose fulfilment would make that practice reasonable. I pursue these issues no further, however. Rather, I reiterate my conditional claim that *if* we employ the notion of moral responsibility at all, we have not found a compelling reason for withholding it from collective entities.

3.6 COLLECTIVITIES AS OBJECTS OF MORAL CONCERN

I now begin the argument that collectivities may enter the moral realm by virtue of being moral patients as well as by virtue of being moral agents. What *happens* to a collectivity is something which can be a matter of reasonable moral concern. I follow a similar procedure to that adopted in relation to responsibility. In this section I outline the *prima facie* case for treating (some) collectivities as objects of moral concern and then in section 7 I consider some objections to that case. Although the question of *treating* collectivities *as* moral agents has now been dealt with and set aside, it will transpire that the case for treating them as moral patients turns in part on considerations which arise from the fact that they *are* agents.

I mentioned in section 3 that non-human animals may be objects of moral consideration, and that is already to populate the moral realm with something besides individual human beings. But it may be thought that calling attention to this case will hardly help to advance the argument for including collectivities under the heading of moral patients. For, of course, both individual human beings and non-human animals are *sentient* creatures. Collectivities are not, so it may be thought out of the question that they should then be reckoned among moral patients.

Will Kymlicka puts forward an argument of that kind in an apposite context, where he is criticising Charles Taylor's contention that a community may have a moral claim for protection, independently of any claims of individual members (Taylor 1987–8). Kymlicka objects:

Groups have no moral claim to well-being independently of their members – groups just aren't the right sort of being to have moral status. They don't feel pain or pleasure. It is individual, sentient beings whose lives go better or worse, who

---

[26] For arguments in favour of that move, see Wallace 1994: 66, 85.

suffer or flourish, and so it is their welfare that is the subject-matter of morality. It seems peculiar to suppose that individuals can legitimately be sacrificed to further the 'health' of something that is incapable of ever suffering or flourishing in a sense that raises claims of justice. (Kymlicka 1989: 241–2)

I find Kymlicka's argument unconvincing, because it is not clear to me why we should tie morality to anything as narrow as sentience. To do so is to ignore many of the less bodily harms that even sentient creatures can visit on one another: such things as deception or offensiveness, for example. These harms are squarely in the moral realm when sentient individuals visit them on one another, but that has nothing to do with their sentience. So why should such harms not also be in the moral realm when they are visited on or by collectivities? (Think how upset politicians get if they think that Parliament has been deceived by one of its members.) In other words, the interpretation of suffering and flourishing in a narrow physical way is *too* narrow to capture many of the concerns of morality. When they are interpreted in a wider way, there is no obvious reason why, say, issues of justice should not arise between collectivities or between a collectivity and an individual.[27]

So much can be said in a negative vein: that the absence of sentience in collectivities is not a sufficient reason to exclude them as patients from the moral realm. Can anything be said in a more positive vein? There is one thing that can be said, though it will not on its own take us far enough. That is that the idea of a collectivity, as such, flourishing is a perfectly intelligible one. Take a football club as one example of a collective entity as defined earlier. Given what a football club is, it is flourishing if it is winning games and championships; and given what the surrounding society is like, if it is doing so in conditions of financial solvency. Such a collectivity's flourishing is a quite distinct matter from the flourishing of the individuals who go to compose it. This is best illustrated by the fact that a given set of individuals may be so hopeless at promoting the aims of the club that the best way to ensure that it begins to flourish again would be to replace them all with other individuals who are more competent at promoting its aims. It will then flourish but they may not. In a similar way, it may be that I may best promote the flourishing of a collectivity to which I belong by driving myself into the ground for its sake. At the extreme, I might literally sacrifice myself so that it can flourish.[28]

---

[27] Notice the shift in Kymlicka's argument from the idea that collectivities have no moral status to the idea that they have no status that might raise questions specifically of justice. These are distinct claims. My own counter-claim is about moral status generally, but I see no reason to agree with either of Kymlicka's claims.

[28] That is an important possibility in the case of collective biological entities (cf. O'Neill 1993: 22).

This point does not take us far enough because the flourishing of a football club is in itself neither moral nor morally significant. Or at least so I would claim. Not everyone would agree. Bill Shankly, the former manager of the English football club Liverpool, once famously remarked: 'Somebody said "Football's a matter of life and death to you." I said "Listen, it's more important than that."' That remark dictates the need to distinguish the claim that assigning collective entities to the moral realm rises to the level of bare conceptual intelligibility from the claim that doing so has some significant degree of plausibility. It is the latter that I am concerned to establish. It is conceptually intelligible that someone should bring fervour, even moral fervour, to the flourishing of a football club, that they should regard it as something of massive importance, overriding what others would take to be the most important moral considerations. It is equally conceivable that someone should take up the same attitude towards the preservation of their family's reputation. But we (or at any rate I) would think that there was something deranged in their doing so, and my assumption is that I shall not convince many readers of the plausibility of assigning collectivities to the moral realm by calling attention to the collective good of a football club.[29]

Now that may raise the suspicion that my achieving such conviction will turn on the contingent question whether there is any collectivity whose flourishing happens to be regarded as morally important both by me and by my readers. However, I now put forward an argument which is intended precisely to minimise that sort of reliance on the particular set of values which anyone happens to hold.

The question is whether there could be some other type of collectivity whose flourishing was more plausibly of moral significance than that of a football club. I suggest that there could be, and I invite the reader to construct their own example, according to the following recipe. Imagine any collective entity whose whole *raison d'être* is to promote or sustain some important moral value. Imagine, for example, that a number of people come together to form an organisation for that purpose: it might be the ending of slavery, the establishment of socialism, the protection of traditional forms of life, the maintenance of an atmosphere of collegiality.

---

[29] Football appears to provide fertile ground for creative thinking. The *Guardian* carried a report in 1997 of a group of Italian anarchists who collectively adopted the identity of Luther Blisset, an English footballer who had had a notoriously disastrous season with an Italian club. They were arrested for travelling on a tram without tickets while simultaneously broadcasting on a local radio station. An editor of the radio station explained: 'Identity and fixity are the enemies of communication and have to be combated by nomadism and collective identity. When the conductor asked for their tickets they replied that a collective identity does not travel with a ticket' (*Guardian*, 15 March 1997, p. 16).

In these circumstances, the collective entity will flourish to the extent that it is succeeding in promoting its aims, and it will be entirely reasonable to regard its flourishing as something *morally* desirable and its enfeeblement as something morally undesirable.[30] Nothing turns on the acceptance of any particular example here, and indeed nothing turns on the *raison d'être* of the collectivity being morally positive. If a group of people formed the Society for the Destruction of Morality this collectivity would enter the moral realm, in the sense defined at the beginning of section 3, because its flourishing would be something morally *un*desirable.

Two objections might be raised to this argument. First, it might be objected that the example is a cheat, since it simply packs in moral considerations which can then be appealed to subsequently to show that the collectivity is a moral patient. Secondly, it might be objected that the example proves too much, since it shows that absolutely anything can be an object of moral concern. A hat or a wastepaper bin could be an object of moral concern if morally significant consequences followed from its destruction – for example, if someone were attached to it for sentimental reasons and its destruction would cause them great distress.[31] But if absolutely anything could be a moral patient, then there would be nothing special about collectivities as originally defined which would be at all germane to their status as moral patients.

I believe that both objections should be resisted. First, if the aim is to establish that some collectivities can be objects of moral concern, as against the view which would confine that status to individual human beings, then it is legitimate to build into an example of a collectivity any particular additional features which might be required to ensure that it has that status. There can be no embargo on endowing the collectivity with properties which turn out to be relevant to the question whether it can be the object of moral concern unless there were some independent reason for such an embargo. To be sure, the concern with what happens to a collectivity in these circumstances will arise from the moral nature of the *consequences* of what happens to it, rather than arising directly and in-trinsically from what happens to it. That is to say, the failure to flourish of

---

[30] There are important distinctions to be made here. A collectivity's aim might be the achievement of some state of affairs not yet extant, or it might be the sustaining of some already-existing state of affairs. In the former case, once the state of affairs had been achieved the demise of the collectivity might be appropriate and unexceptionable. Its flourishing is therefore not necessarily something of moral importance in all circumstances. That is one of many respects in which even morally significant collectivities may differ from human beings.

[31] It might be said that absolutely anything can have moral *significance*, giving rise to moral duties in a roundabout way, but that it is a much more special matter for something to have moral *standing*. Cf. Carruthers 1992: 1.

a collectivity C devoted to realising desirable moral property P will be *bad*, on account of the importance attached to P, rather than *bad for the collectivity C* (or at most, if it *is* bad for C this will because it is bad anyway, rather than vice versa). In that respect the case may differ from the moral concern with what happens to an individual human being, where it may indeed be because something is bad for the individual human being that we can conclude that it is bad. But then, as I have indicated, my claim is not that any collectivity has exactly the same moral status as a human being.

On the other hand, and in answer to the second objection, the fact that a collectivity can be endowed with the property of promoting some moral value indicates why it is especially appropriate to suggest that they enter the moral realm as moral patients and to link this to their agency. Unlike hats or wastepaper bins, collectivities can aspire to, intend to, attempt to and actually produce states of affairs which are themselves morally freighted. It is not definitive of collectivities that they should actually do so, and constituting a collectivity is clearly neither a necessary nor a sufficient condition of being a moral patient. But collectivities have a significantly appropriate potential for acquiring that status, precisely because they share some of the relevant features of individual human beings. What happens to them may be of moral significance because what happens to them may carry implications for what, otherwise, they would be in a position to *do*.

This is the *prima facie* case for assigning collectivities to the moral realm. In the next section I attempt to strengthen it by relating it to a number of suggestions in recent discussion of these issues. They all revolve around the idea that if we endow collective entities with moral importance at all, such importance is merely derivative from the moral importance attaching to individuals. One point that should be stressed is that this idea is not necessarily incompatible with the claim put forward at the beginning of this chapter. The claim *that* collectivities are part of the moral realm is not itself a theory as to *why* they are, and it might be that the explanation as to why they are must be couched in terms of their value to individuals. I shall attempt to cast doubt on that explanation; but I also indicate that, even if it is correct, the entry of collectivities into the moral realm has independent significance.

3.7 COLLECTIVITIES AND PERSONAL GOOD

The unique moral importance of individuals is expressed trenchantly by Philip Pettit in endorsing what he calls *the personalist assumption*, the assumption that the relevant constituency for judging the normative adequacy of political institutions is human beings. He quotes with approval Bentham's advice: 'Individual interests are the only real interests. Take care of individuals; never injure them, or suffer them to be injured, and you will have done well enough by the public' (Bentham 1843: 321, cited in Pettit 1993: 287). Pettit acknowledges the possible rejoinder that many goods are not properties of individuals but rather of corporate entities, goods like the solidarity of a community or the continuity of a culture. His response is that personalism need not be blind to such goods. 'While the goods are not properties of individuals, they are still properties that make an impact on individuals; persons will fare differently, depending on whether they belong to a fractured or solidaristic community' (287).

Christopher McMahon similarly sponsors *moral individualism* and rejects 'the idea that the goods of organizations, understood as distinct organisms, deserve moral consideration' (McMahon 1994: 64). Partly this is held to be because the lives of organisations are so different from those of natural persons. They might in principle last for ever, in which case their claims might simply lose their urgency. Or they may split into two organisations, or readily undergo fission and fusion, in which case we lose a grip on what their interests as organisations actually are. Partly it is held to be because it would be pointless to treat organisations as having moral claims unless they could sometimes outweigh those of individuals. But, McMahon argues:

> Suppose that an organization is threatened with nonexistence because all of its members have discovered more worthwhile ways to spend their time, and no other people are interested in replacing them or would be interested in replacing them in the future. For example, suppose that the only members of a corporation are its employees and they all receive more attractive job offers. It seems absurd that there could be any moral objection to the departure of the members on the ground that the organization will cease to exist if they leave. (65)

John Broome takes up a position similar in a number of respects to that of Pettit and McMahon. He embraces what he calls *the principle of personal good*, 'which says, roughly, that one alternative cannot be better than another unless it is better for someone' (Broome 1991: 131).[32] He then entertains the possibility that something non-personal, such as the

---

[32] Broome adds the slightly puzzling qualification that the principle ought to be prefaced with 'Setting aside goods that are entirely independent of the good of people, ...' (166). However, he makes clear that that qualification is intended to deal with goods such as the survival of some living species which are quite obviously separate from the good of people, and goods of that kind

preservation of a culture, might be thought morally desirable.[33] He suggests that for such a thought to clash with the principle of personal good, it would have to be held that it is sometimes good to preserve a culture even if this is not in the interests of those whose culture it is, nor in anyone else's interests. He argues as follows:

Suppose the progress of materialism breaks up a culture. People have radios and bicycles, and think themselves better off, but they no longer speak their ancestral language and join in communal celebrations. It might be claimed that the results of this development are bad. But would that mean: they are better for the people, but bad all the same? Or would it mean: the people think themselves better off, but actually they are not, because their loss is greater than they think? If the latter, it is simply reminding us that culture is a good, for people, whose value people do not always recognize. If the former, then it is definitely denying the principle of personal good. But the former claim seems implausible to me. Would it really have been better to preserve the culture, even at the cost of denying the people the genuine benefits of material progress? I doubt it. (169)

I now put forward three reasons for finding the line of argument expressed by these thinkers unpersuasive.

First, it relies heavily on an appeal to pre-existing moral intuitions. Perhaps such an appeal is inevitable at some point and in some way in an argument of this kind; but we should take care that it is not too locally based, and it is important to be able to support it with argument. For example, someone in Japan or Korea might not take the *insouciant* attitude that McMahon relies on in talking of the survival of a firm. A collectivity, while not itself being of the kind described in section 6 which has some moral goal as its *raison d'être*, may nevertheless have an admirable history and a present which embodies such qualities as loyalty and honour. And that may be thought enough to make its survival a matter of some (even of moral) importance.

The point here is that initial intuitions may be dislodged, or formed differently, when we realise that a collectivity may be a *locus* of moral qualities even if that is not the reason for its existence. The passing of a firm might be a matter of regret from a moral point of view, even though the role of a firm is the wholly non-moral one of making money. A similar point might be made nearer home with the example of a university department with an illustrious history. Different initial intuitions are likely here because different views are possible about the role of a university

lie beyond the scope of his discussion. His principle is explicitly designed to deal with '[c]ommunal goods, for instance, [which] seem to belong to people together, but not to any individual' (166).
[33] For an example of such a view, see Taylor 1995c.

department. It might be thought that the educative role is itself a moral one, in which case the intuition would be that the demise of a department was morally undesirable. But it might instead be thought that the fostering of *intellectual* virtues was not itself a moral matter, in which case the initial intuition would be that its demise was of no moral concern. But, in a similar way to the case of the firm, that initial intuition might be loosened if it were realised that the department had been the locus of a concern for the well-being of students, the fostering of an atmosphere of friendly and supportive collegiality. It might well then be thought regrettable that it should disappear, even if it does so because all present incumbents find better offers elsewhere.

(Notice how it makes a difference when the locus of moral virtues is a collectivity, even if its virtues gain their importance wholly via their importance for individuals. The set of individuals will be distinct from the set where there is simply an *ad hoc* collection of them. There will be former members of the collectivity to consider, in view of the role which it played in their life and their present feelings towards it. For that reason the continuity of that particular collectivity may be of moral importance as a matter quite distinct from the fortunes of the current members of it.)

Consider how the appeal to intuition works in Broome's argument. He expresses scepticism about the claim that certain developments might be good for people but bad all the same, since they involve the destruction of a notionally non-personal good, a culture. He doubts whether it would be better to preserve the culture at the cost of denying a different kind of good to the people. Hence, he claims, the apparently non-personal good either turns out *not* to be non-personal or else it could not plausibly trump the personal. But the appeal to intuition only supports the conclusion that personal good is not outweighed; it does not support the conclusion that there is no other kind of good involved. Maybe it's true that it *wouldn't* have been better to preserve the culture at that cost. But that does not show that no other kind of good is involved besides personal good. Instead, it might follow from the fact that personal good *always* trumps impersonal or collective goods.

That leads to the second point about these arguments. They ascribe to the sponsor of the moral significance of collectivities a stronger thesis than the sponsor really needs to espouse. They assume that there would be no point in such sponsorship unless the significance of non-individuals were sometimes held to outweigh that of individuals. But that is not so. Consider an analogy to explain why. Suppose you hold a moral theory according to which rights are always trumps. It would not follow that you then had to dismiss the rest of morality as simply redundant. At the very least you would need further theoretical resources to deal with situations where rights simply didn't enter the picture or were equally balanced. In an analogous way, a perfectly tenable position would be to hold that the moral status of individuals was such that it did always outweigh that of collectivities, but that nevertheless there is something there to be outweighed. The moral status of collectivities would matter, for example, when it came to settling issues between collectivities where no individuals' goods as such were at stake, or where individuals' goods were evenly balanced. We might therefore well have reasons for believing that collectivities have moral claims even if these were always outweighed by those of individuals.

The third weakness I perceive in these arguments arises from a concession that they all seem to embody. In each, it seems to be allowed that the *specification* of certain goods is non-individual: solidarity, community, culture, and so on are more abstract than individuals are. But it is held that the explanation of *why* these things are goods must consist in their being good *for* individuals. An analogy may again help to uncover the weakness here.

I may have one of two attitudes towards things that I value: I may value them only *because* I have chosen them or, on the contrary, I may choose them only because I think they have value independently of my choices.[34] As an example of a *choice-dependent value*, I may take up some hobby, for example doing the *Times* crossword puzzle or playing chess, where I don't think there is anything intrinsically worthwhile or valuable in doing those particular things, but I happen to derive enjoyment or absorption or stimulation from doing them. The activities associated with those particular projects, then, would not strike me as having any value if I had not made such a choice: there would be no reason for me to engage in them.[35] On the other hand, there are projects that I may regard as

---

[34] Ronald Dworkin makes a similar distinction between volitional interests, which arise from desires I happen to have, and critical interests, whose importance is not in the same way dependent on my happening to want something (Dworkin 1989: 484–5). See also the related distinctions between valuing and desiring in Smith 1994: 133–5; between intrinsic worth and contribution to well-being in Scanlon 1998: 92; between weak and strong evaluation in Taylor 1995a: 134; and between desiring things because we think them worthwhile and finding things worthwhile because we desire them in Wolf 1997a: 211. Bernard Williams observes that 'if something is important in the relative sense to somebody, this does not necessarily imply that he or she thinks it is, simply, important. It may be of the greatest importance to Henry that his stamp collection be completed with a certain stamp, but even Henry may see that it is not, simply, important' (Williams 1985: 182; cf. Williams 1995a: 189).

[35] Matters are not quite as simple as this makes them appear, however. See chapter 5, section 3.

valuable independently of my choosing them. Here, I don't value them because I have chosen them; rather, I choose them because I think they have value. I might set up and run a soup kitchen for needy people in that spirit. That is, I might regard this as something that has value, something there is reason to do, and not merely reason for someone who has chosen to do it. Projects of this kind rest on *choice-independent values*. Nothing turns on the particular examples I use to illustrate this distinction, of course. Someone could invest the activities I mention with exactly the opposite significance which I have taken them respectively to have and still accept the distinction itself.[36]

This distinction between choice-dependent and choice-independent values and reasons is reproduced in the context of collective entities. I may belong to the lunchtime common-room crossword-puzzle collectivity, which, with its rich combined classical, scientific, philosophical and literary talents, completes the *Times* puzzle in an impressively short time. But I would feel that the world was in no way less valuable for me or anyone else if it did not exist. *A fortiori* I would feel that the world was no less valuable if I quit and went for a swim every lunchtime instead. Alternatively, I may belong to a collectivity whose activities I do regard as having value independently of my choices. Let us suppose that it is an organisation for promoting political or religious consciousness, and let us suppose that I believe that the world *would* be a worse place, maybe for me or for someone else, but maybe just *objectively* worse, if this collectivity did not exist.

By appealing to the existence of choice-independent values we are able to push the origin of value one stage further back from the mere act of valuing on our part: we are able to explain why it is that we should ever come to value one thing rather than another. Analogous considerations can be applied to what Pettit *et al.* say about non-individual goods. When they insist that those goods impact on individuals, what they say is correct. But it doesn't follow that the value of those goods *proceeds from* their impact

---

[36] Susan Wolf takes an altogether sterner line on that. In discussing what gives life meaning, she suggests that some things, such as dedication to music or a political cause, seem suitable for that role while others, such as ice cream, do not. She comments: 'I cannot say that the opportunity to eat it regularly . . . gives me any reason to live whatever. Nor would the ongoing availability of crossword puzzles or mystery novels' (Wolf 1997b: 304). Unless this is taken as a purely autobiographical comment, it seems to me unduly prescriptive in its dismissal of sensory or low-grade cerebral activities. For my part, when I am too feeble to do anything for myself I hope there will be someone else around to spoon ice cream in, and if there is I will consider that that gives me a reason for living. For philosophers a more compelling example might be the enjoyment of the rays of the sun, as Diogenes might confirm. That is a real rather than a flippant example: there are people for whom little else is possible *except* that enjoyment, and they find it sufficient.

on individuals. Rather, we may wish to see those goods promoted and wish to see their benefits accrue to individuals, but precisely because we believe that they are goods independently of that. We don't value them because they are valuable for individuals; on the contrary, we think they are valuable for individuals because we think they are valuable. That seems to me a plausible claim to make about friendship, solidarity, culture and similar things.

These considerations do not themselves support the claim that collectivities are proper objects of moral concern, but they suggest an analogous move which does. If we want to explain why individual human beings themselves are owed moral consideration, rather than simply taking that fact for granted, we have to make reference to what it is *about* them that licenses that claim, and that must involve reference to some state or property or relation, abstractions distinct from individuals themselves.[37] It is in that way that non-human animals, as well as individual human beings, enter the moral realm. A relevant property of human beings to explain why they are granted moral importance is their sentience: they can experience pleasure and suffer pain. Consistency then requires that, *ceteris paribus*, any other entity exhibiting that property enters the moral realm.

But of course sentience is not the only property of human beings which is pertinent to their status as objects of moral consideration. There is a whole complex of other states, properties and relations, such as capacities for self-consciousness, for rich and varied relations with others, the possession of aspirations for the future and the ability to act so as to further them, capacities for loyalty, creativity and amicable or loving relations. Once again, if the value of those states, relations and properties explains the moral importance of human beings, then their exhibition in other entities will, *ceteris paribus*, confer moral importance on those other entities too. If, for example, the capacity for having expectations frustrated is morally important, then it will remain so whether manifested in human beings or in collectivities.

Now there is every reason to hold that some collectivities do exhibit some of the properties in virtue of which individual human beings elicit

---

[37] Other views on this matter are possible, however. Onora O'Neill favours a practical, constructivist approach which 'need not look for a wholly general, theoretical criterion by which to distinguish agents from non-agents, or subjects from mere things' (O'Neill 1996: 93). Jean Hampton argues that if we say that moral regard is to be paid because of some characteristics which a person possesses, 'it turns out to be done not because we have regard for *him*, but because we have regard for that within him which is the carrier of value'. Instead, she prefers the view that 'we simply say that it is our personhood itself which is valuable, and not any particular trait we have' (Hampton 1997: 36, 47).

moral concern, and therefore can be objects of moral concern themselves, well beyond the rather special case where they actually exist to further something of moral importance in the manner suggested in the example of section 6. Committees, or for that matter whole nations, can have aspirations for the future and the capacity to act so as to further them; they can manifest loyalty and trust, and have that loyalty and trust abused; they can be the beneficiaries of generosity or the victims of deception. If it matters morally that these states and relations should or should not obtain, then it will continue to matter morally regardless of whether those experiencing them are individual human beings or collectivities.

I also mentioned at the beginning of section 6 that the case for treating collectivities as moral patients turns in part on considerations which arise from the fact that they are agents. Some of the examples of the previous paragraph indicate why this is so. Collectivities can deliberate, form projects, make decisions and then act in their realisation. Having the power to deliberate and to act necessarily brings with it the power to act for good or ill. But it is also a further standing condition of agency to be susceptible to the thwarting of planned actions (sometimes, though not always, as a result of human agency). This thwarting can happen to a collectivity as well as to an individual. Its happening can be a matter of moral concern in either case, most obviously so where the planned actions themselves have moral significance, thus making the entities in question moral patients. But this particular instance of moral patienthood, being an object of moral concern because of thwarted plans, is possible only because the entity in question is also an *agent*.

It would generally be thought that moral patienthood arising from thwarted plans can exist for individuals even where the thwarted plans are morally neutral. That is, it would be thought that it can be a matter of legitimate moral concern that an agent A is prevented from performing some action X even if the action X itself has no particular moral significance, is neither morally desirable nor morally undesirable. We should note that it is reasonable to hold the same view with regard to some collectivities. For example, it may be thought to be a matter of moral concern if a nation is prevented from acting in self-determination, or if a neighbourhood association is prevented from realising its plan to create a particular kind of environment, even if so acting does not itself carry any moral significance. (Once again, the acceptance of my point here does not turn on a belief that *these particular* collectivities are entitled to moral concern. It is the principle of that possibility that I am arguing for.)

There is a further point. Even if it were true that all moral good is good for people, this is not the same as being good for *individuals*. Take the simplest example, of a couple (cf. Levine 1993: 21). Each individual within it will be morally important, but it is perfectly plausible to regard the couple itself, indivisibly, as morally important. What happens between people, as we significantly put it, may have independent weight. Thus, three conflicting states of affairs may respectively represent what is best for X, what is best for Y and what is best for the couple. X and Y might or might not then subordinate what is best for them as individuals to what is best for them jointly. They might or might not do what is best 'for the relationship'. It may be true that all that is in question in such a case is the good for people, but even so, what is in question in part is what is good for people-as-a-couple.[38]

The recognition or refusal of recognition to the distinct interests of some composite entity of this kind may have substantive and important consequences. In *Griswold v. Connecticut* the US Supreme Court struck down a law prohibiting contraceptives, and it did so on the grounds that the law violated privacy in the sense of intruding into the intimate affairs of a couple. There followed the similar case of *Eisenstadt v. Baird* where the Court also struck down, but its justification for doing so involved a move from the idea of privacy *qua* participant in a relation to privacy *qua* individual. The judgement stated: 'It is true that in *Griswold* the right of privacy in question inhered in the marital relationship. Yet the marital couple is not an independent entity with a mind and heart of its own, but an association of two individuals each with a separate intellectual and emotional makeup.'[39] It is certainly true that a marital couple has no literal heart of its own, rather less clear that it has no mind of its own. What is certainly clear, however, is that a marital couple can reach decisions which the individuals *qua* individuals would not, and it certainly has interests distinct from theirs *qua* individuals.

Moreover, we should not assume that the moral consideration owed to collectivities and their states is necessarily a marginal aspect of morality. That depends partly on how much of people's significant lives are lived in the context of collectivities, and partly on how we elaborate on the values which we take to be of central importance in human life. It is arguable, for

---

[38] 'Some things have value to me and to you, and some things essentially have value to us' (Taylor 1995b: 190; cf. Taylor 1995c: 139).

[39] The cases (*Griswold v. Connecticut*, 381 U.S. 479, 485–486 (1965), *Eisenstadt v. Baird*, 405 U.S. 453 (1972)) are discussed, though for different purposes, in Sandel 1996: 96–7. For discussion of related aspects of the substantive issue see also Cohen 1997.

example, that it is a necessary feature of many central human relations such as friendship and love that there should be a shared understanding involved in them which is not decomposable into X's understanding and Y's understanding (cf. Taylor 1995c: 136–40). If that is correct, then the states of various collective entities will become of fairly central moral concern because of their indispensable role in fostering relations between individuals which are themselves thought of great moral importance.

3.8 CONCLUSION

In chapter 1, section 4 I introduced D1, the idea of qualitative distinctness, the idea that individual persons differ qualitatively from other kinds of entity in certain important respects, such as the capacity for forming intentions and acting on them and the capacity for experiencing a range of emotions and sensations. Associated with that idea is the belief that it is the possession of these characteristics which qualifies individual persons for full membership of the moral realm. Whilst acknowledging that a compendious list of such characteristics could be drawn up which distinguished us from other kinds of entity, I suggested that complications might arise from the fact that some, though not all, of those characteristics are shared by other entities. That is the thought I have explored in the present chapter.

I have tried to follow the strategy of beginning from universal truths about human beings which would be assented to whatever cultural background or philosophical assumptions one began from, and arguing from them to far more contentious conclusions. We thus began from the fact of collective agency. I proposed operating with a generously wide conception of collective agency which extended beyond the case of conscious, intended action. We stand to lose sight of a whole dimension of human action if we leave no conceptual space for actions, either collective or individual, whose character is not necessarily apparent to those whose actions they are. Within that appropriately wide characterisation of collective agency it is then possible to make many pertinent distinctions, such as the distinction between intended and unintended actions, and between conventionally constructed and naturally occurring ones.

The conclusions then are that the actions of certain collectivities are the proper object of moral appraisal because their agency is sufficiently similar to the agency of individual human beings; and that certain collectivities can be the object of moral concern because they exhibit some of the properties in virtue of which individual human beings

themselves elicit moral concern. These claims about the moral significance of what certain collectivities do and the moral significance of what
happens to them does not require that any non-human entity should
be just like a human being. Certainly no collectivities possess moral
importance just *qua* collectivities, in the way in which, arguably, human
beings do *qua* human beings. Nevertheless, I hope to have shown that
there is sufficient overlap in the properties of individual human beings
and collectivities for the doings and the fate of some collectivities to be
morally significant.

If the arguments are sound, the conclusions will apply to any human
society in which human beings form collectivities of the kind described,
which is to say that they will apply to any human society at all. But they
seem peculiarly appropriate in the conditions of modern society. Here,
collective agency is especially powerful. Governments and international
corporations, amongst other collective agencies, have massive resources,
massive powers, and a repertoire of actions which are simply not available
to individual human beings. In these circumstances, a conception of
human agency which concentrates on the case of interaction between
single individuals seems especially inadequate.[40]

In circumstances where such powerful agencies can deliberately and
wittingly act in beneficent or malign ways, a theory of the responsibility
of collectivities is required, and it will have practical consequences. For
example, a clearly worked out account of the conditions in which a
collective agency may be responsible for corporate manslaughter would
give a rationale for claims to compensation – an important possibility
where collective entities are possessed of vastly greater resources. It will
also be of some practical importance to be able to distinguish the case
where a collectivity has acted through some authorised channel from the
case where only an individual has acted. In that connection, Tuomela
provides the interesting example of the Ryti-Ribbentrop Pact. Finland's
President Ryti signed a pact with Ribbentrop, and though the Finnish
government approved of his doing so the pact was intentionally never
taken to the parliament for ratification. In consequence the Finns did

[40] In this connection Galbraith comments, 'The modern corporation or public agency has an
internal intelligence and authority of its own; these are to some extent independent of, or superior
to, those of the persons who are seen, and who see themselves, as in command' (Galbraith 1993:
66). The importance of collective agency in the modern world is a point which is recognised
across a wide political spectrum, ranging from Marx to Hayek. For Marx, the explanation of
the origin of part of surplus-value lies in the results of the cooperation of the collective worker
(Marx 1867: 451–3). For Hayek, social cooperation utilises more knowledge than any individuals
possess (Hayek 1960: ch. 2).

not regard this as a pact which the two *countries* had agreed to, although the Russians did (Tuomela 1989: 252).

I have argued for the inclusion of some collectivities in the moral realm on account of what *happens* to them, as well as the inclusion of some on account of what they *do*. The view that only individual people can be the objects of moral *concern* seems to me an unnecessarily parochial one, and it does not gain extra plausibility merely from the fact that it is the most commonly encountered view in our own parish. As Brian Barry remarks, 'It rules out appeals on behalf of God, Nature, History, Culture, the Glorious Dead, the Spirit of the Nation or any other entity unless that claim can somehow be reduced to terms in which only individual human interests appear' (Barry 1983: 124). Moreover, I have suggested that a proper understanding of the grounds for attaching moral importance to individual human beings themselves provides cognate grounds for attaching moral importance to some collectivities.

Suppose, now, that none of the arguments for attaching moral significance to collectivities are convincing. Even then, it is plain that the fact of participation in collective action carries significance for practical reasoning in general. Individuals themselves can take non-moral but practical decisions about the contributions they make to collective action. They can decide to join or not join a committee, to take part in or not take part in a team's activity, to collaborate or not collaborate with fellow workers. Further reflection is therefore called for, the better to understand the ways in which individuals may identify with or dissociate themselves from what is done in a collective context. It is to that issue that I now turn.

CHAPTER 4

Practical collective identification and dissociation

The topics of this chapter are active *identification with* and *dissociation from* collectivities of the kind defined in the previous chapter. In the case of individual action, an individual may either engage wholeheartedly in what they are doing, identifying with the project they are executing, or they may engage in a curmudgeonly way, where their heart is simply not in the project (perhaps because they are coerced into it). At the extreme, their mental dissociation from their action may result in their ceasing to perform that action at all. An analogous range of attitudes from commitment to dissociation may also accompany an individual's engagement in collective action.

The exhaustive options in the relevant possible relations between individual and collectivity are described; the importance of keeping a theoretical space for the option of dissociation is argued for; and three forms of collective identification (*primitive, mediated* and *pure collective identification*) are distinguished. The aim is to draw out some of the implications for practical reasoning which follow once the existence of collectivities is recognised. In particular, I shall suggest that the model of the individual agent forming plans on the basis of individual preferences is too impoverished to account for all the practical reasoning which is called for: the option of collective identification is in certain respects *sui generis*. I shall introduce an initial, rudimentary description of collective identification – *the first approximation* – and then as the chapter proceeds I shall attempt to pinpoint a number of respects in which it requires elaboration, modification and amendment.

4.1 THE RANGE OF POSSIBILITIES

Collective membership is necessarily relevant to questions of practical decision-making. The awareness that one is a member of a collectivity is the awareness that one is *acting* in a particular way, and it is always possible at least in principle to raise the question whether to *go on* acting in that way. The claim is not that when one discovers that one is a member of a collectivity one necessarily does raise for oneself questions like 'Do I want to be acting as I am?' or 'Have I any good reason for doing this?' Rather, the point is the doubly modal one that it *must* be *possible* to raise such questions, although in the event one may for all kinds of reasons fail to do so.[1]

It is possible to take a stronger view. Christine Korsgaard argues: 'Reflective distance from our impulses makes it both possible *and necessary* to decide which ones we will act on: it forces us to act for reasons' (Korsgaard 1996: 113; italics added). She adds that 'in one sense no human action can happen without reflective endorsement. When people skip reflection or stop too soon, that is a kind of endorsement, for it implies that the work of reflection is done' (161). Thomas Nagel agrees. He raises the question why a reflective self must decide anything, rather than simply being a passive observer. His answer is that it is the very same self which reflects and decides. 'Given that the person *can* either try to resist or not, and that he is now self-conscious, anything he does will imply endorsement, permission, or disapproval from the reflective standpoint' (Nagel 1996: 201).

This view seems to me *too* strong. Even though it may be true that it is one and the same self which reflects and decides, these are distinct activities and either of them may occur without the other. My reflection may be idle or ironic and detached in nature, and may entirely fail to influence the way in which I act. In that case, the reflective self need not be giving permission for the actions of the acting self: it simply remains aloof. Equally, of course, I may act impulsively or unwittingly, without any reflection at all. But when reflection has occurred, the accompanying awareness and knowledge of my own actions at least gives the opportunity for endorsement or disapproval of them.

When you become conscious of the collectivities you are a part of and the actions which they and you engage in, then, you may not reflect any further on those facts or arrive at any attitudes towards them and you may not act any differently. But a rational agent would undertake some appraisal of that kind. Since we are not merely agents but reflective agents, we are capable of doing this. I shall argue, moreover, that this capacity is part of a wider capacity to reflect on the characteristics which

---

[1] A similar kind of double modality occurs in Thomas Nagel's claim that 'Whenever one acts for a reason ... it must be *possible* to regard oneself as acting for an objective reason' (Nagel 1970: 96–7), and in Onora O'Neill's claim that 'reasons for action *must* be held *capable* of being followed or adopted by others' (O'Neill 1996: 57).

define us and to decide, either in practice or in attitude, whether or not to acquiesce in their so defining us. We may, within limits, decide who we are and what sort of agents to be; and that includes as an important possibility the decision whether to act singly or collectively. To adopt a phrase of Susan Hurley's, we do not have to take the unit of agency as fixed and it would be irrational to do so. We can achieve more, and can avoid some well-known difficulties connected with the Prisoners' Dilemma, if we are prepared to act, say, as a *pair* in certain situations where untoward results will follow if we do not do so (Hurley 1989: 145–7; cf. Sugden 1993).[2]

Collective identification and collective dissociation are properly seen as representing two polar extremes in the matter of one's relation to collectivities: as contraries rather than as contradictories. Between them lies a great deal of territory, including the area occupied by witting or unwitting indifference, unthinking acquiescence and even a failure consciously to distinguish oneself from the corporate entity as part of which one acts (one may simply be *immersed* in it).[3] In a slightly procrustean way we might plot the exhaustive possibilities in the matter of one's relation to collectivities as follows. Either one is engaged in some collective action or one is not; and either one actively identifies with the action or one does not. This gives a total of four exhaustive possibilities, where E signifies engagement in action and I signifies active identification:

	I	*NOT-I*
E	*E/I*	*E/Not-I*
NOT-E	*Not-E/I*	*Not-E/Not-I*

All four possibilities are fulfilled, though some are of more interest than others and some of the four contain crucially distinct variants within them. Of least interest is the bottom right-hand quadrant, *Not-E/Not-I*. Many people unknown to me, in many faraway parts of the globe, are

[2] Sugden has the nice example of a handbook for players of bridge. Someone might object that they had reason to follow the book's advice only if they had reason to think that their partner would. But that is to miss the point that such handbooks are written precisely for people who are prepared to think and act as a team, rather than for people for whom any act of collaboration is problematic (Sugden 1993: 85).

[3] Unthinking acquiescence may, of course, bring its own rewards. For example, a corporate organisation may give a greater reward to someone who simply identifies with it rather than questioning its beliefs and policies, even if it is true that the outcome of such questioning would be a conscious affirmation of its beliefs and policies. Reflective support may be less useful to the corporation than unthinking support. Cf. Galbraith 1993: 68.

engaged in collective activity which I know nothing about and *a fortiori* have no attitude towards. In such a case my state instantiates *Not-E/Not-I*, but nothing of any consequence follows and the case is desperately uninteresting. By contrast, I am particularly concerned with cases where I am part of some collectivity, am not simply immersed in it and have raised for myself the question whether to identify with or dissociate from it. That leads to a concern with *E/I*, the phenomenon represented in the top left-hand quadrant, engagement in collective activity accompanied by active identification, and with one variant of *E/Not-I*, the cluster of phenomena represented in the top right-hand quadrant, namely cases where I do not merely fail to identify with the collective activity but where I positively dissociate myself from it. (Mere failure to identify would be exemplified by the phenomenon of the unwitting clique described in chapter 3, section 2. Failure to identify occurs in such a case because the individuals engaged in the collective activity are unaware that they are so engaged, as a consequence of which the choice of identification or dissociation does not present itself.)

At first sight it might seem that the bottom left-hand quadrant, *Not-E/I*, must represent an empty category. After all, if I am not engaged in collective action, how can any question of my identifying with it arise? But this would be a mistake. A trivial and a serious example illustrate why. It is common for football fans to identify with the actions of the team they support. They speak of how the match turned around after *we* scored the equaliser. They are not participants in the team's collective actions but they speak as if they were.[4] In a similar way, it sometimes happens that people feel a shared sense of guilt, taint or responsibility for actions performed by some group to which they belong even if they were not themselves involved in the performance of the actions. Americans who played no part in the massacre at My Lai may feel guilt or taint in that connection, as may Germans who were not themselves Nazis when they contemplate the Holocaust. They feel that a significant point is expressed in the thought that, after all, *we* were responsible for those events (cf. May 1992: 152).

Mention should be made of a further phenomenon of collective identification which falls outside the matrix but is of importance. In chapter 3,

---

[4] It might be objected that in an extended sense the fans *are* participants in the actions since their presence and vocal encouragement are causally instrumental in achieving the desired outcome. But this way of speaking is adopted even by fans who are nowhere near the scene of the action and therefore do not even play this minimal causal role. In these circumstances, therefore, the identification does occur with actions to which the fans are not party.

section 2 I introduced the category of *potential collectivities*. In these cases I am not engaged in collective action because there is none such to be engaged in. Nevertheless, I may still identify with a potential collectivity. I indicated in that section how people's consciousness of a potential collectivity might be influential in determining their actions: the knowledge that a group of other people *could* act collectively in a certain way might lead a spectator with such knowledge, for example, to forestall just that possibility. Such is the *external* view of a potential collectivity. What we should now notice is that an *internal* view of a potential collectivity may also play a significant role in an individual's thought and action.

There is an analogy between an individual's identification with a potential collectivity and an individual's thought about potential individual action. In the latter case, the individual may form a conception of a possible action, judge that there is some reason in favour of performing it and move to do so. In the former case, they may form a conception of a possible collective action and judge that there is some reason in favour of it. They cannot then move to perform it. Partly this is because the performance of a collective action is never an option for an individual,[5] but also because the circumstances for their participation in collective action are *ex hypothesi* not in existence where the collectivity in question is only a potential one. But what they can do (and what it is reasonable for them to do) is take whatever steps they can to create those circumstances, to create a state of affairs where they and others do jointly perform the collective action in question.[6]

Thoughts about potential collectivities can play a creative and innovative role in the life of human agents. For example, a number of people may recognise that they form a potential collectivity capable of preventing some harm; and that recognition may itself play a role in their actually forming themselves into the relevant collectivity. People are starving, they might say, but if we joined together to organise a relief operation we could achieve the ending of this state of affairs in a way in which none of us individually could do.[7] Or consider disputes among Marxists and post-Marxists about the relative significance of such dimensions as class,

---

[5] Except in the necessarily special case, noted in chapter 3, section 1, where one person is authorised to act on behalf of the collectivity.

[6] Compare what Nagel says about those predicates which provide reasons: 'Such a predicate provides reasons both primarily and derivatively: primarily, for things to which it applies, and derivatively, for things which promote that to which it applies primarily' (Nagel 1970: 47).

[7] The example is Larry May's. He adds to it the more contentious claim that 'the potential members of these groups often must first recognize that they share responsibility for the harms, in order to feel motivated to form structures allowing for collective action' (May 1992: 105).

gender and race. In a familiar dialectical move post-Marxists will complain that Marxists wrongly privilege class against other dimensions, and Marxists will reply that, while these other dimensions may carry their own significance, they have not played the role that class divisions have in the structure and development of history. This dialogue may simply be conducted at cross purposes. The primary point of the post-Marxists may be not explanatory but normative: not to explain why history has developed in a particular way but to indicate where the interests of different groups of people lie and therefore what reasons they have for acting in various ways. In that vein they might argue that people distinguished in terms of non-class characteristics have not played the role in history which classes have played precisely because such people have been oppressed in ways which made unlikely their organisation into effective collective agents. In other words, their point may be to distinguish *potential* collectivities by reference to the characteristics and interests of those who would compose them. If that is correct, then the absence of groups characterised in non-class terms as major historical agents would not prejudice the claim that they have reasons to *become* major agents. As the post-Marxists might say, in an ironically *tu quoque* spirit, *es kommt darauf an sie zu veraendern,* the point is to change the state of affairs which has obtained historically so that groupings other than class groupings begin to control events. The debate would then have to proceed on the terrain of explicitly normative considerations pertaining to practical reasoning – an outcome which seems to me entirely in keeping with Marx's own aspiration to change the world rather than merely interpreting it. It does not follow, of course, that the post-Marxists would have a better case than the Marxists on this terrain. I pursue some of those complications in chapter 5, section 6.[8]

4.2 COMMUNITY AND IDENTITY

The topic of this chapter is distinct from but overlaps with discussion familiar from the liberal/communitarian debate. The concept of a community is a protean one. At the very least it must designate some kind of commonality; but *what* is shared in common, and to what degree, is a matter of alternative interpretations. It may be a question of common origins, beliefs, values, aspirations or interests.[9] On some understandings,

---

[8] For further discussion see Graham 1992: 57–60; Levine 1987: 5; Levine 1993: 13–15; and Offe and Wiesenthal 1985: 170–220.

[9] For reliance on some of these different dimensions of commonality, see for example Kukathas 1996: 80–104; Sandel 1982: 148–53; and Taylor 1982: 25–30.

therefore, the idea of community may designate only *passive* features of people's lives and situation. But though communities need not, they may, as a matter of fact, constitute a collectivity, an agency of the kind specified in the previous chapter. Where they do, questions of identification will arise in exactly the same way as for any other collectivity. I can in principle raise the question whether to act as a constituent of that community.

Indeed, the process of appraisal, leading to possible endorsement or dissociation, has application over a much wider area than just that of collective existence. That process is available not just where I become conscious of some collective (or for that matter, individual) action that I am involved in, but wherever I discover that some predicate is true of me. Wherever I discover not just what I am *doing* but what I *am*, I can in principle raise the question of whether or not to acquiesce in what I have discovered.[10] More general considerations therefore need to be taken into account here, since the discovery that I am a member of a collectivity is simply one form taken by the discovery that a predicate is true of me.

The first step in arriving at an adequate understanding of collective identification is to distinguish it from simple identity. Consider some well-known passages from communitarian literature. Alasdair MacIntyre says that

we all approach our own circumstances as bearers of a particular social identity. I am someone's son or daughter, someone else's cousin or uncle; I am a citizen of this or that city, a member of this or that guild or profession; I belong to this clan, that tribe, this nation. Hence what is good for me has to be the good for one who inhabits these roles. (MacIntyre 1981: 204–5)

He also says that where the virtue of patriotism is in question it 'requires me to regard such contingent social facts as where I was born and what government ruled over that place at that time, who my parents were, who my great-great-grandparents were and so on, as deciding for me the question of what virtuous action is' (MacIntyre 1984: 93).

Michael Sandel, in criticism of a 'deontological ethics' which insists that we view ourselves as independent selves, refers to

loyalties and convictions whose moral force consists partly in the fact that living by them is inseparable from understanding ourselves as the particular persons we

---

[10] I can in principle always raise that question, but sometimes the answer to it will be 'You cannot, even in principle, decide to divest yourself of that predicate. It is necessarily attached to you.' The constraints on practical decision-making implicit in that answer will concern us in chapter 5, section 4.

are – as members of this family or community or nation or people, as bearers of this history, as sons and daughters of that revolution, as citizens of this republic. Allegiances such as these . . . allow that to some I owe more than justice requires or even permits, not by reason of agreements I have made but instead in virtue of those more or less enduring attachments and commitments which taken together partly define the person I am. (Sandel 1982: 179)

Now there is something importantly correct in these claims. If the arguments in chapter 2 were sound then it will be impossible to give an exhaustive account of who or what I am merely by the use of one-place predicates. Any significant description of me will by implication include causal links to other human beings, in terms of either causal consequence or causal precondition. Indeed, even to describe me as a human being is implicitly to rely on at least two-place predicates, since a human being is the result of the actions of parents. And if the arguments in chapter 3 were sound then at least part of my identity will be given by an enumeration of the collectivities to which I belong. Part of what I am is a member of a given family, or committee, or trade union, or church, or class, when part of what I do is act as a constituent of such bodies. By extension, part of what I am will be given by reference to the various attachments mentioned by these authors, whether or not the entities with which the attachments are associated actually constitute collectivities in the sense defined in the previous chapter.

But there is a great difference between passive identity of that kind and *active, practical identification with* collectivities. We might say that practical identification with a collectivity consists in *associating myself with its decisions and actions, on appropriate occasions attempting to think and act as if for the collectivity itself, and taking its good as my own, treating it as I would treat my own individual good.* I shall refer to this as *the first approximation* to an account of collective identification: it will turn out to be in need of various elaborations, modifications and amendments.[11]

Practical identification, taken in the sense specified in the first approximation, goes beyond simple identity since it involves endorsement of a practical attitude rather than just recognition of a fact. A similar extension is involved in the passages quoted from MacIntyre and Sandel, when I do not merely recognise that I am a member of different communal entities but adopt certain specifically moral obligations in that connection.

---

[11] The topic of such collective identification is a recognisably Rousseauean one, of course. For pertinent comments, see Levine 1993: 81.

Now the analytical distinction between identifying oneself *as* a member of some entity E and actively identifying oneself *with* the entity E might readily be conceded. But one way of interpreting these passages is as holding that the two nevertheless go together, that the factual description of oneself as a member of E licenses some kind of inference to the practical decision to accept E-related obligations, actions or whatever. (Notice the 'Hence' in the first quotation from MacIntyre and the strongly modalised claim that what is good for me *has to be* the good for a member of E.) This is an altogether more questionable claim, even if one sees nothing wrong in general with moves from factual premises to practical conclusions. I now proceed to question it.

4.3 IDENTITY AND DISSOCIATION

The claim that identity and identification coincide is not without a degree of plausibility. After all, it is a striking fact about predicates used to describe social roles that they seem to carry with them some specific range of both obligations and interests. For example, being a son or daughter or parent carries with it the idea of a set of obligations and interests. So, it seems, does being a teacher or a neighbour or a cyclist. Predicates used to describe collective membership are a sub-class of such social predicates, so the same will apply to them. To be a member of a team, it seems, will equally carry with it the idea of certain characteristic obligations and interests.

What are we to make of this apparent connection between social roles and obligations or interests? We might treat it in a relatively circumspect way, as Martin Hollis does when he suggests that roles are sets of essentially normative but only quasi-moral expectations, so that less than 'pukka' moral obligations are attached to them (Hollis 1998: 111–16).[12] Or we might adopt the less qualified position expressed by Christine Korsgaard: 'You are a human being, a woman or a man, an adherent of a certain religion, a member of an ethnic group, a member of a certain profession, someone's lover or friend, and so on. And all of these identities give rise to reasons and obligations' (Korsgaard 1996: 101). I want to suggest two distinct reasons for greater circumspection in the matter.

First, both Hollis and Korsgaard recognise that a multiplicity of the relevant predicates may apply to a person, and that fact carries with it the

---

[12] Hollis notes that such 'quasi-duties', often arising in connection with kinship, patriotism, nationalism and fundamentalist religion, can serve to unite insiders in a sense of their superiority to outsiders (117).

possibility of conflict. The obligations associated with parenthood may conflict with the obligations associated with citizenship. (Do I turn my son or daughter in when I discover that they are dealing in hard drugs?) The interests associated with being a cyclist may conflict with the interests associated with being a taxpayer. (Do I forego benefits I might obtain from my income in order to contribute to the cost of traffic-calming measures?) That kind of clash provides the site not just for problematic reasoning about interests but also for many instances of moral agony. It provides, too, one reason why practical judgements cannot be inferred from truths about social roles. At most, *prima facie* or *pro tem* judgements could be inferred.[13]

Even these weaker inferences become insecure, however, in the light of the second reason. I put it first in terms of the *interests* associated with a given predicate, then I suggest that it also applies to *obligations* associated with a given predicate. In the case of interests, if the predicate 'concentration camp inmate' or 'registered unemployed person' applies to me, then it might be said that certain interests will be associated with the possession of those characteristics: an interest in staying on good terms with the camp commandant, an interest in seeing the level of income support maintained. But these limited interests, as it were, are in effect displaced by an overriding interest in shedding the characteristics in question, an interest in living outside a concentration camp, an interest in getting a job or joining the seriously rich *un*registered unemployed people. Associated with some of these predicates, then, are what I have elsewhere called *escape-interests*, an interest in that predicate's *ceasing* to be true of me, which eclipses any more confined interest arising from the fact that it *is* true of me (Graham 1986b: 26). The predicate provides material for a practical decision, but it does so in the form of providing me with reasons for choosing to *change* my identity in the relevant respects.

It might be objected that the original, limited interest remains at least as a *prima facie* practical implication of the predicate and that this is displaced only by further information about the circumstances of the agent, in which case practical implications can after all be read off the applicability of a predicate relating to a social role. The answer to this is twofold. First, it is already a sufficiently serious matter if only

---

[13] Or perhaps even *pro tanto* judgements, in terms of which it might be possible to judge that I ought (in respect of my role as a parent) to do x and that I ought (in respect of my role as a citizen) to do not-x (cf. Hurley 1989: 130–3). However, there are grounds for thinking that *pro tanto* reasons too would lapse in the light of the second argument I give for dissociating practical decisions from the occupation of a social role. For further discussion of *pro tanto* reasons, see chapter 6, section 3.

prima facie inferences are possible, since in that case the bolder, unqualified conclusions about what follows from occupancy of such a role will no longer apply. But secondly, we can distinguish cases where an escape-interest follows directly from the nature of a description and cases where it follows only together with some further specification of the particular circumstances in which it applies. The descriptions 'victim of racial discrimination' and 'dependant on income support' illustrate the distinction: the former of its very nature carries an escape-interest whereas the latter does so only given certain contingent truths about the treatment of such dependants in certain circumstances (Graham 1996a: 138).

If someone may have a reason for distancing themself from some social role and the interests associated with it, an analogous point can be made in terms of obligations. Certain obligations and duties may be associated with a predicate, but if the predicate in question is 'concentration camp commandant' then its applicability to me does not give me a reason to discharge those duties but rather a reason to rid myself of the predicate. Hollis's circumspection is entirely apposite. And though the point has been made by reference to a particular moral value (the undesirability of anyone's being a concentration camp commandant) it does not depend on subscription to any particular values. It requires only a recognition that there are or may be cases where it would be morally undesirable for anyone to carry out the duties associated with a particular social role. My argument is therefore an analytical one about the conceptual distinctions needed for an adequate view of the phenomena about which people take up moral attitudes.

Sometimes, of course, actual escape may not be an option. I may be trapped in a role or a collectivity and have no alternatives but to participate in some form of collective action which I think there is reason not to perform. For example, I may be a coerced member of a collectivity, such as a conscientious objector conscripted into the army. In that case the psychological escape afforded by dissociation may become particularly important. This may be the only avenue available for sustaining my sense of who I am, not in the literal sense of what predicates are applicable to me but rather in the sense of what values I endorse. The preferable avenue may be to *act* in a way which manifests my commitment to particular values, but if that is not an option then at least I can take up an *attitude* which reflects it.

The Patti Hearst case is instructive in that regard. Patti Hearst was abducted by an obscure group called the Symbionese Liberation Army and subsequently took part in armed raids with its members. It would be possible to take part in these collective actions while reminding oneself that the participation was coerced and that one did not endorse what was being done. The ironic twist in this case is that the evidence of security video footage suggested that she was in fact a willing participant, and an audio tape was heard on radio in which she announced her conversion to her captors' views and denounced her parents. It is a reasonable assumption that in this case the failure to dissociate in attitude was a consequence of brainwashing. In less extreme and less isolating circumstances, collective dissociation in attitude may be available. Thus, imagine a number of individuals who belong to a collectivity consisting of slaves. Membership of the collectivity is oppressive for them, and they might form within it a distinct collectivity devoted to furthering their escape-interests, their interest in securing a state of affairs where they were no longer slaves. Relevant shared experience could play a role there – they would not simply be cut adrift from any sense of identity by the act of dissociation in attitude – but without the accompanying characteristic of acquiescing in their own oppression, as would be the case if they simply identified with the slave collectivity.

Communitarians tend to be at best ambivalent in their acknowledge-ment of my ability to distance myself from the values implicit in the descriptions that apply to me. MacIntyre, for example, allows that 'rebellion against my identity is always one possible mode of expressing it' and does not insist 'that the self has to accept the moral *limitations* of the particularity of... forms of community'; but he still maintains that 'the self has to find its identity in communities such as those of the family, the neighbourhood, the city and the tribe' (MacIntyre 1981: 205). Sandel similarly allows that as 'a self-interpreting being, I am able to re-flect on my history and in this sense to distance myself from it'; but he too maintains that 'the distance is always precarious and provi-sional, the point of reflection never finally secured outside the history itself' (Sandel 1982: 179).

The strength of the case for allowing identity and identification to co-incide should be acknowledged. The values of our family, neighbourhood or tribe exert an enormous causal influence over our practical decisions. This is so not just in the sense that we are much more likely to opt for and value certain courses of action if we are surrounded by other peo-ple who do so, but also in the sense that the norms and standards and forms of reasoning by which we make practical decisions are likely to be similarly influenced. Departure from the values of our background and the identity which it gives us may not be practically possible. Daniel Bell asks (rhetorically), 'Is it possible for an Inuit person from Canada's far North suddenly to decide to stop being an Inuit, or is the only sensible response to recognize and accept this constitutive feature of her identity?' (Bell 1993: 10) If departure is possible, it may nevertheless carry severe penalties, as may happen, for example, with a departure from traditionally expected gender roles (cf. Sandel 1996: 111–15). Moreover, some form of recognition by our fellow human beings is important to us; and whereas recognition can be taken for granted during our occupancy of a traditional role, there is no such guarantee if we forsake a traditional role in favour of some other one which we simply construct for ourselves (cf. Taylor 1992: 34–5). The importance of identity in the sense in play here is attested to by the chilling example of the Kosovo Albanians who were stripped of their identity in a fairly literal sense on leaving Kosovo: no objects or documents remained with them which would indicate who they were. That might be thought an apt image for the idea of making practical decisions from some detached, mid-air position, rather than from the vantage point of the norms and standards with which we grew up. In any case, it might be said, why place so much emphasis on possibilities of dissociation when there may be nothing wrong with the values of our background in the first place?

Many of these observations are well taken, and some of them will concern us in chapter 5. It is certainly true that we have to make practical decisions from *somewhere*, in other words with certain standards and values and with a certain assumed identity; there is no mid-air position from which to do so. But it does not have to be from the community that we find ourselves in or that we grew up in. (We should never forget that we may be more or less lucky in that regard.) Not only that, but the fact that we have grown up with certain values is in itself *no reason whatever* to endorse them. If they have something to be said for them then they have something to be said for them, but that something does not include, even as a part, the fact that we were imbued with them.

Seyla Benhabib has suggested that the moral point of view arises precisely when people raise the question 'under what conditions can we say that these general rules of action are valid not simply because it is what you and I have been brought up to believe or because my parents, the synagogue, my neighbours, my tribe say so, but because they are fair, just, impartial, in the mutual interest of all?' (Benhabib 1992: 6) My concern is with validity in a wider sense than Benhabib's, since it is a concern with *any* kind of good reason rather than necessarily a specifically moral one.[14] But her point applies in the wider sphere of good reasons in general. To have a good reason for identifying with our community, more is required than simply that it is *ours* or simply that we *do*.

That point applies all the more clearly in the pluralist circumstances described in chapter 1. We know that we subscribe to the values that we do chiefly because of the circumstances in which we have been brought up, and we therefore know that had we been brought up in different circumstances we would hold different values. We are also acutely aware that we are surrounded by diverse cultures where people do subscribe to other values than ours and that exactly the same is true of those people as is true of ourselves. These facts ought to disturb us more than they do and ought to impress on us the importance of being able to give a reasonable justification of the values we hold, separately from the contingencies which explain how we come to hold them.[15] As Susan Hurley puts it, human beings are 'self-determining agents, who have the capacity and the responsibility to determine, in part, their own identities. The irrationality of failing to do so cannot be avoided by declining responsibility for who one is, by treating the identities of persons as a fixed brute fact' (Hurley 1989: 158).

It is perhaps worth stressing that what needs to replace mere unthinking assimilation of the values surrounding an agent, and the identity implicit in them, is *justifiable* selection either of these or of alternatives, rather than *mere* selection. With certain provisos the mere fact that I have chosen certain values does not have any reason-conferring power.[16] There may be good reasons for identifying with a collectivity even where I do not choose to do so, but equally there may be an absence of good reasons where I do choose to do so. This too is a matter to address more fully in the next chapter, but what can be said here is that just as mere unthinking acquiescence does not give a good reason for identification

---

[14] And after all, we may fail to find many rules of action which exhibit the extremely demanding feature of being in the mutual interest of *all*; the world may simply not be arranged in a way which accommodates that. There may be irreconcilably conflicting interests, or we may be surrounded by zero-sum games. Benhabib herself seems to acknowledge the difficulty of specifying wholly general interests (cf. Benhabib 1992: 48).

[15] For serious discussion of these issues, see Cohen 2000: 7–19 and Scanlon 1998: 336–8.

[16] I suggested in chapter 3, section 7 that there could be such choice-dependent values in the trivial case of a hobby which I take up even though I do not believe the activity has any intrinsic worth: I do not choose it because it has value, but rather it comes to have value for me simply because I have chosen it. The fact that these cases are so marginal underlines the inappropriateness of allowing mere choice to carry such weight in the present context, where so much more is at stake. But for further complications in the question of choice-dependent values see chapter 5, section 3.

neither does mere choice. The choice must itself be guided by appropriate considerations (whatever they turn out to be).

4.4 PRIMITIVE AND MEDIATED COLLECTIVE IDENTIFICATION

So far, we have the first approximation to a description of collective practical identification and an argument that there is a need in principle for rational assessment of such identification. The argument has proceeded mainly via the negative claim that dissociation from some existing identification may have to be contemplated. In this section I begin the elaboration of the first approximation by describing two forms which collective identification can take: primitive and mediated. (Pure collective identification is described in section 5.)

In *primitive collective identification* I associate myself with the actions and decisions of a collectivity because, and to the extent that, I believe that they advance my individual goals.[17] This case provides one model and a very limited conception of how an individual can come to identify with a group's actions. The model is important because it shows how collective identification can lead to 'mutually beneficial cooperation, [in which] each agent cooperates to advance her own aims' (McMahon 1994: 103). The limited nature of this form of identification is apparent in

The Principle of Collective Rationality. One has reason to contribute to a cooperative venture that produces something that one regards as good if its total value to one when one's contribution is added to those of the others who have contributed or will contribute exceeds the cost to one of contributing. (104)

The identification is limited because although it involves a commitment to a collective project, the commitment is born of entirely individual reasons. Indeed, one person's reason for the commitment may be quite different from another person's just because their goals are different. You and I may be committed to the collective project of painting a house, but our respective reasons for that commitment may be my wanting a painted house and your wanting to get some exercise.[18]

It is consistent with recognising this limited form of commitment to collective projects to take the view that no other form is even possible. Thus, McMahon argues with regard to democratic decision-making that

---

[17] The very act of joining a collectivity may be seen as an expression of identification, and withdrawal as an expression of dissociation. For the historical importance of this kind of identification with a collectivity, see Pizzorno 1981: 256–8.

[18] The example is from Bratman 1992: 329, though he uses it to illustrate a different point.

'if the members of a group are to defer to democratic decision making because of its epistemic properties, then, they must be able to regard it as a way of obtaining a better understanding of what they *as individuals* have reason to do' (McMahon 1994: 145). The implicit contrast with what they have reason to do as individuals is with what they have reason to do *as a collective body*.

Primitive collective identification is entirely congenial with standard forms of rational choice theory, whether in the general form of assuming that rational agents act in a maximising way to achieve their objectives, whatever those objectives happen to be, or in the more specific form of assuming that rational agents act in pursuance of their narrow self-interest.[19] All the same, primitive identification is not nugatory: it changes the range of reasons open to an individual agent. Suppose, for example, that I have some goal G and that I also have empirical evidence that the Society for the Promotion of Goal G, of which I am a member, is better at achieving that goal than I am. Then, in so far as this is my objective, I have reason to identify with that collectivity and to accord its decisions greater weight than my own unaided judgements. The existence of such a collectivity makes a substantive difference to the practical reasons available to me.

The stage is then set for potential conflicts between the different reasons available to me. Suppose, more particularly, that the goal G in question is the serving of my interests. Then, so far as pursuit of my interests is directly concerned, I have a reason to identify with the collectivity. But it is common to attach a premium to autonomy, in the sense of retaining for oneself the discretion over how to act in such matters rather than ceding that discretion to other agencies. To the extent that I do place a premium on autonomy in this sense, I have a reason to act on my own individual judgement. Well and good if I exercise my autonomy by choosing to identify with the collectivity in these circumstances; not well and good if I do not.

The idea of an individual's interests is not unproblematic, and the introduction of mediated and pure collective identification (and later arguments) will suggest some reasons why. The idea of *mediated collective identification* can be introduced in the following way. In order for me to pursue my self-interest, whether according to my own judgements or by identifying with a collectivity designed for that purpose, it must be clear who or what this 'self' is whose interests are to be pursued. We have

---

[19] For recent discussion of such theories, and their connection with the model of *homo economicus*, see Brennan and Lomasky 1993.

seen, in the previous section, some of the sources for reaching clarity on that question in the stock of social descriptions which may apply to me. Now I may reasonably care about what happens to me not in all my particularity but under such specific limited descriptions, and this opens up the possibility of identifying with a collectivity because of what *we* are able to achieve or because of what is being done *to us*, where the relevant plurality is identified by some characteristic which I share with others. For example, I share some characteristic C with a number of other people and we come to form a collectivity. I then associate myself with the acts of the collectivity, and this association is mediated by a concern for what happens to someone with characteristic C. In that spirit my motivation to identify with a collectivity can extend beyond my bare individuality, as it were. For example, I might as a coloured person become a member of the National Association for the Advancement of Colored People.

Notice that this process of collective identification might proceed along one of two routes. First, we might for various reasons *ourselves* judge that some characteristic C has significance: either because we have ourselves endowed it with significance (we have, for example, just constituted ourselves as the team wearing red ties), or because we believe it has some intrinsic significance (people with impaired vision share certain problems and certain interests in common).[20] Or, secondly, while regarding C as having no significance in itself, we might be compelled to invest it with significance because *other people* treat those of us who possess that characteristic in a particular way (for example, we are victimised because of our race or our sex). To adopt a particular terminology, we might regard the characteristic C as carrying *original* significance or *reactive* significance, depending on whether the significance originates with some independent judgement of the agent or is attached to a characteristic in reaction to the behaviour or attitudes or judgements of others.[21] In either set of

[20] The contrast introduced here between original and reactive significance is therefore distinct from the contrast between choice-dependent and choice-independent values. What is essential for original significance is simply that the significance be judged to be present by the agent themself, whether as a result of their decision and *fiat* or as a result of their being moved by antecedently existing considerations. Hence original significance can arise both from choice-dependent and from choice-independent values. But where the antecedently existing considerations are composed of the judgements of *other* agents, then the significance becomes reactive rather than original, in the terminology adopted here.

[21] For discussion of phenomena which fall under the description of reactive significance as defined here, and in particular of the role which awareness of a common enemy or oppressor can play in creating common interests and joint actions, see Elster 1986b: 150–3; May 1987: 39–40; and Sartre 1960: 353–7. The distinction between original and reactive significance is applied to the constraints of necessity discussed in chapter 5, section 4.

circumstances we may join together and form a collectivity which exists to protect or further the interests of those who possess characteristic C.

Whichever route the process of identification travels along, whether through the significance which we ourselves attach to C or through the significance which other people attach to C, there is a further important distinction. I might be concerned about what happens to other people with characteristic C because that is a good empirical guide to what is likely to happen to me, since I have characteristic C. Alternatively, I might be concerned because, taking an objective and detached view, I find it objectionable that this should happen to *a person* with characteristic C.[22] The difference can be brought out in this way. Suppose there is a collectivity for protecting Black people from disrespectful treatment by others. Suppose, however, that while many Black people suffer from such lack of respect, Black people who travel in chauffeur-driven cars stand a much better chance of avoiding it, and that I fall into the latter group. If my concern arises simply out of the empirical connection between being Black and being treated disrespectfully, then I may lose any reason for associating with such a collectivity. But if it arises out of a more general and detached concern for the treatment of people with characteristic C then a certain kind of solidarity is appropriate and a certain kind of vicarious harm may befall me. If it matters to me that a C-person be treated in a certain way, then it matters to me *whether I am that person or not.* I care about a category to which I belong, so I care about what happens to anyone in that category. If Jones is shown a lack of respect *because* they possess characteristic C, then lack of respect is shown to someone whom I am like in the relevant respect.

Larry May offers an account of solidarity similar to but also distinct from the kind I employ here. He argues that individual members of a group who are not directly harmed

can be said to be indirectly or vicariously harmed in that their status is adversely affected by what has occurred to their fellow members. Either solidarity characterizes the feelings of the members toward each other, thereby creating empathetic reactions of all to the harm of some members, or indiscriminate treatment of individual persons as group members by outsiders creates a risk of similar treatment of all members of a group. (May 1987: 115)

The distinctness in May's account lies in the fact that, where empirical grounds for fearing similar treatment are absent, he postulates a *feeling* of

---

[22] That kind of objectivity and detachment has been informatively described by Thomas Nagel, in everything from Nagel 1970 to Nagel 1986.

solidarity as explaining the grounds of identification. That seems to me an incomplete and rather *ad hoc* explanation unless a reason is given for entertaining such a feeling, for it leaves room for the question why one should not just divest oneself of the feeling and in that way avoid harm. In contrast, if we link the feeling with a judgement about harm from a detached standpoint in the manner which Nagel has described, this provides a reason both for the identification and for the accompanying feeling when someone else with characteristic C is harmed.

Primitive and mediated collective identification differ considerably in terms of the surrounding attitudes which accompany identification with the actions of a collectivity. What they share in common, however, is that in both the identification is motivated by a concern for individuals and states of individuals. I now move to a form of collective identification which does not in the same way grow out of a concern with individuals.

4.5 PURE COLLECTIVE IDENTIFICATION

Consider an analogy employed by thinkers as diverse as Marx and Rawls, the analogy of an orchestra (Marx 1867: 448–9; Rawls 1972: 523–4 n. 4; cf. Dworkin 1990a: 329 and Searle 1995: 23). An orchestra is a collectivity according to the definition given in chapter 3, section 1. When I play in an orchestra the significance of my actions is properly captured only by reference to the collection of other musicians with whom I act; what the orchestra does is distinct from what we as individual agents do (it can produce an orchestral sound); and the orchestra persists as an entity while its composition out of a particular group of individuals changes.[23] Now it can matter to me that an orchestra I belong to plays well. How are we to understand that kind of concern? It may, of course, be fairly extraneous. It may matter to me because I need my mind to be taken off a bereavement or the end of a disastrous affair, or because I want to be associated with a successful orchestra for the glory this will bring to me. But the concern may be more intrinsic to the orchestra itself. It may matter to me that the orchestra plays well because I value such achievements.

---

[23] Despite the impressive example of the multi-instrumental jazz musician Roland Kirk, the phenomenon of the one-man band is a rather dubious counterexample to the contrast between what an individual does and what an orchestra does. But the analogy of a choir would be an even more striking example of the second feature of collectivities. The quality of tenderness evinced by a 100-strong male voice choir singing a lullaby *pianissimo* could not be matched by the most perfect soloist.

Even then, the intrinsic value placed on some collective activity may be construed as more or less distinct from individuals and their concerns. Rawls introduces the orchestra analogy in the course of defending contract theory against the charge that it must view social institutions instrumentally, as a means by which individuals can pursue their own personal ends more effectively. On the contrary, he says, 'human beings have in fact shared final ends and they value their common institutions and activities as good in themselves. We need one another as partners in ways of life that are engaged in for their own sake, and the successes and enjoyments of others are necessary for and complimentary [*sic*] to our own good' (Rawls 1972: 522–3). Taking inspiration from Humboldt, he suggests that this connects with the fact that, although we cannot develop all of our own talents, we can appreciate those of others.

> We are led to the notion of the community of humankind the members of which enjoy one another's excellences and individuality elicited by free institutions, and they recognize the good of each as an element in the complete activity the whole scheme of which is consented to and gives pleasure to all . . . As a pure case to illustrate this notion of social union, we may consider a group of musicians everyone [*sic*] of whom could have trained himself to play equally well as the others any instrument in the orchestra, but who each have by a kind of tacit agreement set out to perfect their skills in the one they have chosen so as to realize the powers of all in their joint performances. (523–4)

Many forms of life share the characteristics of social union, 'shared final ends and common activities valued for themselves', including science, art, families and friendships. But Rawls thinks the analogy with games is clearest, where a 'good play of the game is, so to speak, a collective achievement requiring the cooperation of all' (525–6).

Now Rawls shows here how one might identify with a collective activity for its intrinsic worth rather than for any extraneous reason. But although the collective activity is valued for itself, that value nevertheless seems to be rooted in the successes of other *individuals*, the good *of each*; and it is then strictly the powers of *each* rather than the powers of *all construed as forming a collectivity* that the orchestra is formed to realise. But the orchestra analogy can be employed in a different way: it may be a site for enjoying not the excellences of other individuals but the excellence of the collective entity itself. It is what *we* achieve that matters to us. And this may be a substantively different matter from developing my excellences and enjoying those of others. It may be just the rapport that is set up in collective playing, the monitoring of what is happening with other players and the adaptation to it and the reciprocity which that engenders, which we value. Here it is the perfection of what happens *between* players that we value, rather than what happens to each of them considered individually. What we value here, therefore, is distinct from anything which is expressed in a concern for individuals as such or individuals sharing some particular property.

I attempted to establish the case for the existence of irreducibly plural agency in the previous chapter. The further possibility which identification with collective action brings with it is that of an irreducibly *first person* plural agency: an indivisible *we* as agent. The first approximation of such identification described it as, amongst other things, *taking the good of the collectivity as my own*. In other words, it attempted to clarify the case of collective identification by assimilating it to the case of individual agency. We can now see that this is an oversimplification. In so far as I value what *we* can achieve collectively, this is not appropriately regarded as *my* achievements or *your* achievements or even as *my-and-your* achievements. It is *our* achievements which are valued, and these are my and your achievements only to the extent that we think of ourselves as participants in the plural agent which we compose. The strategy of assimilating collective identification to the case of individual commitment may be partly helpful in the case of primitive and mediated identification (only partly helpful because even here the idea of individual agency must of course be supplemented by the idea of irreducibly plural collective acts); and indeed at a number of points in the remainder of this chapter I shall draw points of comparison between the collective and the individual case, just as I did in setting up the idea of collective agency in the previous chapter. But such assimilation misses something important about the case of pure collective identification. Here the commitment of identification is not helpfully assimilated to the individual case because the commitment is to something *indivisibly* plural, or at least something *undividedly* plural. Whereas the commitment involved in some forms of collective identification is based on a connection with individual commitments and concerns, in the pure form it is not. Here plurality is of the essence.[24]

Plurality potentially enters in in three different ways. There is, first, the irreducible plurality attaching to the description of the action itself,

---

[24] Cf. 'One's fellow group members, though individually other than oneself, create together with oneself a single joint commitment that functions as a motivating force for all. It creates the conditions of appropriateness of the term "we", which refers to self and others only insofar as they are joined together through the medium of a single – supra-individual – thing, a joint commitment. Reaction to the deeds of one's group is thus not best characterized as reaction to self, as reaction to others, or as even to self plus others, but rather as reaction to a distinct and distinctive entity – the plural subject – with a *sui generis* relation to both self and others' (Gilbert 1996: 383).

the irreducible plurality which is definitive of collectivities of the kind discussed in the previous chapter. There is, secondly, the irreducible plurality involved in describing my commitment, which is not extraneous or arising from some personal goal that I have, but rather a commitment to *our* activity. And there is, thirdly, the potential for plurality in that I may be one of a number of co-agents who themselves all choose to identify with the collective action for intrinsic reasons.

In chapter 3, section 2 I resisted the idea of making the presence of *intention* a condition of collective action as such, on the grounds that familiar examples could be cited, such as that of the unwitting clique, where the relevant features of collective action are present but where intention is absent. But it now turns out that there are circumstances in which it will be of some significance that the performance of a collective action is, as a matter of fact, accompanied by intention. Where a number of individual agents commit themselves to a collective project for no extraneous, individual-related reasons, they may regard themselves as *jointly* so committed as a unit. From that point onwards it will be necessary to recognise my commitments, your commitments and, as a third and separate matter, *our* commitments (cf. Gilbert 1996: 7; Hollis 1998: 83).

The orchestra analogy was introduced in order to make clear the idea of pure collective identification, but it would be an error to suppose that this form of identification attaches only to some particular *kind* of collectivity. *Any* collective entity can elicit *any* of the different forms of identification, primitive, mediated or pure. What is common to the different forms of identification is a basic commitment to the actions of the collectivity, and that can occur in any connection. What differentiates the different forms is the accompanying set of attitudes surrounding the commitment. Thus we saw that there might be, so to speak, either extraneous attitudes surrounding the commitment to the orchestra or attitudes expressive of a commitment to the success of the orchestra as such. Pure collective identification may occur in connection with *any* collectivity: one which is seeking to realise some non-moral good, one which is seeking to realise some moral good or, indeed, one seeking nothing more elevated than to promote some irreducibly collective interest shared by its members. Moreover, although the orchestra analogy is useful in casting light on a number of aspects of collective identification, the analogy also has particular features, concerning the role of the individual's actions as part of the collectivity, which may even make it potentially misleading in other respects.

Action (episodic rather than current action) is definitive of membership of collectivities of the kind discussed in this book. (This is not to deny, of course, that collectivities of a different kind from those discussed here may be based on shared *experience* rather than shared activity.) But action has a distinct role in collective *identification*. Recall the suggestions in the first approximation that identification with a collectivity involved *associating myself with its decisions and actions* and *on appropriate occasions attempting to think and act as if for the collectivity itself.* Just as membership of a collectivity does not require that one act as part of it on every single occasion when it is acting, so identification with a collectivity does not require that one associate oneself with every single one of its acts. (The orchestra analogy may obscure the important point that identification does not require endorsement of all the actions of a collectivity, because there is as a matter of fact likely to be such total endorsement in this rather special collective context.) To put it one way, although collectivities are defined in terms of agency, there is a difference between identifying with the collectivity itself and identifying with what it does on any particular occasion. But an initial decision to identify with a collectivity will render it inappropriate, and perhaps even incoherent, thereafter to engage in deliberation over whether to identify on *every* occasion.

There is a helpful analogy with the individual case at this point. Imagine a ratiocinative individual who decides, after weighing the reasons on both sides of a practical question, to do X. They do not then stop and allow the considerations on the other side of the decision, which they have already accounted for and dismissed, to get in the way of their acting in accordance with the decision to do X, or at least it would be irrational of them if they did. In a similar way, it is part of the idea of commitment to a collectivity that you do not allow yourself to engage in reconsideration of your commitment at every turn. Of course, you may wish to do so from time to time, and there may be cases where you do not want to endorse a particular action of the collectivity's but you would not want to withdraw from it either. But the apparent commitment to the collectivity would be nugatory if a decision had to be made *de novo* on every single occasion of its acting.

The idea of association with a collectivity's actions which is mentioned in the first approximation must therefore be construed as being stringent enough to make a difference to an individual's discretion in practical decision-making, but not so stringent that they are left with no discretion where any and every action of the collectivity itself is concerned. Commitment really is commitment: it does not leave things just as they were before. But commitment is not absolute: there must be possibilities of reviewing it. In this way collective identification carries implications for the question of how far the idea of personal autonomy can or should extend. At the very least, collective identification is incompatible with the retention of personal autonomy on every occasion when the collectivity acts.[25] (The orchestra analogy also brings out clearly that to associate oneself with the decisions and actions of irreducible collectivities is *necessarily* to commit oneself to certain kinds of collaboration and coordination. There is no *separate* step after deciding to produce an orchestral sound which consists in the further decision to collaborate with others.)

Further elaboration is needed of the thought in the first approximation that collective identification involves *on appropriate occasions attempting to think and act as if for the collectivity itself*. It is perfectly satisfactory to say that *thinking* and *acting* for the collectivity are expressive of the commitment implicit in identification: they are two of the most obvious ways of displaying to others, and indeed to oneself, the allegiance one has embraced. (The qualification 'as if' is necessary because, except for the special case of authorised action on behalf of the collectivity, an individual cannot literally think or act for the collectivity.) But that raises the question of which occasions are to count as *appropriate* for these purposes, and it prompts the familiar challenge arising from a standard instrumental theory of rationality, the challenge of the free rider. There are many contexts where it seems that one can raise the question *what is the point* of acting for the collectivity? If others can be relied on to carry out the collective action, why not take a free ride? If there will be sufficient effort from others' actions to ensure that the hosepipe ban is effective, or that the preferred candidate gets elected, or that the much-needed revolution occurs, why do *I* need to join in? What is the point of needless effort, above what is required for the successful outcome? And once that thought is planted the danger is, of course, that the prospect of collective action is undercut, since any individual agent can reason in the same way.[26]

Thinkers sympathetic to the non-reducible importance of collective action have rightly resisted this train of thought. Hurley and Sugden, for

---

[25] The idea of collective identification is particularly important as a resource for coping with a sponsorship of autonomy so unqualified that it threatens to engulf any thought of democratic commitment. For contrasting views on that question see Wolff 1976 and Graham 1986a: ch. 6.

[26] The possibility of this challenge may actually be obscured by the orchestra analogy, because here the actions of constituent individuals tend not to be causally redundant or optional in the way in which they are elsewhere. All the same, I have been reliably informed of instances of miming, even in quite well-known orchestras.

example, both suggest that the model of a part/whole relation may be more apposite than a cause/effect relation in this context. Hurley says: 'It is wrong to assume that an act can only be rationally required in virtue of *its* causal consequences; it can also be rationally required in virtue of its constitutive relationship to a valuable form of agency – or, one might say, in virtue of its *constitutive consequences*' (Hurley 1989: 148). Sugden says:

To act as a member of the team is to act as a *component* of the team. It is to act on a concerted plan, doing one's allotted part in that plan without asking whether, taking other members' actions as given, one's own action is contributing towards the team's objective . . . It must be sufficient for each member of the team that the plan itself is designed to achieve the team's objective: the objective will be achieved if everyone follows the plan. (Sugden 1993: 86)

While these suggestions seem to me welcome, there is nevertheless a residual tendency in both Hurley and Sugden to revert to causal conceptions of individual participation in collective action. Hurley goes on:

[I]t may be rational to participate in a form of collective agency because of the valuable causal consequences of that kind of agency, even if one's individual act of participation does not in itself have the best possible causal consequences but rather merely helps to realize the valuable form of collective agency in question. (Hurley 1989: 148)

Sugden goes on:

It is essential to the idea of acting as a team member that one does not choose an action *because*, taking the actions of other members as given, that action has good consequences. But the actions which one chooses for other reasons may still have good causal consequences, and one may act in the expectation that one will cause these consequences to come about. (Sugden 1993: 87)

In Hurley's case the language of *helping to realise* something is clearly causal. In Sugden's case it looks as though he wishes to retain the importance of the causal aspect of the individual's act but to insist that the bringing about of effects must not be the *intention* of the individual. In both cases it looks as though it has been thought important to allow that *some* causal contribution follows from the individual's act, though it need not be the direct causal contribution which might at first be thought essential. Such a view seems to me to allow too much influence to the conventional wisdom of the standard instrumental conception of reason found in rational choice theory. Why not allow that an act's being constitutive or being a component does not require elucidation in terms which connect it to causal consequence at all?

My suggestion for how we should understand the idea of opting to think and act as if for the collectivity on appropriate occasions, separately from bringing about effects, is this. The reason for *joining in* collective action may be to obtain a particular result. The reason for *identifying with* the actions of a collectivity is to display allegiance and commitment, and one of the most obvious ways to display allegiance and commitment is by joining in the collective action. One can therefore have a reason for joining in the collective action *regardless of whether one's individual action has a causal role in furthering the goals of the collectivity itself.* Identifying oneself *as* a member of the collectivity is an obvious way of identifying oneself *with* the collectivity, and since the collectivity is after all defined in terms of the actions of its individual members this is the most obvious way of identifying oneself as a member of the collectivity. Of course, this process can be represented as a means/end process: affirming who you are or where your allegiances lie is your end, and you act as you do to achieve it. But there need be nothing in this which involves bringing about consequences or helping to realise something. The language of constitution is entirely appropriate: your opting to act as part of the collectivity just *is*, or constitutes, a way of affirming your commitment, it does not bring that about as some separate effect.

Note that this process helps to explain both the intelligibility and the oddity of the examples mentioned in chapter 4, section 1 where someone identifies with a collectivity even though they do not take part in its activities: examples where football supporters identify with their team's exploits, or where people evince vicarious responsibility for what their nation has done. Precisely because opting to act for the collectivity is an obvious way of displaying commitment to it, it is intelligible that people should speak in terms of what *we* have done as a means of displaying such commitment. But precisely because they have not acted in the collectivity in these cases, it is both understandable and odd that they should speak in that way.[27]

---

[27] Brennan and Lomasky argue that one is morally responsible not just for what one brings about and intends but also for what one endorses or identifies with (Brennan and Lomasky 1993: 187). Perhaps the way of speaking encountered in these examples occurs as a kind of homage to what I take to be a more widely held view that causal responsibility is a necessary condition of moral responsibility. Some people believe that in the circumstances of these examples, moral responsibility must be assumed even if one was not instrumental in bringing about the result in question. Because they believe so strongly that moral responsibility must be assumed here, even though the condition of causal responsibility is not fulfilled, perhaps this leads them to speak *as if* it were fulfilled.

4.6 CONCLUSION

What I have examined in this chapter is the commitment or the refusal of commitment which may accompany an individual's participation in collective action. On the one hand, commitment and dissociation in the case of collective action are bound to possess features in common with commitment and dissociation in the case of individual action. On the other hand, the common ground is bound to be less than total. Collective identification is necessarily different from individual identification – necessarily so, since collective action is involved and that is irreducible to and different from individual action. Collective identification immediately introduces the possibility of a concern with states of a collective entity rather than just the state of individuals, whether the agent or others. But, as we have seen in the range of primitive, mediated and pure collective identification, a variety of other considerations may be present in such identification. *What* is identified with is necessarily collective; the reasons for the identification may or may not refer exclusively to collectivities or collective properties.

Accordingly, although there will be an ineliminable reference to collective action in any form of collective identification, in some forms of such identification the explanation of the reasons for identification may conform impeccably to whatever individualist account of motivation is favoured. That is to say, in these cases collective identification can be explained in terms of an individual's conceiving a particular goal and taking efficient steps to realise it (with an optional extra assumption that any such goal must connect with the agent's own interests). We might also strain for such conformity in the case of pure collective identification, but there is no reason to do so. It is perfectly intelligible that there are circumstances where the reasons for identification with a collectivity terminate in considerations about the collectivity itself. It is not some state of an individual agent which explains the identification, nor is the identification necessarily explained by an individual agent's selecting some goal, since the identification may be exercised by a collective agency which itself selects goals.

It is important to remain alive both to the similarities and to the differences between collective identification and more purely individualist accounts of motivation. Some, at least, of the reasons for collective identification may be of exactly the same kind as those accompanying identification with individual action; and, in consequence, the motivations which are available for collective identification are not necessarily different from those which are available in the case of individual action. They may range similarly from the aim of realising some state of the agent themselves, to realising states in the agent and/or others, to realising some abstractly stated end whose connection with the states of individual human beings is indirect or possibly even absent altogether.

At the same time, we are individual human beings who live part of our lives as members of collectivities, and there is no reason why we should not find the original source of motivation in such collectivities rather than in that portion of our lives which is non-collective. There is no good reason to insist on any kind of reduction of collective identification to individual motivation. The individual and the collectivity are not separate; so there is no reason to feel that a bridge must be built between them, and motivational considerations brought back across the bridge from the individual to the collectivity.

I have therefore attempted in this chapter to remove any mystery from the idea of collective identification by enlarging our understanding of that idea and introducing greater conceptual clarity into it. But I hope that a further consequence of the discussion is to have introduced an element of mystery into the idea of individual, and especially self-interested, motivation. Given the possibility of dissociation, as much for individual as for collective action, and given the possibility of escape-interests arising from descriptions attaching to an individual, the idea of simply reading off conclusions about self-interest from a description of the predicates attaching to an individual is far from unproblematic. The relation between collective identification and self-interest is further discussed in chapter 6, section 3. In the meantime, the existence of collective identification as a separate form of rational motivation adds to an already complicated picture of the influences on practical reasoning.

CHAPTER 5

Practical reasoning: sources and constraints

In the previous chapter I discussed an agent's active identification with or dissociation from the different characteristics they possess. This possibility of identification or dissociation reflects the dual aspect of a reflective agent's circumstances: on the one hand, the need for active decision over whether given identifications are reasonable; on the other hand, the need to proceed from a particular set of existing characteristics in arriving at decisions. In the present chapter I attempt to increase understanding of the background against which agents might choose to identify with or dissociate from some set of properties which characterise them.

The stress in the previous chapter was on the capacity of choosing either to retain or to relinquish features which are part of an agent's identity. Some of the discussion of the present chapter should serve to remove a misleading impression which may be encouraged by that stress, namely the impression that there is an option for human agents to change everything about themselves or their circumstances. It is obvious that this is not the case and that they must operate within the constraints set by factors over which they have no control, factors which cannot be changed by them. A proper place must be found for both the sources of and the constraints on practical reasoning.

Having attempted to establish in earlier chapters the independent significance of collective agents, I here argue that there is no reason to take individual agents as in any overall sense more basic than collective ones. I suggest that both kinds of agent face calls on their attention from a multiplicity of sources and that in selecting from these sources such agents are in a permanent state of uneasy equilibrium. They cannot conduct practical deliberation in some abstract way, divorced from facts about their own situation; but nor are they confined to their own situation in reaching practical decisions. There will be constant interplay between what you are and what you decide to do. I also introduce some conceptual distinctions to clarify the nature of the constraints governing practical reasoning. I outline constraints of necessity and constraints of precondition, and I indicate the central place occupied by constraints of materiality.

5.1 SINGULAR AND PLURAL REASONING

The question of reasons for acting will arise for any entity which is both capable of acting and capable of acting reflectively. We have seen that both requirements are met by some collectivities of the kind discussed in chapter 3. Some collectivities deliberate, weigh pro's and con's, and decide to act in one way rather than another. Accordingly, we can raise both for individuals and for collectivities the question of what sorts of reasons would weigh with them in deciding how to act, in so far as they were deciding rationally. The answer will not necessarily be the same in both cases. That depends on a matter not fully dealt with in chapter 3: the exact extent of the similarity between individuals and collectivities, the extent to which the relevant properties of individuals are present either literally or in analogue form in collectivities. For, of course, the exact range of reasons open to a reflective agent will turn not just on the fact that they are a reflective agent but also on exactly what sort of reflective agent they are. I shall argue for a strikingly high similarity in the range of sources of practical reasoning available respectively to individuals and collectivities.

In that regard, however, it may be felt that there is an important asymmetry between singular and plural agency. It might be argued, for example, that singular agency is more basic and that therefore the category of reason for acting applies primarily to individuals and only derivatively to collective agents. After all, it may be said, the locus of decision is in the end the individual; and whereas I may decide to join or not to join in some collective venture, I cannot in the same way decide not to act as an individual, at least not in any way short of acquiescing in my own demise as an agent altogether. Collective agency, it may be felt, is both derivative and optional in a way that individual agency is not.

Some comments of Susan Hurley's appear to support such a position. She argues:

While there are undoubtedly fruitful analogies to be pursued between the relations of persons to their subsystems and the relations of social groups to the persons who are their members, nevertheless familiar bodily-individuated persons remain the normal units of rational agency; in trying to understand various failures of self-determination, we take the personal unit of agency as our starting point. (Hurley 1989: 157)[1]

She suggests that 'it is only against the background of the normal starting point assumptions, which locate agency in the biological individual, that the exceptional cases [such as collective agency] make sense' (319). As she puts it,

[F]or persons the question arises: what kind of agents, among those possible, should there be, and what kind of agent should I therefore be? Persons can see themselves as various possible kinds of agent, and as co-operating in various forms of collective agency with other individual agents; and persons can take steps towards realising certain of these possibilities as opposed to others. (157–8)

I have already expressed misgivings about the idea of simply ascribing priority to the individual over the collectivity in matters of agency, and I argued that each is primary in a number of distinct ways (cf. chapter 3, section 4). Those misgivings have application in the present connection. We find ourselves as constituents in collective agencies of certain descriptions just as we find ourselves to be individual agents of certain descriptions. In a whole range of contexts, from nation states to families via cliques, professional and neighbourhood associations, clubs, teams and committees, our existence as constituents in collectivities is as real as our existence as individual agents. In both cases, the agency may be something of which we are aware to a greater or lesser extent, something that we self-consciously opt for, or something we simply *find* that we are doing; in both cases, we can in principle (and sometimes in practice) decide to cease identifying with the agency. The members of a collectivity may indeed collectively decide to disband (as opposed to deciding individually or even collectively to *leave* the collectivity). In this extreme case as well as others, collectivities can be self-determining, just as individual agents are. Of course a decision to disband is not equivalent to the members' acquiescing in their own demise as individual agents, but it is precisely analogous to their doing so. Thus far, therefore, there are no grounds for supposing that the category of reason for acting applies only in some derivative way to collectivities.

I said that Hurley appears to support the view that collective agency is somehow derivative. Yet she expresses another view, mentioned briefly

---

[1] It is not uncommon for theorists who are sympathetic in general to the idea of collective agency to insist, nevertheless, on its derivative nature as compared with the agency of individuals. See, for example, May 1987: 70 and Scheffler 1995: 232; and, for further discussion, Graham 2000: 49–61.

in chapter 4, section 1, which is at least in tension with that. She refers to
the irrationality of taking the unit of agency as fixed. In dealing with the
Prisoners' Dilemma and similar problems, she argues that it is irrational
of the prisoners not to act *as a pair* and thus do better for themselves, and
an insistence on taking the unit of agency as fixed itself contributes to
the irrationality which needs to be explained (Hurley 1989: 145). In that
case, what is it that determines the appropriate unit of agency in given
circumstances? The answer is this:

What makes an individual as opposed to some collectivity the wrong unit of
agency in particular cases is whatever makes co-operation with the members of
some groups possible and beneficial, with respect to whatever shared or separate
goals are specified, in the circumstances at hand . . . This will vary according to
one's substantive goals and ethical views. But one fails to understand the radical
character of the question if one is tempted to ask: beneficial assuming the unit of
agency to be the individual or the group? Again, the question is in effect about
which possible unit of agency . . . *ought* to be realized, given whatever goals are
specified; it cannot be non-question-beggingly answered by presupposing that
one or another unit is to be taken as given. (147)

Hurley's claim that we should not take the unit of agency as fixed
seems to me correct. Indeed, it seems to follow from the fact that we
have options of collective identification and dissociation as outlined in
the previous chapter: there might be reasons for quitting a collectivity
to which one belonged or for joining one to which one did not belong.
As I have indicated, however, it will not only be individual agents who
may have reasons for not taking the unit of agency as fixed. A collectivity
can raise the question what agencies there should be just as well as
an individual can. Less secure, at least without further explanation, is
the implicit claim that the reasons for identifying with or dissociating
from a particular agency will depend on whatever goals are specified.
As it stands, that seems to leave the goals themselves beyond rational
criticism. But if the goal is one which it is unreasonable to have, then
it will be equally unreasonable to join forces to achieve it. We should
therefore no more take goals as fixed than we should take the unit of
agency as fixed.

At this point, however, someone might object that we shall be in an
unacceptable state of flux unless we take either goals or the unit of agency
as fixed. This thought may be what motivates the line taken by Robert
Sugden in response to Hurley, that 'the idea of rational choice is not
meaningful until the unit of agency has been specified' (Sugden 1993: 87
n. 23). How should we respond to this objection? If we are sufficiently

impressed with the idea that there may be good reasons for changing the unit of agency and also good reasons for changing an agent's current goals, the temptation is to suppose that there must be some third thing which might serve as a fixed point against which to measure agency and goals. If we do not find such a third thing, how can a process of rational assessment ever start? This dilemma, I believe, is one sign of that uneasy equilibrium mentioned earlier which is characteristic of practical rationality. Things have to get worse before they can get better, and we now have to recognise the full diversity of sources of practical reasoning available to individuals and collectivities.

5.2 THE DIVERSITY OF SOURCES

What an agent has reason to do will depend at least on facts about *the agent itself* and facts about its *surroundings*. But within that very broad framework the sources of practical reasoning are irreducibly diverse. An individual agent's consideration of themselves will include at least the following: characteristics of a relational and non-relational kind; characteristics which they possess inescapably and characteristics which they possess escapably; cutting across these divisions, characteristics which they share with others; and, cutting again across all these divisions, the characteristics of any collectivities to which they belong. All of these are potential sources of reasons for acting, but not necessarily in a straightforward way. As I argued in chapter 4, section 3, the applicability of some description to me raises, but does not itself settle, the question of whether I have reason to acquiesce in it. From the fact that I am an X (e.g. a taxpayer) it does not follow that I have reasons to do what an X does; it may follow instead that I have reasons to cease being an X. But any agent must *begin* from facts about themselves, and in that sense those facts will be a source of reasons for acting. So far as an agent's surroundings are concerned, these will include at least features of the non-animate environment and features of the social environment in the form of facts about other individual agents and collectivities. As well as these aspects of themselves and the world as they both are, the individual agent will also form conceptions of themselves and the world as they might be. On the basis of all of these thoughts, they may form intentions to act so as to further the interests of themselves, or of some other individual, or of some collectivity. Or they may form the intention to act in accordance with some abstract value. They may choose either to act in a way which they believe to be important antecedently of any choices they have made or to act in a way whose importance arises precisely from their choices.

We should note that *every source of practical reason mentioned* in the previous paragraph is available not just for individual agents but also for some collective ones. Though it is not definitive of collectivities that they are reflective or that they have a good, many do as a matter of fact possess such features; and this opens up the possibility of their having reasons for acting which are identical in kind to those available to individuals, in so far as both collectivities and individuals possess the characteristics which generate them. Where collectivities do possess these features, they can pay attention to their own characteristics, to those of similar agents, and even to those of any collectivities to which they belong (a committee may belong to some larger collective body, for example). They can act to further their own interests or those of some other individual or collectivity; they can act to promote some abstract value; and they can value a course of action for choice-dependent or choice-independent reasons. Such processes as deriving reasons for action from your states and your relations with other agents and their states, as well as deriving them from aspirations to unrealised states of the world, can all be reproduced in the case of collective agents.

A further layer of complication is added when we bear in mind that it is not just collectivities and individuals, in the non-collective part of their existence, which have reasons for acting. It is also individuals *qua* members of collectivities, when they have identified, reasonably, with some collectivity and are so to speak thinking and acting as for that collectivity. In that sense, individuals will have further derivative reasons for acting as a result of the forms of collective identification described in the previous chapter.

The upshot for an individual agent is the potential for a multiplicity of different reasons for acting, from a multiplicity of different (and different kinds of) sources. The point is illustrated nicely by an observation of John Searle's that when I am in a restaurant I am a citizen, an owner of money, a client and a bill-payer (Searle 1995: 35). All of these descriptions of an individual agent will generate reasons for acting (and, it may be, reasons for *different* actions); and descriptions of the individual agent are themselves only one source of reasons for acting. There will be no shortage of reasons for acting; the problem will be in ordering them in some way so that final judgements can be made and action results.

But the idea of equilibrium is more apposite than the idea of ordering, if the latter is thought to signify some kind of hierarchy of reasons.

Consider some of the possibilities here. I may have a reason for resisting tax impositions which is generated by the description of me as a taxpayer, but a reason for encouraging them which derives from my membership of a collectivity committed to improving facilities for cyclists, and another reason for encouraging them which derives from my commitment to furthering a fairer division of the earth's resources. I may have a reason for engaging in a regime of training which derives from my chosen project of becoming a boxing champion, but a reason for not doing so which derives from obligations which I acknowledge to spend my spare time with my children. I may have a reason for keeping a promise to meet a friend next Friday, but a reason for missing the appointment and spending that afternoon in some interesting activity which the Collectivity for Interesting Activities, of which I am a member, has just decided upon. Examples could be multiplied indefinitely, and I do not here put forward any argument to establish a formula for ordering such reasons. Of course, one such reason must be allowed to prevail on a given occasion if action is ever to result; but there are no obvious grounds to suppose, for example, that reasons from a particular source, such as a description of the agent, or an abstract value, or a chosen goal, will necessarily always prevail over those from another source.[2]

On the other hand, it is a pertinent feature of human agency, in the case both of individuals and of collectivities, that it normally extends over more than one occasion of action. In consequence, the dominance of a particular reason, or of reasons from a particular source, is not something which must obtain on every occasion. This leaves room for the possibility that all the different sources are kept in some kind of equilibrium. A successful and integrated human life will require that an agent is responsive to reasons from all of these sources, rather than being responsive to reasons from one source to the exclusion of those from other sources; and an averagely continuous life will afford the opportunity for such responsiveness. Reasons which fail to prevail on a given occasion may get their chance on subsequent occasions.

At least we can hope that it will be possible to support a potential reason from one source, relative to another source which is taken as fixed *at that point* (but not necessarily at other times). For example, suppose that I am uncertain whether a given description which applies to me generates a straightforward interest or an escape-interest.[3] That question

---

[2] But aren't *moral* reasons supposed to prevail over those from any other source? Yes they are, but it is difficult to find an intellectually compelling case for that supposition. See chapter 6, section 1.

[3] For the distinction between straightforward and escape-interests, see chapter 4, section 3.

might at least be settled relative to my membership of some collectivity. Thus, the description of me as needing to sell my labour power might generate an escape-interest if it turned out that my being in that state made me a member of a collective entity which was uniquely capable of instituting a set of non-exploitative social relations where such a need was no longer present.[4] In a similar way, if I am uncertain whether to identify with some collectivity to which I belong, this might be settled relative to some abstract value to which I am committed. I might, for example, decide to identify with or dissociate myself from the nation to which I belong depending on whether it furthers or hinders mutual respect among people of different ethnic backgrounds.[5]

In the light of these possibilities, we arrive at a conclusion which is at least partly in the spirit of Hurley's view described in section 1. The strategy of not taking the unit of agency as fixed is adopted; but simply as one variant of a more general strategy of not taking *anything* as fixed in an absolute sense, while having to take something as fixed in a relative sense. No practical reasoning can take place without *something* being taken as fixed within the context of that piece of reasoning. What is taken as fixed for the purposes of that reasoning may be the character of the agent, the character of the agent's environment, the reasonableness of a given goal, or one or more of a number of other factors. This is exactly analogous to the fact that in *theoretical* reasoning some premises must be accepted without question if any inferences are ever to be made. But just as any such accepted premise may be open to question outside of that context, so any consideration which is taken as fixed within the context of a piece of practical reasoning may itself become the subject of a practical decision on another occasion.[6] More remains to be said, however, about both the freedoms and the constraints which we face in coping with the diversity of reasons for acting, and the remaining sections of this chapter address these matters.

---

[4] For discussion of that particular case, see Marx 1867: 439–54 and Graham 1992: 97–103.

[5] The possibility of measuring the deeds of a collectivity against some abstract value indicates one way in which there might be a reason, beyond mere membership, for identifying with a collectivity to which I belong.

[6] Cf. '[A] sensible contractualism, like most other plausible views, will involve a holism about moral justification: in assessing one principle we must hold many others fixed. This does not mean that these other principles are beyond question, but just that they are not being questioned at the moment' (Scanlon 1998: 214). The fact of a diversity of sources for reasons to act can cause problems for an instrumental theory of rationality, especially in terms of how a rational agent is to order diverse preferences. For discussion, see Brennan and Lomasky 1993: ch. 9; Gauthier 1986: ch. 2; Goodin 1986; and Hampton 1998: 169–75.

5.3 CHOSEN PROJECTS

In chapter 1, section 1 I described the notion that in modern conditions of life we must be the authors of our practical decisions in a strong sense, and I suggested that choice and decision are in any case hardly separable from human action at all. But there is an ambiguity lurking here, which was briefly alluded to in chapter 1, section 2. It might be true both (i) that the world does not make us do things, that we must ourselves opt for courses of action and carry them out, and (ii) that a rational agent would act solely in accordance with the dictates of the world, because reasons for acting can be derived from descriptions of the world as long as we understand 'descriptions of the world' in a suitably generous sense. It is not easy to judge whether or not (ii) is true, and this returns us to unresolved questions about the role of an agent's choices in providing reasons for acting.

To couch the issue in those terms is perhaps suggestive of a dialectic which occurs in the liberal/communitarian debate and of the rival images associated with the two forms of theory. In speaking of the image associated with each form of theory I refer not necessarily to the propositions to which a theorist is explicitly committed, but rather to the view which is liable to be produced or at least encouraged in the minds of those who encounter their theories, by the descriptions and propositions to which the theorists *are* committed.

For liberalism, 'the self is prior to the ends which are affirmed by it; even a dominant end must be chosen from among numerous possibilities' (Rawls 1972: 560). The image liable to be produced by this thought is that of the lone individual, starting with a clean slate and looking for considerations *ab initio* which can be inscribed on it. For communitarianism, a shared communal end is 'not a relationship [people] choose (as in a voluntary association) but an attachment they discover . . . ' (Sandel 1982: 150). The image liable to be produced by this thought is that of the community-embedded individual for whom practical reasoning is a matter of ascertaining truths about their identity rather than making decisions, for whom 'agency consists less in summoning the will than in seeking self-understanding' (152).

The virtue of the liberal image is to stress that agents do have something to *decide*, that there are choices to be made in acting for reasons and that there is a need actively to seek out and embrace sources which can be used for arriving at ends. Its defect is to leave the impression that there might be some position of pure characterlessness from which such decisions might be made. The virtue of communitarianism is to stress that agents do indeed act from a position of embeddedness in rich social contexts characterised by commitment to particular values. Its defect is to leave the impression that those contexts remove the need for critical assessment and judgement in acting for reasons. But neither form of theory quite addresses the issue we have now arrived at. I have argued in chapter 4, especially section 3, that choice and decision, rather than mere consultation of current allegiances and identities, are necessary for rational practical reasoning; but that does not tell us whether or not such choice and decision, if carried out rationally, involve any original input from the agent rather than an acknowledgement of what the facts, generously construed, demand. It does not answer the following question: *Does the fact of my choosing a particular course of action carry any weight on its own as a reason for so acting?*

In chapter 3, section 7 I drew a contrast between choice-dependent and choice-independent courses of action: those that I may value only *because* I have chosen them (such as doing crossword puzzles) and those that I may choose because I think they have value independently of my choices (such as running a soup kitchen). Now it is arguably pleonastic to say that *I myself* value something which I have chosen: an agent's choices, it might be said, are as a matter of conceptual necessity indicative of what they value. Whether that is correct or not, however, the sharper question is whether the choice of an action on my part can itself really *give me a reason* to carry it out. That question is a genuine one because, of course, people may exercise their decision-making powers in silly or even positively malign ways. Suppose, for example, that I choose to drink a can of paint or to become a hitman for the Mafia (cf. Cohen 1996: 183 and Hollis 1998: 161). Does my act of choice itself give me a reason in either case? It may seem an unwelcome conclusion that I acquire reasons for engaging in these activities by virtue of choosing to do so: in the first example because, from all other points of view except my having chosen it, there is nothing to be said in favour of the action and plenty to be said against it; in the second example because it looks suspicious if I can acquire reasons for doing morally awful things just by virtue of making a particular choice.

Theorists vary in the extent to which they are prepared to limit the independent importance of choice in the light of this difficulty. Christine Korsgaard, for example, asserts the importance of autonomy in the following terms: 'The reflective structure of human consciousness requires that you identify yourself with some law or principle which will govern your choices. It requires you to be a law to yourself. And that is the source of normativity' (Korsgaard 1996: 103–4). This strong commitment to the role of the agent's own choices appears to be qualified when she says: 'Certainly I am not saying that reflective endorsement – I mean the bare *fact* of reflective endorsement – is enough to make an action right' (161). But in explicit consideration of difficult cases like that of the person who chooses to become a Mafia hitman she stresses the importance of choice and decision in a way which appears to eclipse the importance of other, independent considerations altogether. She says that

... there is a real sense in which you are bound by a law you make for yourself until you make another ... There is a sense in which these obligations are real – not just psychologically but normatively. And this is because *it is the endorsement, not the explanations and arguments that provide the material for the endorsement*, that does the normative work. (257; italics added)

In contrast, other theorists give a more qualified role to choice and try to bind its importance to other, non-chosen, factors. Raz suggests that '[a]utonomous life is valuable only if it is spent in the pursuit of acceptable and valuable projects and relationships' (Raz 1986: 417). Will Kymlicka argues similarly:

Liberals aren't saying that we should have the freedom to select our projects for its own sake, because freedom is the most valuable thing in the world. Rather, it is our projects and tasks that are the most important things in our lives, and it is because they are so important that we should be free to revise and reject them ... (Kymlicka 1989: 48)

He adds: 'Saying that freedom of choice is intrinsically valuable suggests that the more we exercise our capacity for choice, the more free we are, and hence the more valuable our lives are' (48). But that, he concludes, would be absurd, because in fact a life of constantly changing choices would be empty of commitment and therefore *less* valuable.

In fact, these last difficulties do not follow from positing the intrinsic value of choice. After all, we might hold that something was intrinsically valuable but not in unlimited quantities (salt is valuable, but it doesn't follow that the more the better); we might recognise, for example, that it needed to compete with *other* things of intrinsic value. Moreover, it is not sufficient simply to say that it is our projects which are the most important thing in our lives. This does not bring out *why* it is important that we should choose them rather than simply having them allocated to us, and it raises familiar problems of paternalism. Indeed, it leaves us with the question whether choice can be thought important *per se* or not.

Consider the following suggestion. It might be said that we are faced with a situation more complex than my stark contrast between choice-dependent and choice-independent values allows, one which is better represented by a series of gradations. At one extreme there will be actions which are intrinsically important, such as helping people in distress or ensuring that I don't neglect my own well-being (*i-actions*). At the other extreme, there will be actions of a clearly trivial nature, at least in normal circumstances, such as wearing a green shirt (*t-actions*). But in between these extremes there will be actions which, while not necessarily being intrinsically important, are worthwhile, such as playing music or walking in beautiful countryside or responding pleasantly to people in casual encounters (*w-actions*).

This suggestion might then be extended to address our present question in the following way. It is plain, it might be said, that i-actions do not need any choice on my part for me to have a reason for performing them, whereas t-actions do need something like that. But, the suggestion continues, the situation is less clear-cut with w-actions. In a weak sense it may seem to follow from an action's being worthwhile that I have some reason to perform it; but we shall rightly feel that w-actions are to a large extent optional and interchangeable: not as much as t-actions, perhaps, but certainly in a way that i-actions are not. Hence, this suggestion concludes, there is a great deal of fertile ground between the two extremes, ground where my choosing an action may carry weight as a reason for performing it. The agent's choice, it might be said, makes all the difference between one optional and interchangeable activity and another: here, choice really is productive of reasons for acting.

This suggestion seems to me to carry problems of its own and to be misleading in the way it is stated, but for all that to carry an important insight. It carries problems of its own in so far as it implies that there is a category of trivial actions such that there are no considerations, beyond my choice, which have a bearing on whether or not I have a reason to perform them. If my claims in chapter 2 (The indistinctness of persons) were correct, that is not so. On the contrary, my performing such actions may have massive implications for other people's lives via a consideration of causal precondition (see chapter 2, section 2). In that case, even in the marginal area of apparently trivial actions there will be reasons for and against performing them which are distinct from the matter of the agent's choice to do so. That is not the point I wish to press here, however.

The insight in the suggestion is misleadingly stated because it is made to appear that choice is all on its own reason-producing. Bear in mind the point made in section 2 that reasons for acting will come from a number of irreducibly disparate sources. Typically, the problem is not a shortage of reasons for acting but a superfluity; and an agent may be confronted with a situation where there are many incompatible actions which they have reason to perform, actions which may be either equally valuable or all valuable but in incommensurable ways. One reason (or set of reasons) must prevail if action is to result at all, and it is in these circumstances that choice has a vital role. It has the effect of a casting vote, as it were, and breaks the logjam; and once such a vote has been cast, everything changes. But in these cases it is not the *mere* fact of choice which gives an agent a reason for acting; it is the fact of the agent's having chosen from antecedently existing reasons.

The answer to the question whether choice is important *per se* therefore seems to me to be this. It might be claimed in the case of t-actions that it is important *per se* on the grounds that in these cases there is no other consideration which can incline an agent to one action rather than another. Even if that claim were correct, it would provide only a very limited context in which choice was important. My suggestion, however, is that choice is also important where there are *too many* considerations to incline an agent to one action rather than another. This includes not only w-actions but also i-actions. There are reasons to relieve physical pain, to ensure that everyone is decently housed, to maintain self-esteem, and so on. All are worthy, but in a particular situation it may be that not all can be realised. Choice will not be important here *per se* if that means 'whatever else is true', since its role presupposes that other reasons for action obtain; but it will have a role to play which cannot be discharged in any other way and without which action simply cannot result.[7]

It remains to add, here as elsewhere, that all of the claims made in this section apply to *agents* and not just to individual agents.[8] There can

---

[7] For similar discussion, see Raz 1986: 388–98 and Scanlon 1998: 118–20. Raz suggests that choice is analogous to promising in changing the situation and sometimes, though not always, tilting the balance in a particular direction. Scanlon makes a distinction between the broad sense of rational aims, which includes all those aims which an agent would have reason to have, and the narrow sense, which includes all those which they actually have insofar as these are rational. The narrow sense then preserves a role for choice while also preserving a 'critical' element. See also Nagel's discussion of 'reasons of autonomy' in Nagel 1986: 166–71.

[8] Against this it might objected that, whereas individuals have an automatic interest in living their life according to their own choices, collectivities do not. Scanlon suggests that 'the life of a rational creature is something that is to be *lived* in an active sense – that is to say, shaped by his or her choices and reactions' (Scanlon 1998: 124–5). Surely I have myself allowed in chapter 3 that

be and are collectively shared projects which are central in people's (collective) lives; the same questions can arise as to whether the mere fact of those projects having been (collectively) chosen carries any normative weight; and the same answers can be given in terms of the circumstances in which choice may have a role to play. As a corollary, tensions are bound to arise if major moral significance is attached to the role of choice, as it frequently is. Most frequently it is thought important that choice should remain with individuals, but, as I have noted in earlier discussion, there is also attachment in some contexts to the importance of choice remaining with a collectivity. A national right to self-determination[9] is an obvious and important example, but in many more mundane contexts it could plausibly be argued that choice should remain with some collectivity. (It is for the club to decide where to take its annual outing, it is for the neighbourhood committee to decide whether the children's playground should be re-sited, and so on.) Since the aspirations of individuals and collectivities can conflict, there will be circumstances where difficult decisions have to be made about which entity's choices are more important.

5.4 CONSTRAINTS OF NECESSITY

In this and the two following sections I introduce some conceptual distinctions to clarify the nature of the constraints which face us as agents. In the previous section I raised the possibility that the facts of the world, in some suitably broad sense, might dictate what we had reason to do. Whether they do or not, what is much clearer is that the facts certainly *constrain* what we have reason to do. In one way, at least, the role of constraints in practical reasoning seems to me to be necessarily underappreciated in rational choice theory. According to Elster, 'There is no alternative to rational-choice theory as a set of normative prescriptions. It just tells us to do what will best promote our aims, whatever they are' (Elster 1986a: 22). Any theory which just tells us to do what will promote our aims leaves those aims themselves uncriticised. But criticism

many collectivities are not rational in that sense? Some, for example, are entirely unconscious agents. Surely, then, the claims in this section will not apply to them? The point is well taken that collectivities exhibit a great diversity and some share far fewer properties with individual human agents than others do. My response to it is essentially the same as the argument I put forward in chapter 3 about the moral status of collectivities. *Some* of them have the status of rational agents, and for those which do the arguments of the present section will apply, just as they do to individuals.

9 That is an idea which stands in much need of elaboration, of course (and the *moral importance* of an entity's autonomy is distinct from that entity's having a *right* to autonomy). See Miller 1995: ch. 4; Raz 1984: 190–5; and Waldron 1993: 339–69.

is sometimes required, because not everything is a reasonable aim, not everything is achievable.

Though much about me and my circumstances is alterable, much is not. For example, there will be multiple constraints making it irrational for me to conceive the aim of becoming the world's greatest 25-year-old ballerina. Some pertinent descriptions of me denote what I am *inescapably*. My place of birth, my nationality as defined by birth, and my racial origin are all matters which are beyond the reach of practical decision. Agents may distance themselves mentally from such inescapable features of themselves or their environment, they can engage in counterfactual speculation or fantasise about such features being different, but they cannot escape them in reality. Factors of that kind therefore really do place limits around practical aspirations. Any feature of an agent or their circumstances which cannot itself be the subject of a practical decision I shall refer to as a *constraint of necessity*. It is always irrational to conceive a practical project whose realisation would involve the reversal of a constraint of necessity. I now offer a number of clarifications and distinctions as an aid to understanding the idea of that kind of constraint.

We can distinguish between *conceptual* and *causal* constraints of necessity. It is a conceptual necessity that I cannot make myself into a Neanderthal creature (since there would be nothing of the essential me left) but a causal necessity that I cannot make myself into a world heavyweight boxing champion. The status of the constraint is a secondary matter, however, since it would be irrational of me to conceive a practical project that flew in the face of *either* type of constraint.

We should also distinguish between a genuine causal constraint of necessity, which renders some project causally *impossible*, and any factor which renders a project causally *realisable but only at great cost* or by disturbing many other causal networks. Thus, it is not causally impossible for me to change my shirt, my house, my country of residence, or my sex, though these different options vary enormously in the degree to which they would produce consequential changes elsewhere in my life. Within the range of causally possible projects we should therefore recognise a spectrum running from 'causally possible with relatively little disturbance' to 'causally possible but only at the cost of great disturbance'. These differences will certainly weigh with a rational agent: they provide the material for decisions about how important a particular project is and whether its pursuit justifies making great changes elsewhere. But what is causally possible, even at great cost and with great disturbance, does not actually *preclude* as the constraints of necessity do.

A further clarification of the idea of the constraints of necessity consists in distinguishing between *necessity* and *permanence*. Factors which *we* are powerless to change may still vary, only in ways which are beyond our control. A clear and poignant example of this is age. We cannot change our place of birth *or* our age; but the latter, unlike the former, constantly changes in a relentless and uniform way that we can do nothing about (cf. Rorty 1984: 154). That form of change is something which an agent is constrained by and cannot alter. It is necessity, therefore, rather than permanence *per se*, that functions as a constraint.

One final clarificatory distinction. I have described any factor which cannot itself be the subject of a practical decision as a constraint of necessity. There will be innumerable features of agents and their circumstances which cannot be altered, but which are of no conceivable relevance to any question of what to do. It is obvious that it will not be worth describing a factor in terms of the constraints of necessity unless it has some salience to practical decisions. There are then two interestingly different ways in which a factor can acquire such salience: via *original* or *reactive significance* (cf. chapter 4, section 4). A constraint assumes original significance where the significance originates with the independent judgement of the agent themself. For example, they make the decision to value and celebrate (or, as it may be, to revile and deplore) some ineradicable feature which they possess. A constraint assumes reactive significance where an agent endows it with significance in response to the actions or attitudes of others, and would not otherwise choose to attach any significance to it. The difference between original and reactive significance is illustrated by the difference between agents' choosing to become part of a Black Pride movement and their needing to regard their race as significant as a means of protecting themselves from white racists.

These observations and distinctions are intended to increase our understanding of the *concept* of a constraint of necessity. Clearly, it will be partly a matter for empirical investigation to decide on which factors meeting the conceptual specification of constraints of necessity are of any particular significance in particular circumstances. It will be plain that race falls into the important category in many actual circumstances, as does nationality.[10] In any event, as the examples indicate, constraints of necessity may arise from an agent's collective existence as much as from any individual characteristics which they possess. Such constraints

---

[10] Nationality is actually ambiguous. Where it is defined by reference to place of birth then this constitutes a constraint of necessity; but where it is defined by reference to citizenship then that is something which agents may choose to change, at least in principle (cf. Barry 1983: 134–7).

are also often highly germane to practical reasoning, despite not being changeable themselves by human action. They may provide agents with excellent reasons for trying to change what *other* agents are doing, and it may also be important for agents to own, so to speak, what cannot be changed.

Are there significant constraints of necessity which do not depend on the vagaries of circumstance, which constrain *all* agents under all conditions? In order to find any, we should have to look at the most general and inescapable features that reasoning agents possess. Christine Korsgaard has suggested that such a constraint is to be found in our very humanity itself and that it contains powerful implications for practical reasoning.

Her argument begins from the assumption that practical reasoning requires an identity: '[T]he principle or law by which you determine your actions is one that you regard as being expressive of *yourself*' (Korsgaard 1996: 100). 'A view of what you ought to do is a view of who you are' (117). She contrasts this conception of practical identity, a conception 'under which you find your life to be worth living and your actions to be worth undertaking' with a theoretical conception, 'a view about what as a matter of inescapable scientific fact you are' (101). She then argues that, whereas most of our identities are contingent and can be shed, our identity as human beings, practical reasoning animals, is not contingent and cannot be shed.

What is not contingent is that you must be governed by *some* conception of your practical identity. For unless you are committed to some conception of your practical identity, you will lose your grip on yourself as having any reason to do one thing rather than another – and with it, your grip on yourself as having any reason to live and act at all. But *this* reason for conforming to your particular practical identities is not a reason that *springs from* one of those particular practical identities. It is a reason that springs from your humanity itself, from your identity simply as *a human being*, a reflective animal who needs reasons to act and to live. (120–1)

The powerful implications which are held to follow include the derivation of morality itself simply from the fact that we are practical reasoners.

[I]f you are to have any practical identity at all, you must acknowledge yourself to have a moral identity – human identity conceived as a form of normative practical identity – as well.... What makes morality special is that it springs from a form of identity which cannot be rejected unless we are prepared to reject practical normativity, or the existence of practical reasons, altogether... (125)

This moral view of oneself then influences practical reasoning in a pervasive way. She associates herself with the following view:

We could, with the resources of a knowledge of human nature, rank different sets of values according to their tendency to promote human flourishing. If values are associated with ways of conceiving one's identity, then the point will be that some ways of thinking of our identity are healthier and better for us than others. The basic claim here would be that it is better for us to think of ourselves, and more essentially to value ourselves, just as human beings than, say, as men or women, or as members of certain religious or ethnic groups, or as the possessors of certain talents. (117)

She cites Mill's arguments about the damaging effects on men of identifying themselves in terms of gender and Rawls's arguments for the enhancement of a sense of self-worth through regarding talents as a social resource, suggesting that they are meant to show that 'societies which accord equal value to human beings as such are better *for* people and that this is one reason to have them' (118).

I am to a large extent in sympathy with the *sort* of project that Korsgaard is engaged in: it seems fairly clear that our identity as human beings is a constraint of necessity of the required permanent and inescapable kind, and that it will set limits to what we can accept as good reasons for acting. It is less clear, however, that the more particular conclusions which she wishes to reach can be arrived at in the particular way she follows.

I shall have more to say about the relation between morality and practical reasoning in general in chapter 6, and it may in any case not be entirely certain what features a reason must have to qualify as a *moral* reason; but it must at least be possible to believe that there are reasons for doing X, that there is something to be said for doing X or that doing X is worthwhile, without this implying a specifically moral attitude on the part of the believer. Moreover, it is at best an exaggeration to say that every such reason itself constitutes a view of one's identity. Korsgaard's remarks wrongly suggest that an agent's reasons for acting must in a more than trivial way reflect back on their own life, whereas some of the principles governing my actions will be an expression of my self only in the trivial sense that they are expressive of a person who has decided to act in such-and-such a way. If the introduction of morality proceeds via a premise which connects all reasons (non-gratuitously) with a view of one's identity as a human being, then the introduction will fail on that ground if on no other. To put it one way, my practical judgements are *mine* but their source may be something quite other than myself: my circumstances or the reactions and treatment I receive from others, for example.

Korsgaard's stark distinction between practical and theoretical conceptions of identity is also unhelpful here. (It is too suggestive of that other stark contrast between *is* and *ought*.) What you are, as a matter of inescapable scientific fact, may itself furnish material for practical reasoning. Our actual external circumstances, as opposed to our own identity, could not possibly be ignored in assembling reasons for acting, but as soon as notice is taken of them some of Korsgaard's more specific conclusions are in jeopardy. It may be better *in abstracto* to think of ourselves as human beings than as, say, men and women, workers and capitalists, or rulers and ruled; but the circumstances we find ourselves in may make it imperative for us to focus most strongly on the less inclusive descriptions. The reactive, rather than the original, significance of the less exclusive descriptions may be responsible for that. We may long to be able to think of ourselves just as human beings; but if others constantly treat us in certain ways on account of some more specific properties we possess, such as our gender or our ethnicity, then it will not be better for us to think of ourselves just as human beings. On the contrary, we may need to join together under the more specific descriptions for reasons of self-protection. At the limit, that may be necessary if we are to survive as human beings at all. If you find yourself in the middle of a pogrom, better to think of yourself as a Jew since that will give you a better chance of reaching circumstances where you may persuade others to treat you just as a human being and not as a Jew. Accordingly, it may be *true* that societies which accord equal value to human beings as such are better for people, but yet *false* that it is better, in the circumstances we are in, to think of ourselves primarily as simply human beings rather than under some more specific descriptions. Thinking of ourselves primarily just as human beings may be highly desirable but simply premature until others have begun to think of us, and to treat us, in those terms.

I should emphasise, however, that what I have expressed misgivings about here is the particular set of implications which Korsgaard attempts to derive from a consideration of the constraints of necessity imposed on us by our humanity. That our humanity constitutes a universal constraint of necessity seems to me obviously correct, but it is another matter how we elaborate on that idea. In section 6 I suggest that an alternative aspect of our humanity, our materiality, provides us with a more plausible way of elaborating on the idea of our humanity as a constraint of necessity.

5.5 CONSTRAINTS OF PRECONDITION

All human actions have preconditions and, like the constraints of necessity, those preconditions may be either causal or conceptual. It is a causal precondition of my cycling to work that I should have ingested a certain quantity of food; it is a conceptual precondition of the same action that I should have the use of a bicycle (or tricycle or unicycle or other conceptually appropriate means of transport). It will be irrational of an agent to opt, without further ado, for a given course of action if one or more of its preconditions is unfulfilled. Where that is the case, the agent must either ensure the fulfilment of the precondition or abandon the aspiration to that course of action. Preconditions of action therefore constitute a constraint on practical reasoning.

The question can then be raised, as in the case of constraints of necessity, whether there are any constraints of precondition which constrain *all* agents in all circumstances, independently of their particular character, situation or projects. If there are, this will be of considerable significance, and not only in connection with practical reasoning. In the context of pluralism described in chapter 1 the identification of universal constraints of precondition may be useful for making comparisons among different cultures. Those cultures may be assessed according to the extent to which they make provision for the satisfaction of universal preconditions for action, and if the preconditions really are universal this will avoid the prejudice which would be involved in judging a culture *either* according to its own standards *or* according to the standards of some rival culture. It may also be possible to assess different distributional principles by reference to universal constraints of precondition in a way which is free from philosophical or cultural bias (cf. Sen 1992: ch. 3).

There are a number of theories in the philosophical literature which specify and enumerate properties more or less similar to what I have termed the constraints of precondition. Some examples follow. The most obvious is Rawls's theory of primary goods: 'things that every rational man is presumed to want' which 'have a use whatever a person's rational plan of life' (Rawls 1972: 62; cf. 396). The assumption is that 'all citizens have a rational plan of life that requires for its fulfillment roughly the same kind of primary goods' (Rawls 1993: 180 n. 8; cf. 75–6). The list of primary goods from Rawls's later work comprises basic rights and liberties; freedom of movement and free choice of occupation; powers and prerogatives of offices in political and economic institutions; income and wealth; and social bases of self-respect (181).

Len Doyal and Ian Gough claim that 'since physical survival and personal autonomy are the preconditions for any individual action in any culture, they constitute the most basic human needs – those which must be satisfied to some degree before actors can effectively participate in their form of life to achieve other valued goals' (Doyal and Gough 1991: 54). They also suggest that

physical health can be thought of transculturally in a negative way. If you wish to lead an active and successful life in your own terms, it is in your objective interest to satisfy your basic need to optimise your life expectancy and to avoid serious physical disease and illness conceptualised in biomedical terms. This applies to everyone, everywhere. (59)

As part of his Principle of Generic Consistency, Alan Gewirth suggests: 'Freedom and well-being are necessary goods for each agent because they are the generic features and proximate necessary conditions of all his action and generally successful action, and hence are needed for whatever purpose-fulfillment he may seek to attain by acting' (Gewirth 1994: 28).[11] Particular cultures, he claims, can then be judged in relation to how far they provide these goods for everyone (36–7).

John Kekes argues that there are 'universally human, historically constant, and culturally invariant needs created by human nature' and that these 'primary values' stand in contrast to secondary values, which vary with particular traditions and conceptions of the good life (Kekes 1994: 49). He draws up a list of candidates for the position of primary values falling into physiological, psychological and social categories, and argues that these primary values 'constitute a context-independent ground for settling some conflicts among values' (50).

Bernard Williams raises the question, 'Is there anything that rational agents necessarily want . . . merely as part or precondition of being agents?' (Williams 1985: 55). His reply is that they necessarily want freedom. As agents, we want certain outcomes and we want to be able to produce them. We must then want not to be frustrated in such endeavours, for instance by interference by other people. (For Williams this claim is one premise in an argument designed to hoist us into the moral world. He rejects the argument but he does not reject the claim itself.)

Of course, it is possible to take up a sceptical stance on the very existence of any universal preconditions of the kind specified in these theories.

---

[11] The Principle of Generic Consistency is expounded at length in Gewirth 1978: chs. 1–3. See also Beyleveld 1991.

In that spirit, Michael Walzer argues: 'There is no single set of primary or basic goods conceivable across all moral and material worlds – or, any such set would have to be considered in terms so abstract that they would be of little use in thinking about particular distributions' (Walzer 1983: 8; cf. Bell 1993: 69). I shall say something more about such scepticism in section 6 but, even leaving it aside, there are a number of general problems in producing a convincing theory of universal constraints of precondition.

For one thing, there are circumstances in which suicide may be a rational project.[12] Perhaps the only realistic prospect in someone's life is a future of unending torment, and in those extreme circumstances all they have reason to do is end their life. Or they may correctly calculate that the best way of advancing some cause which they judge to be more important even than their own life is to sacrifice themselves for its further-ance. Self-immolation by Buddhist monks during the Vietnam War or by Jan Palach during the Soviet occupation of the former Czechoslovakia are cases in point. These examples remind us of the very wide range of possible courses of action for which agents can have good reasons. Where agents have good reasons for bringing about some state of affairs which does not involve their own continued existence, it is difficult to argue that they have any continuing reason for sustaining the precon-ditions of their continued existence. Nevertheless, cases of suicide are peripheral and exceptional, and it would still be worthwhile to formu-late universal preconditions of action which at least cover the standard case of a rational agent with a continuing interest in acting in the world. It would simply have to be conceded that there was a slight loss of gen-erality if the formulation failed to cover cases of suicide. We should note, moreover, that even in these peripheral cases the agents will need what-ever is necessary for their continued existence up to the point of their performance of this last act.

There are problems beyond this peripheral area, however, again aris-ing from the very wide range of actions which may be favoured by a rational agent. The richer and more specific the list of preconditions which a theory contains, the more exposed it is to the objection that it is appropriate only for particular courses of action or ways of life associated with them – the objection, in other words, that it speaks not to univer-sality but only to some implicitly favoured set of individual or cultural assumptions. That has been a familiar objection to Rawls's doctrine of primary goods. One of the earliest criticisms was Thomas Nagel's, that

---

[12] Kekes considers the significance of this possibility (cf. Kekes 1994: 50).

Rawls's list of primary goods implicitly favoured a liberal individualist agenda in which 'the best that can be wished for someone is the unimpeded pursuit of his own path, provided it does not interfere with the rights of others' (Nagel 1973: 10). Michael Sandel similarly mentions, but does not pursue, the possible objection that Rawls's view 'is implicated too deeply in the contingent preferences of, say, Western liberal bourgeois life plans' (Sandel 1982: 27).

The question is not whether the goods on Rawls's list are *desirable*. It seems clear, for example, that self-respect and its social bases are desirable for all agents in all circumstances. The question in this context is not even whether Rawls can fairly claim to have shown that the primary goods are desirable from a set of universal considerations. The question is, rather, whether the primary goods can be shown to be indispensable to all human action. That seems doubtful, not least because Rawls's list contains an uneasy combination of universal and culture-specific features of human life. For example, it is difficult to see how something as specific as a free choice of occupation could be thought to be a precondition of all rational plans of life, when occupations are a phenomenon peculiar to particular forms of society and even within our own there are rational agents whose lives do not involve any occupation as such.[13]

Certainly if a theory of universal preconditions is to have any leverage in a pluralist context, then it must avoid parochialism both in form and in content, as I pointed out in chapter 1, section 3.[14] We cannot presuppose particular views of the good life or make philosophically and/or culturally contentious assumptions about the particular property in question if it is to be invoked in assessment of differing cultures. Given this and the problem of the very wide range of projects which a rational agent can embrace, it will be a sensible strategy to opt for relatively simple and general features as universal preconditions.

Health, as sponsored by Doyal and Gough, seems a promising candidate. Yet even here there is a difficulty. There are people who want to achieve particular goals even at the cost of the loss of longevity or the risk of falling prey to disease. (For that matter, there are people whose aspirations are not for anything which they or their own culture would really call an active and successful life: they might, for example, aspire to

---

[13] This would be true, for example, of people in our own society with sufficient wealth that they choose to live their lives in other ways than any involving an occupation. They might devote themselves to voluntary good works or to sybaritic indulgence, or to a mixture of the two. None of these activities amounts to, or has as a precondition, the holding of an occupation in the ordinary sense of the term. See Graham 1996a: 141–3.

[14] Parochialism in form is discussed in chapter 6, section 1.

achieve a certain contemplative state. In that case, Doyal and Gough's claim about universal preconditions would be at best a conditional one. *If* you want to lead an active life, then you need the following...) The difficulty is dramatised in the case of the philosopher Brentano, who said that he welcomed his blindness since it enabled him to concentrate on his philosophy. These cases suggest that placing a priority on health does not have the universal reach which might at first be thought. It may be rational to opt for some goal whose achievement is actually incompatible with health as normally construed.

Doyal and Gough acknowledge the difficulty presented by cases like these and reply: 'Such arguments ignore the fact that Brentano had to possess enough physical health to acquire the conceptual tools neces-sary to respond to his disablement in the enhanced way he claimed' (Doyal and Gough 1991: 316 n. 6). That reply perhaps enables them to retain some version of their original claim about health being a universal precondition, but its content has changed and its interest is somewhat reduced. The concept of health involved in the claim has contracted and now appears to amount to no more than whatever physical state might be necessary for the carrying out of the envisaged actions. Compare, for example, the idea of the need to optimise life expectancy mentioned in their original claim about what applies to all agents. If 'optimise' means maximise, then the claim is clearly vulnerable to counterexamples: peo-ple may rationally have life plans of sufficient importance that they imply a lifespan shorter than if they did not. It is not rational to take longevity as trumping any other aim. But if 'optimise' means something else, then the danger of tautology is apparent. It will be universally true that agents need to ensure that their life lasts long enough to carry out their plans; but that might turn out to be very short indeed: for example, if their plan is to leap on a grenade in order to save their comrades. The danger then is that the claim about what is a universal precondition of action will lapse into a tautology. It will amount to saying no more than that all actions have as a precondition the maintenance of a state in which the agent is enabled to carry out the actions in question.

Freedom or liberty is an obvious alternative to health as a universal precondition, but related problems arise here. The point is illustrated by Philip Pettit's claim that liberty is 'capable of commanding the allegiance of the citizens of developed, multicultural societies, regardless of their more particular conceptions of the good' (Pettit 1997: 96). It is the ideal of liberty specifically as non-domination which Pettit believes can play this role, and he recognises the possible objection that such an ideal is not neutral and will not command universal allegiance. He responds:

People in some traditions may display an ideologically nurtured desire to subject themselves to this or that subgroup: to those, for example, of noble birth, priestly role, or patriarchal status. But to my eye this requires the suppression of a deep and universal human desire for standing and dignity, and the elimination of a robust and healthy disposition to feel resentment at such pretensions of superiority. And even if I am wrong about that, what is certainly true . . . is that someone who is content to live in the mainstreams of a contemporary, pluralistic society is bound to treasure the ideal of not being dominated by others. Embrace the life of a sect who abase themselves before some self-appointed guru and you will see little in the idea of freedom as nondomination. Embrace the life of a contemporary, pluralistic society and you will see much. (96–7)

There are at least two problems here. First, the passage seems to imply that *any* subjection to another person is unacceptable. But that is almost certainly not what Pettit intends: he will surely allow that you can sometimes subordinate your will to that of another but that you should not do so where this results in their having *arbitrary* power over you (Pettit 1997: ch. 2). Someone may then believe that, let us say, a priestly role is a legitimate one and does not fall into the arbitrary category. In that case, they may agree at some level with Pettit, but not at a level which allows him to use uncontentiously the kind of examples he does to illustrate the idea of non-domination, and so not at a level where he gets any purchase on the disagreements arising from *de facto* pluralism discussed in chapter 1, section 1. Sects which worship gurus often exist *within* a contemporary pluralistic society, and that is precisely what gives rise to some of the problems mentioned in the earlier discussion. We are not given here a reason which *anyone* could adopt for embracing the ideal of non-domination, only the assertion that for anyone who has *already* embraced it a certain kind of problem will not arise.

But the second and more immediate problem for our present discussion is this. The sponsorship of liberty specifically in the form of non-domination is a clear departure not just from neutrality but also from a universal starting point. Separately from whether liberty in that form is desirable, it is certainly not a universal constraint of precondition. It is plain that even a slave is capable of many instances of human agency. A human agent is, quite simply, capable of many courses of action even while in a state of domination. To be sure, there is plausibility in making liberty, under a minimal construction of liberty, a constraint of precondition. Problems of free will and determinism aside, it is a necessary condition of human action that the agent be capable of selecting a possible course of action and initiating it. But it will be a fallacy of equivocation to argue from this truth to the conclusion that agents have a universal need for liberty under some other construction.[15]

There are, then, some formidable difficulties in articulating a convincing story about universal preconditions. None of them should lead us to conclude that there are no such preconditions. But we need to focus on conditions sufficiently close to all action to qualify as universal, yet not so close that it becomes uninformatively tautological to describe them as preconditions of action itself.

5.6 MATERIAL CONSTRAINTS

Beginning, now, from the truism that we are material creatures with material needs I want to suggest that this fact generates constraints both of necessity and of precondition. Acceptance of the truism might itself be questioned on Cartesian sceptical grounds, I suppose; but it is reasonable to say that the claim that we have a body is at least less contentious than, for example, the claim that we have a soul (cf. Williams 1993: 26).[16] Certainly it is reasonable to say that problems of practical reason arise only in circumstances where we have agreed that we *are* material organisms acting in a material world.

Our materiality, like our humanity, constitutes a constraint of necessity. It is a non-alterable characteristic which must be taken into account in all practical reasoning. The needs arising from this materiality place a limit on the aspirations it is rational to nurture, because the state which gives rise to those needs cannot be shed. Unlike our being at a particular spatial location, for example, our existence as material creatures cannot

---

[15] This fallacy seems to me to be committed by Doyal and Gough in their discussion. They raise the difficulty against their own position that survival and autonomy cannot be *goals* of human action if they are preconditions of it: we cannot 'need to achieve the very things which our achievement of anything presupposes' (Doyal and Gough 1991: 54). Their reply is that the human capacity for action is one of degree, so that 'the woman who is trying to increase her understanding of her actions and their consequences through working during the day and going to school at night will hardly appreciate the news that she already possesses the autonomy which she is working so hard to increase. Her goal is the capacity to do more of the things which she deems significant within her culture than she is capable of at present.' There is a basic need 'to *sustain* or *improve*' autonomy (55). It may seem that a fallacy of equivocation is avoided if different degrees of the same idea of autonomy are involved, as is suggested here; but that seems to me to be an illusion. In the sense in which any agent must understand the nature of their actions as a precondition of acting, courses at night school are not necessary for that precondition to be fulfilled. In the sense in which such understanding is desirable, it is not a precondition of any action.

[16] For anyone who believes we possess immortal souls, our rational practical aspirations are limited by our materiality only *while* we are embodied. That is still a considerable constraint, however.

itself be the subject of a practical decision preparatory to any further practical plans. We are, in a word, stuck with it.

Our materiality also constitutes a constraint of precondition. It is a consequence of our being the kind of creatures we are that our survival from one moment to the next depends on the satisfaction of a range of material needs, a range which expands as we conceive of more extended forms of action whose execution takes more than a moment. Thus, my scratching my nose in a moment depends on an uninterrupted supply of oxygen to my brain; my posting a letter tomorrow depends on my receiving sustenance sufficient to support my continued biological functioning; my completing a philosophy paper in the course of the next month depends on my meeting a wider range of needs, including the need for shelter and clothing to protect me from the elements. In addition, the latter two actions also depend on the availability of a range of material objects which I can employ in various ways, and that will be typical of most actions above a low level of triviality.

I leave aside here the question of whether our materiality is a conceptual or a causal constraint. Suppose that we came across creatures which were in many respects similar to us, but they were able to carry out their plans of action without needing to meet material requirements as we do, in the form of providing ourselves with food, clothing, shelter and other necessities. Should we be prepared to call them people? I am not sure, but it is at least clear that this is not our condition nor will it become so in any foreseeable circumstances. What is equally clear is that material constraints are universal: all human agents must satisfy certain material needs as a precondition of exercising their agency in any matter whatsoever. This is not a local truth which might fail to hold in some other place, or for some agents, or for some projected plans.

Indeed, the material constraints reach beyond action and constrain all aspirations. They go beyond what any *agents* must concern themselves with and speak to what any human *beings* must concern themselves with. They will apply, for example, to someone who has no interest in acting at all but aspires simply to experience certain states: they too must concern themselves with the meeting of their material needs for this aspiration to have any chance of success. Satisfaction of material needs is a prerequisite of any life at all. This greater generality of material constraints means that they are less intimately connected specifically with the concept of action itself (unlike, say, the constraints of freedom or autonomy), and there is correspondingly less danger of its being uninformatively tautological to describe them as constraints on action. But so far as action itself is concerned, their reach is complete. They govern not merely permissible conceptions of the good or rational plans of life: they govern all actions whatever.

All of these claims about material constraints might be true but yet carry no great significance. As I pointed out in section 4, it is not worth describing a factor in terms of constraints unless it has some salience to practical decisions. But, given the nature of human existence, our materiality could hardly have greater salience to practical decisions. It is a contingent fact of enormous consequence that the satisfaction of material needs is a central rather than a peripheral or negligible part of a human life. It is central partly because these needs must be met *recurrently*. Suppose that we were capable of settling the satisfaction of our material needs in the first fifteen seconds of our existence, so that we no longer had to concern ourselves with nourishment, providing sheltered habitation, or clothing to protect ourselves against the elements, and we could simply go on to give our life a chosen shape free of all those concerns. Our lives would then be utterly different, because in life as it is those needs make themselves felt for as long as a lifetime, since life literally ceases if they go unmet. Material constraints are perennial constraints.

They are also central for a further reason. The satisfaction of material needs requires resources. People are differently placed with regard to possession of the appropriate resources, but generally speaking we do not live in a world where they exist unowned, as if we could simply appropriate them separately from entering into relations with other human beings. At least for many people the constraints of materiality operate in the form of making it necessary for them to enter into some relation of dependence with someone who can provide them. In our immediate social context this will often involve taking employment in order to gain access to them via monetary transactions, or else occupying an intimate relation with someone who does that.[17] Employment itself, if it has this role of solving the resources problem, is standardly not a peripheral aspect of someone's life. Hence, material constraints are central in the further sense that, for many people, the activities they must engage in in order to satisfy their material needs are themselves central in their lives. (For people who possess a large fortune, however, material constraints will not be central in their life in this way.)

---

[17] Robert Goodin notes that across the world the arrangement for the (normally contributory) old age pension presupposes that 'everyone is either in work or is in a stable, long-term liaison with someone else who is' (Goodin 1992: 198).

In section 5 I mentioned Michael Walzer's scepticism about the idea of culturally neutral primary or basic goods, and it might now be objected that the postulation of material constraints is itself not free from any problem of cultural bias. Walzer argues:

A single necessary good, and one that is always necessary – food, for example – carries different meanings in different places. Bread is the staff of life, the body of Christ, the symbol of the Sabbath, the means of hospitality, and so on . . . If the religious uses of bread were to conflict with its nutritional uses – if the gods demanded that bread be baked and burned rather than eaten – it is by no means clear which use would be primary. (Walzer 1983: 8)

Now we must tread carefully here, since Walzer's chief concern is with specifically distributional questions, and it appears from the context that he may have the question of *moral* primacy in mind. But certainly we should resist any temptation to generalise his point so far as the constraints of materiality are concerned. A demand on the part of the gods that all foodstuffs be burned would be self-defeating for any continuing relation between rulers and ruled, as would obedience on the part of the people. The explanation for this enables us to develop one, culturally unbiased, sense in which the use of food as food is primary.

Recall the distinction invoked in section 4 between the *original* and *reactive* significance which some consideration may have, depending on whether its significance (i) originates with the independent judgement of an agent themselves or (ii) arises in reaction to the behaviour or attitudes or judgements of others. What the case of materiality illustrates is that a factor may carry significance independently of human attitudes altogether. To the categories of original and reactive significance we need to add (iii) the category of *brute* significance. As well as things which are important to us either because we ourselves independently judge them to be so or because we are compelled to do so as a result of someone else's investing them with importance, there are also things which are important to us *whether we or anyone else thinks they are or not*.

To illustrate, if I have conceived the ambition to become the heavyweight boxing champion of the world I may (i) experience regret and pain if I find myself spending all my time watching new wave French films instead of attaining a degree of physical fitness, a pain which might be entirely inappropriate if I had not invested this project with a certain importance. In contrast, there are circumstances where (ii) I would suffer the pain of social opprobrium if I bore a child out of wedlock. The importance attaching to this state is something dependent on social attitudes, and I may have to take it into account regardless of what my own attitudes are on the matter. But in contrast to both of these cases would be (iii) the pain associated with falling off a cliff. Our materiality and the importance we must attach to it are analogous to the latter kind of pain. It is important whatever we think about it, and whether we think about it or not. That makes its importance, in itself, an objective consideration, and to that extent beyond the reach of any particular culture (though of course there can be crucial cultural variation in the way that the objective fact is perceived and theorised). It does not depend on agents' perception either of the world or of themselves: their material need-satisfaction constitutes a constraint whatever they may think, whatever culture they may belong to, and whatever their culture may *say* about it. It carries rational motivational force quite generally. You may be interested in projects far removed from any consideration of material need-satisfaction, but if you are to be interested in any projects at all you must be interested in *that* project.

The brute significance of materiality, for all human beings in all conditions, regardless of their particular aspirations and regardless of their own conception of things, makes it an excellent candidate for the role of criterion for arbitrating among different cultures and theories of reasons for acting. It has the required universality discussed in chapter 1, section 3, picking out features possessed by all human agents in all circumstances rather than those encountered only in some cultures; and the description of the constraints of materiality is couched in minimally contentious language, not depending on any particular set of moral values, for example. Just as any reasonable agent, whatever their projects and commitments, will attend to their material circumstances, so, if we wish to judge different social environments in terms of their conduciveness to the realisation of human plans, we can raise questions about their provision of the material prerequisites of human action, questions which may be a long way from the views or conceptions or values evident in those social environments themselves. We shall be entitled to ask, for example of environments which might see themselves primarily in religious or political terms, what their organisation implies for the meeting of material needs, how their inhabitants must relate to one another in that regard, what sort of human beings result from the arrangements for meeting material needs, and so on. This opens up the possibility of criticism of some such environments in terms other than those in which they primarily see themselves (for example, that human agents, whatever their particular aspirations, must enter into degrading or inhumane relations in order to be in a position where they can pursue their plans), but not in terms which represent the prior prejudicing of some cultures at the expense of others.

The constraints of materiality raise many more issues than can be pursued in this book. The centrality and significance of our materiality can be interpreted in a number of ways, not necessarily consistent with one another, which challenge traditional philosophical categories and perspectives. There is, for example, the complaint that the individuals of traditional state of nature theory are presented without regard to their materiality, as if they were disembodied and disembedded creatures, and that this has serious consequences for our understanding of their situation and the problems that confront them. A recognition of their inevitable materiality might then be invoked to object to the exclusion of issues of nurture and reproduction from discussion of public life (cf. Benhabib 1992: 152–7 and Okin 1991 67–90). For questions of pluralism and the politics of recognition there is the general suggestion that culture, and respect for culture, may not be comprehensible in abstraction from the dynamics of political economy (cf. Rorty 1984: 152–6). We need a philosophical theory of our materiality before we can deal with these matters, and my aim here has been to argue the need for such a theory rather than to provide it.

Among the issues which such a theory would have to address is the question whether our existence as *consumers* or as *producers* is more basic to our materiality. It may seem obvious that it must be our role as consumers. After all, there can be no exceptions to the fact that we must act to meet our material needs; and although it will be true of us *as a species* that we must act to produce the means of satisfying these needs, it need not be true of each and every individual. In other words, a certain kind of parasitism is possible, a state of affairs where some meet their material needs through becoming beneficiaries of the productive efforts of others. Appearances may be misleading here, however. Productiveness is itself a less than transparent notion, and in any adequate theory would have to lose its association with the crude idea that production necessarily involves the creation of a material object. On a more generous construal, where productiveness consists in making some contribution or other to the production of what is necessary for material creatures, while it will still not be true that every human being is productive, many more will be so than might at first be thought.[18]

---

[18] For elaboration of that point, see Graham 1989.

More importantly, it would also be necessary to clarify the sense of basicness in question when it is asked whether being a consumer is more basic than being a producer. For a given set of people, the fact that they had to produce in order to put themselves in a position where they could consume might certainly be freighted with more significance for their lives than the fact, simply, that they had to consume. Disentangling all this would not be easy, but doing so would be necessary to arrive at a sound conclusion about the precise significance of the constraints of materiality for reasoning agents.[19]

It may be advisable to enter a caveat about my claims in this section. The stress on the role of our materiality in creating constraints of necessity and precondition is not a claim about the relative importance of material as against other (such as cultural or spiritual) aspects of life, where importance is taken to imply degree of value. (Such a claim *could* be made, but it is inherently likely to appeal more to *l'homme moyen sensuel* than to philosophers.) Nor is there any hint of a crass materialism which would eulogise an ever greater consumer culture. On the contrary, the constraints of materiality, as I have suggested, must be taken account of because they have such an influence over those parts of our life which are *not* concerned with securing satisfaction of material needs, and which may indeed be valued more highly by us. Both in terms of the proportion of our lives taken up by activities which in one way or another enable us to satisfy our material needs and in terms of the sort of people we become as a result of the social relations defining our material activity, the influence of our materiality is enormous. If the rest of our life matters to us, then we should scrutinise very closely anything which has such a profound effect on what matters to us.

5.7 CONCLUSION

In this chapter I have attempted to consolidate some of the claims of earlier chapters. I have suggested that there is a high degree of similarity between the nature of agency in individual human beings and the nature of agency in collective entities. Neither should be taken to be primary in any overall fashion, and both are subject to practical reasons from a wide variety of sources. That fact emphasises the importance of the need

---

[19] For the importance, in a particular historical context, of the shift from identifying oneself as a producer to identifying oneself as a consumer see Sandel 1996: 224–5. For discussion of some of the difficulties in too readily identifying being a beneficiary of others' productive efforts with being an exploiter or a parasite see Graham 1989; Graham 1999a; and van Parijs 1995: ch. 5.

for judgement, decision and choice on the part of reasoning agents. So far as concerns the importance which is attached to the role of choice, I have suggested that good reasons for acting cannot be derived *merely* from the act of choice, but that the act of choice can play a significant role in circumstances where a number of other considerations antecedently provide reasons for acting.

Among the considerations antecedently relevant to practical reasoning will be those which do not so much provide reasons for embarking on particular practical projects as constitute constraints on them. Constraints of necessity and constraints of precondition will figure in the practical reasoning of all human agencies at all times and places. A general specification of those constraints can be given; the construction of a substantive theory about the constraints which operate in particular circumstances will depend in part on detailed empirical investigation to see which factors meet the general specification (albeit investigation which must be informed by judgements about what is worth mentioning as being a constraint).

One substantive claim, however, which can be made in advance of detailed empirical investigation is that the constraints inseparable from our materiality constitute significant constraints both of necessity and of precondition. Rooted in the nature of human life itself, regardless of the social attitudes, beliefs and conventions obtaining in a particular situation, is the requirement to satisfy a whole range of material needs on a continuing basis. This inescapable requirement is so central in human life that rational agents will ask themselves, with regard to *any* projects which they adopt, 'What are the material needs which must be met for me to persist as an agent and for me to achieve this particular project? What implications for my life follow from the meeting of those needs? What other activities are required for meeting them and what effects will they have on the agent I become as a result?' We know, not as a result of detailed empirical investigation but as a general empirical fact, the fact of causal interconnection whose significance was discussed in chapter 2, that the satisfaction of one person's material needs inevitably involves their entering into complex interrelations with many, many others. The business of dealing with the constraints of materiality under which any given agent stands, therefore, generates many complicated questions about other people's lives besides those of the agent concerned.

Since the constraints of our material needs obtrude themselves into any project whatsoever, and since the meeting of those needs involves complex interactions among large numbers of people, it follows that the very idea of human agency is already deeply social in character. From a consideration of universal and uncontentious facts about the prerequisites of human agency, we arrive at a conclusion which further questions the acceptability of D2 from chapter 1, section 4, the idea of the distinctness of persons as separateness, and the associated intuitive idea introduced there that the best state of affairs is one in which as many distinct people as possible are carrying out their plans as successfully as possible. In one clear sense arising from our materiality, human lives are not separate at all; they are connected, and, as it may well be, connected in ways of which we are not even aware. The realisation of any plan of action whatever that I may conceive of will involve other people, because of the material prerequisites of pursuing it. In that way, many other people, and their plans, are already implicated in the plans of any given, apparently distinct, agent.

The substantive claim about the brute significance of our material-ity to our practical reasoning constitutes a timely reminder. We live in an unprecedentedly self-conscious age where self-perceptions and self-conceptions receive a great deal of attention. There are good reasons for this, not least because our lives may be crucially affected by those features of ourselves which carry reactive significance, as well as by those features which we endow with significance from our own choice. Our lives may be crucially affected by the way in which others see us, and that is a good reason for making those perceptions part of our own self-awareness (without necessarily endorsing them). But lying beneath the identities we choose or have forced upon us there are facts about our condition which make their significance felt whatever we or others think. Material facts are facts of that description.

CHAPTER 6

Practical reasoning and morality

At the beginning of this book I observed that my main concern was to work out what followed from our existence as social creatures for practical reasoning in general, rather than what followed specifically for morality. I have, however, attempted at various points to relate my discussion to moral thinking, if only because moral thinking is so pervasive. Thus, in chapter 3 I suggested that there was as much reason to ascribe moral responsibility to collectivities as there was to ascribe it to individuals, and I suggested that collectivities could be objects of moral concern in similar ways to individuals. In the present chapter I attempt to relate earlier discussion to moral thinking more systematically. I entertain the suggestion that morality has a pre-eminent role in questions of practical reasoning and, without attempting to settle whether the suggestion is correct, I call attention to some of the questionable presuppositions on which it rests, note the diversity of roles which morality plays, and indicate some of the difficulties in forming a vocabulary consistent with the suggestion until we are sure that it is correct. I also point out a number of respects in which our thinking about morality may be affected by the conclusions of earlier chapters. This includes a return to the idea of pure collective identification discussed in chapter 4, section 5, and a consideration of its relation to the polarity of altruism and self-interest.

6.1 THE CHALLENGE OF MORALITY

Consider the following challenge. It might be objected that, precisely because morality has not been at the centre of my concerns, any conclusions about practical reasoning which we may have arrived at can be no more than provisional. After all, it might be said, morality itself is the supreme source of practical reasoning: it serves to trump any lesser conclusions about what to do and how to behave. Indeed, on some interpretations morality will provide us with reasons for acting which are independent of the vagaries of human circumstances altogether, whether those of a particular person or those of the species itself. Recall Kant's claim in that spirit that 'the grounds of obligation must not be sought in the nature of man . . . but *a priori* solely in the concepts of pure reason' (Kant 1785: 5, cited in Cohen 1996: 172).

Moreover, this objection continues, it is not hard to see how morality comes to have this central role as the supreme source of practical reasoning. Recall the intuitive idea described in chapter 1, section 4 that the best state of affairs is one in which as many distinct people as possible are carrying out their plans as successfully as possible. But, this objection suggests, the intuitive idea must be supplemented because of the wayward behaviour which results from the natural tendencies of human beings. Some plans of some distinct people encroach in unacceptable ways on the plans of other distinct people. Morality, it may be said, then plays the vital role of exercising a constraint over such wayward behaviour.

This view gains expression in the claim that morality is 'a system of a particular sort of constraints on conduct – ones whose central task is to protect the interests of persons other than the agent and which present themselves to an agent as checks on his natural inclinations or spontaneous tendencies to act' (Mackie 1977: 106). Such a device as the making and keeping of promises, for example, 'makes possible mutually beneficial cooperation between people whose motives are mainly selfish . . .' (110).[1] As Comte, the coiner of the term altruism, puts it, 'The chief problem of human life [is] the subordination of egoism to altruism . . . The whole of social science consists therefore in duly working out this problem, the essential principle being the reaction of collective over individual life' (Comte 1851–4: 400).

The challenge of morality, as sketched here,[2] rests partly on claims about the nature of human behaviour and attitudes and partly on claims about the nature of the institution of morality itself, its role and purpose. The claims about human nature are expressed imprecisely and can be interpreted in crucially different ways. It is hardly contentious to hold that people sometimes act selfishly or egoistically; more contentious to

---

[1] Mackie invokes Protagoras, Hobbes and Hume as historical figures adopting a similar approach. It should be noted, however, that not everyone identifies morality with the need to counter egoism by altruism. For further discussion, see Rogers 1997 and Slote 1995.

[2] It might possibly be objected that the sketch is too closely related to a specifically Kantian conception of morality. But then much recent moral philosophy has been Kant-inspired in the relevant respects. See Williams 1976: 1.

hold that this is mainly how they behave; and most contentious of all to hold that this is their essential nature or that they are bound to behave in this way. The employment of such claims in philosophical argument is problematic both because of their crucial vagueness and because of their vulnerability to refutation. As Rawls observes, beyond bits of wisdom to the effect that we should not rely too much on scarce motives such as altruism, there is not much to go on because history is full of surprises (Rawls 1993: 87). Certainly when the claims are taken in their most contentious interpretation they are more easily stated than argued for. Indeed, it is unclear exactly what *form* of argument is appropriate in their justification. Any attempt at *a priori* justification is likely to look circular and tautological (since the many instances of non-selfish behaviour which occur will be re-described as 'really' selfish, but without any good independent reason for such re-description); yet it is not obvious how one would begin to accumulate empirical evidence in a form which makes a convincing case for their truth.[3]

The claims about the institution of morality also need modification. That morality stands in *some* relation to action can hardly be gainsaid. But it is easy to oversimplify and present the relation as being stronger than it actually is. Consider statements such as the following:

... [ethical standards] are *normative*. They do not merely *describe* a way in which we in fact regulate our conduct. They make *claims* on us; they command, oblige, recommend, or guide. Or at least, when we invoke them, we make claims on one another. When I say that an action is right I am saying that you ought to *do* it; when I say that something is good I am recommending it as worthy of your choice. (Korsgaard 1996: 8–9)

Politics and ethics (whatever else they may be, however else they may be understood) are domains of *activity*. The reasoning we bring to them must be *practical reasoning*, that is reasoning which we and others can use both in personal and in public life not merely to judge and appraise what is going on, not merely to assess what has been done, but to guide activity. (O'Neill 1996: 2)

It is only because so many practical principles are embedded in characters and institutions, so have become received views, that it can sometimes *seem* that fixing on a description is all that is required. But the moral life is a matter of action, not of connoisseurship ... to appraise is not in the end just to converge

---

[3] For discussion, see Sen 1987: 18–22. The natural home for the most contentious claims is economics. Sen expresses doubts about the security of the claims in that context, suggesting that they have typically been based on some special theorising rather than empirical verification and that more plausible theories to explain economic behaviour have been developed. For more general discussion of the dubious status of the claims, see O'Neill 1998: ch. 12.

on agreed descriptions of cases: it is also to affirm that cases that fall under agreed descriptions are to be dealt with in this or that way. (O'Neill 1996: 88)

For all positive moralities and other practical precepts . . . are concerned, directly or indirectly, with telling persons how they ought to act, especially toward one another. (Gewirth 1994: 27)

These statements seem to me to exaggerate by ignoring the fact that there is, so to speak, a contemplative side to morality. Part of morality has the role of expressing moral responses (I should be happy to say: recording moral facts), and though such responses *may* connect indirectly with action they do not have to. We reach, for example, moral conclusions about what sort of person Julius Caesar was or about whether X has subjected Y to a regime of bullying. Over a wide area, morality is concerned in this way with moral assessment and appraisal of various kinds, appreciation and evaluation of character, of states, and indeed even of actions; but moral appreciation is not itself necessarily action-directed. The point can be made in terms of the moral vocabulary. The most general expressions such as *ought* or *right* and *wrong* are those most obviously linked to action. But richer and more specific expressions such as *gentle, courageous, treacherous, considerate, helpful,* may be employed in the interests of reaching some appraisal which is not connected to action. To say that morality is a matter of action rather than connoisseurship is then to compress together two distinct points: that descriptions of the world do not, or do not necessarily, tell us what we should do, which may be true; and that moral claims always have the role of telling us what we should do, which is false.[4]

Given the fact that morality does not have a connection with action as intimate as this, then an account of practical reasoning which allots no special place to morality does not come into conflict with morality in the same way as it would if morality itself really were nothing other than a form of practical reasoning. It is fairly obvious that not all practical thinking is moral thinking: there can be reasons for doing something

---

[4] The view which I am characterising as positing too strong a connection between morality and action is very widely held. For opposing views, see for example Murdoch 1970 and Taylor 1995a. I should add that Korsgaard's position is more nuanced than the quotation given in the text implies, but not in a way which affects the question at issue. She argues that it is not merely ethical concepts which have normative force. Concepts such as knowledge, beauty and meaning, she suggests, 'all have a normative dimension, for they tell us what to think, what to like, what to say, what to do, and what to be' (Korsgaard 1996: 9). But the broader the sense of normativity invoked – not merely doing, but thinking and the rest – and the wider the set of concepts over which it is spread, the less special will specifically moral concepts be in the matter of normativity (at least without some further argument as to their unique position).

which are self-interested, legal, aesthetic and so on. If it is also true that not all moral thinking is practical thinking, then, to put it metaphorically, there will be an area where a theory of practical reasoning and morality pass each other by rather than coming into head-on collision.

But it may now be felt that these considerations do very little to meet the challenge of morality raised at the beginning of this section. All that really comes out of them is that a theory of practical reason which is not itself moral does not fall foul of *the whole of* morality. It may be agreed, then, that we should not exaggerate here by ascribing to the whole of morality features which characterise only part of it. But then the objection can be made that at least *part* of morality is concerned with guiding conduct, and that is agreed on all sides. And that, it might be held, is all we need for morality to pose a challenge to a theory of practical reason in the way envisaged at the beginning of this section.

There is some justice in this complaint, and I now try to pinpoint what should be conceded to it and what not. The dilemma is expressed by Christine Korsgaard in the following terms:

Human beings are subject to practical claims from various sources – our own in-terests, the interests of others, morality itself. The normative question is answered by showing that the points of view from which these different interests arise are congruent, that meeting the claims made from one point of view will not neces-sarily mean violating those that arise from another. And that in turn shows how the threat is conceived. The threat is that the various claims which our nature makes on us will tear us apart . . . The concern is that morality might be bad or unhealthy for us . . . We reply to the challenge by showing that morality's claims are not going to hurt us or tear us apart. (Korsgaard 1996: 60–1)

These comments illustrate a fact which is obvious enough from the history of moral philosophy but which was not made explicit in the way the challenge of morality was laid out earlier: it is widely felt that the institution of morality is necessary for human beings but also that there is something intellectually problematic in securing its position. There is, in that way, a challenge *to* morality which morality itself has to meet. Nor is it universally thought that its position *should* be secured if it is taken to be an essential part of morality that it should override other consider-ations. It is a well-known theme in Bernard Williams's philosophy that if morality requires someone to abandon projects which give their life meaning then morality itself is to be rejected (though something broader, ethics, is to be retained).[5]

---

[5] See, for example, Smart and Williams 1973 and Williams 1976. For discussion, see Nagel 1986: ch. 10; Scheffler 1982; and Wolf 1997b.

Consider how the matter may be couched in terms of vocabulary.[6] In a famous and influential article Elizabeth Anscombe suggested that the moral *ought* should be given up, since it had lost its original connection with a divine law conception of morality and retained only a 'mesmeric force' (Anscombe 1958: 192, 195).[7] On the face of it, it might seem that this is an impossible demand to make, since it is precisely the expression *ought* and cognate expressions which carry the action-guiding burden of morality. How could that part of morality retain its connection with action, how could it tell us what we ought to do, without a suitable vocabulary? Now there is a reply to that, but it comes at a price. It might be said that the action-guiding burden could be carried by the richer and more specific terms described earlier (*gentle, courageous, treacherous*, and the rest). Thus, you might settle any issue of how to act 'by considering whether doing such-and-such in such-and-such circumstances is, say, murder, or is an act of injustice; and according as you decide it is or it isn't, you judge it to be a thing to do or not' (201). In that way you might proceed directly to an action-guiding conclusion without the need for any term like *ought* to carry that message.

Why does this solution carry a price? Because if we allow the action-guiding role to more than one such specific term, there is the possibility of conflict between them. Suppose that some putative course of action involves injustice but that the only alternative to it involves cruelty. Then I could not endow the term *cruelty* with the same strongly action-guiding role as the term *injustice*. I could not judge an act involving cruelty a thing not to do at the same time as judging an act involving injustice a thing not to do. Or at least I could do so only on pain of leaving no course of action or inaction to which I would be able to commit myself in these circumstances. So either we must allow only one such specific term to carry the decisive action-guiding force which a term like *ought* is thought to have; or, if we allow such decisive action-guiding force to more than one specific term, we must contemplate the possibility that the vagaries of the world will cause us to end up in situations where practical paralysis results.

The obvious solution to this difficulty is to allow the terms in question a less strongly action-guiding role, so that some kind of summation can take

<hr />

[6] For one attempt to couch some of these issues in terms of the varied moral vocabulary, see Graham 1975. For more recent and systematic argument, see Williams's account of thick ethical concepts in Williams 1985: 128–30.

[7] Compare Jean Hampton's suggestion that 'the symbol representing the normative necessity operator might be a hand with an outstretched forefinger, representing the directive gesture of a supreme commander' (Hampton 1998: 107).

place when all relevant descriptions of putative courses of action have been gathered in. In other words, we might insist that these terms do have some action-guiding force, but something weaker than the unqualified force of indicating 'a thing not to do'. They might, say, carry the force 'a thing *there is some reason* not to do'. We could then, in theory, collect all relevant descriptions attaching to the various options for action in a given situation, and make some final decision on what is the thing to do on that basis. (One option involves injustice but generosity, another involves cruelty but honesty, and so on.)

To clarify the different action-guiding forces which a given term might possess we could introduce a system of subscripts: G to indicate that the term has some general force in guiding actions, that it denotes, in general terms, the *sort* of thing not to do (but not necessarily *the* thing not to do in these circumstances); and D to indicate that it has a more decisive force in guiding actions, that it does denote, precisely, the thing not to do. Under these conventions, the claim concerning an act of injustice expressed by Anscombe, that it is a thing not to do, would be represented by the assertion that it was an act of injustice$_D$, while the weaker (and on my view more acceptable) claim that it was a thing there is some reason not to do would be represented by the assertion that it was an act of injustice$_G$.

But two points should be noticed about this. First, if we operate with a vocabulary governed by G-subscripts, it looks as though an *ought* vocabulary has to be smuggled back in at the point where a summation takes place in the light of the collection of relevant G-subscript descriptions attaching to alternative possible courses of action. The summation has to be expressed in a way that differentiates it from judgements which do not have the same kind of finality for the purpose of guiding action. One of Anscombe's complaints about the moral *ought* is that it carries the suggestion of a verdict, and that where there is no judge or law the idea of a verdict does not make sense (Anscombe 1958: 195). But precisely what is required in this context is a verdict in the sense of a *decision*, and the term *ought* or something similar will be necessary to express such a decision. Otherwise, we are left simply with a stock of descriptions indicating what is to be said for and against alternative courses of action, but not a decisive judgement which can then actually determine what action is to be taken.

The second point is that once it has been conceded that richer and more specific terms can be used in an interim way towards a final judgement, the question can be raised why we should not assume that exactly the same is true of the moral *ought* itself. Under the suggested conventions, the claim that one morally ought to do something could be represented either by the assertion that one ought$_D$ to do it or by the assertion that one ought$_G$ to do it. Why assume, without further ado, that it is properly represented by the former rather than by the latter? In other words, why assume that what you ought to do from a moral point of view is necessarily what you ought to do all things considered?[8] Why not, indeed, introduce a further M-subscript so that what ought$_M$ to be done denotes a summation of descriptions of what there are reasons to do from a moral point of view? The ought$_D$ formulation could then be preserved for denoting overall decisions about what to do, which might or might not coincide with what to do from a moral point of view.

I make no pretence here to answering the question of whether the pressure from morality can converge with the pressure from other sources, in the manner that Korsgaard hopes. Nor do I have any theory to settle the question of whether moral considerations can legitimately be taken as overriding other considerations. It would be presumptuous to pretend otherwise in a book which is any case devoted to other topics. My concern in this section has been to argue that unless or until these matters are settled, we should not form our views of practical reason in a way which presupposes that they have been settled, nor should we arrange our theoretical vocabulary in a way which prejudices the possible outcomes of debates on these questions.

6.2 SOCIAL EXISTENCE AND MORALITY

More needs to be said, however, to correct a mistaken impression which may be left by my remark in the previous section that there is an area where a theory of practical reasoning and a theory of morality pass each other by, rather than coming into head-on collision. After all, in my earlier discussions I have been at pains to stress that a proper appreciation of our social nature does carry implications for moral thinking; it will not do now, therefore, to leave the impression that they can just be kept out of each other's way.

Consider, then, how some of the problematic aspects of morality are affected by the arguments of earlier chapters. There is a general assumption in thinking about morality that, although it has a role in adjudicating at some points amongst the conflicting interests of individuals, at other

---

[8] Bernard Williams argues in a similar vein that obligations generated by morality are never final practical conclusions. They are an input, and one way of securing the protection of important interests, but only one kind of ethical input at that. See Williams 1995b: 205.

points it does not need to do so. In other words, there is the thought that morality does not engross the whole of our life and there would be something wrong if it did. (It is a familiar complaint against utilitarianism that if we tried to live according to its precepts we should never be off duty, because there would no situations where it did not apply.) The problem then is to distinguish in some rationally defensible way between the area where morality legitimately holds sway and the area where it does not. The attempt to do so by appeal to the distinction between an area where no one other than the agent is causally implicated by the agent's actions and an area where such implication is present is notoriously problematic, and I attempted to render it more problematic in chapter 2 by introducing a further dimension to the fact of causal interconnection in the form of causal precondition. There may be nothing wrong with the aspiration of not allowing morality to engross the whole of our life, but our social nature creates more complications than are generally recognised for the case we might set out for realising that aspiration. We fail to appreciate how pervasive causal connection is if we leave causal precondition out of our calculations.

The challenge of morality described in section 1 rested on the assumption that the jostling interests amongst which morality must step in and adjudicate are all *individual* interests; but in chapter 3 I suggested that collectivities shared enough of the characteristics in virtue of which individuals entered the moral realm for collectivities to enter the moral realm in their own right. Collectivities can be the locus of beneficence, loyalty, cruelty, pride, shame. They can be the perpetrators or victims of deception, they can deliver or experience generosity, they can develop their autonomy or have it thwarted.[9] What a collectivity does and what happens to it are then things which can *matter* from a moral point of view. This claim, as I pointed out, does not require that any non-human entity should be just like an individual human being – only that there is sufficient overlap in relevant properties. It does not require, so to speak, that any collectivity should be capable of committing all of the Seven Deadly Sins or infringing all of the Ten Commandments.[10]

---

[9] Autonomy bridges the distinction between moral agency and moral patienthood discussed in chapter 3. Collectivities can deliberate, form projects, make decisions and then act in their realisation. Hence their sharing of the moral realm *qua* agents with individual human beings. The thwarting of autonomy can happen to a collectivity as well as to an individual, and its happening can be a matter of moral concern in either case, thus making them moral patients. But this particular instance of moral patienthood is possible only because the entity in question is also an *agent*.

[10] Ronald Dworkin makes the point that an orchestra *only* has a musical life, it does not have a sex life or blood pressure or worries, and in the same way a nation may have a political life but not a

If this claim is correct, it helps to explain the problematic nature of inferences from D1, the thesis of the qualitative distinctness of persons discussed in chapter 1, section 4. Where it is held that there are only individuals with their individual interests, then the role of morality could be seen as solely concerned with the adjudication of such interests, and the idea of sacrificing the interests of an individual to those of some other kind of entity must simply be thought to involve some kind of error. If, however, as I attempted to establish, there are irreducible collectivities, if they may have an irreducibly collective good, and if sometimes that collective good may be a moral or morally significant good (either because the collectivity is formed explicitly to promote a moral good or because there are states of the collectivity which replicate morally significant states found in individuals), then the role of morality cannot be exhausted solely in paying attention to the interests of individuals. The question of weighing the rival demands of individuals and collectivities is a genuine one, and it has a place on the moral agenda as well as elsewhere.

It might be felt that this last suggestion is either absurd or sinister; for surely morality is an institution for the benefit of people, and how in that case could it happen that the interests of people should become displaced by some other kind of consideration? But this reaction is based on two misunderstandings. First, as I argued in chapter 3, section 7, it is already a familiar part of moral thinking to place value on abstract considerations such as loyalty, truth and the like. It is therefore not a new departure in this sphere to place value on something other than an individual human being, and in any clear-headed morality it is already an open question whether the demands of the individual must always trump any other consideration in all circumstances. Secondly, we must bear in mind that the entry of collective entities into the moral realm already inhabited by individual human beings is not like the addition of six more objects to six objects already in a room. Collectivities are themselves composed of individual human beings and nothing more, so it is not some kind of sinister and ghostly entity, quite separate from people, which is being introduced into the moral realm. Indeed, even if we confined ourselves only to considering each individual person's well-being and gave no independent weight to the well-being of any collectivity, we should still need to consider persons not just as individuals but also as members of collectivities, since that is in part what they are. What is good for

---

sex life (Dworkin 1989: 495–7). It must be broadly true that collectivities as such do not have sex lives, though exception would have to be made of a collectivity whose *raison d'être* was collective sexual activity, as in the practice of orgies.

them *qua* individual may not be the same as what is good for them *qua* member of a given collectivity, and balancing and trade-offs may be called for.

6.3 SOLIDARITY, ALTRUISM AND SELF-INTEREST

In chapter 4, section 5 I described a form of identification with a collectivity which is unmediated by considerations to do with oneself as an individual, a form of solidarity which is indivisibly plural in its character. In this section I explore further the motivation for solidarity in this form and discuss its relation to moral motivation.

The terms 'collective interest' and 'collective self-interest' are frequently used to refer to the interests shared by a number of individuals *qua* individuals. In that sense a number of shipwrecked people might be said to have a collective interest in survival, where this means that each of them has an interest in their personal survival, an interest which may be mutually interdependent with a similar interest on the part of other individuals. In contrast, what is involved in the solidarity of pure collective identification is a commitment to a collective interest where this refers, rather, to the interests of the collectivity considered as such. The interests of a team or an orchestra are distinct from those of the individuals who compose it. How, then, might we explain a commitment on the part of those individuals to further the good of a collectivity to which they belong?

In discussing the example of team loyalty, Martin Hollis suggests that solidaristic identification with the team might be taken in one of two ways, each of which leaves the rationality of the identification relatively problematic. Either it just *happens* that what each individual wants most is that the team does well – which looks a pretty arbitrary and fragile state of affairs, and therefore isn't much of an explanation as to how individuals might rationally opt for teamwork in the first place. Or they 'obey norms which put their team first blindly, and untroubled by critical doubt' – in which case blind obedience makes them sound more like ants than intelligent human beings (Hollis 1998: 109). Hollis's own preferred option is that individuals might act for the good of a collectivity via the medium of a *generalised reciprocity*: they will do so if enough other members of the collectivity are doing so, and in the recognition that A may help B because B helped C. Vendettas and baby-sitting circles, in their very different ways, illustrate such generalised reciprocity (127, 147;. cf. Levine 1993: 63–6).

In support of his own preferred option, Hollis says

> There are, I think, two robust ways of conceiving of teams and hence of actions
> done for the good of a team. One is to think of the team as an entity transcending
> its members, with a good which transcends and determines theirs. The other
> is to think of team membership as a constitutive relation between what are still
> separate people. (Hollis 1998: 138)

Now if these ways of conceiving teams exhausted all the possibilities, we
might well find the first conception so unattractive and implausible that
we would opt for the second. If we did so, we could then make sense of
commitment to the team in terms of Hollis's generalised reciprocity. But
notice that if we do so we stay at the level of relating individual goods
to one another, rather than relating individual and irreducibly collective
goods to each other. We deny ourselves the resources which would be
required to explain solidarity in the form of *pure* collective identification.
But if some of my earlier arguments were sound, then the two ways
of conceiving of teams which Hollis describes are neither exhaustive
nor exclusive. We can (and should) create a hybrid third conception by
combining elements from each.

First, since teams are one instance of the irreducibly collective agency
described in chapter 3, there are indeed good reasons for thinking of
them as transcending their members. Teams are capable of acts of which
individuals are not capable, their conditions of survival are different from
those of individuals, and there is a whole level of significant description
of our social world which would quite simply be missing if we did not
employ the vocabulary of irreducible collectivities. Moreover, taken in
one sense it will also be reasonable to say that such entities, as well
as transcending their members, have a *good* which transcends that of
their members. The good of a team is to be successful *as a team*, winning
games and championships and trophies. That good transcends that of the
members in being distinct from, and not reducible to, anything which
can be regarded as an individual's good *qua* individual. (I argued in
chapter 3, section 6 that, at the extreme, the way to ensure that a *team*
flourished might be by making sure that the individuals composing it
at a particular time did not – by kicking them out and replacing them
with members more capable of doing what was necessary for achieving
the team's good.) Where the idea of transcendence is taken to express
this kind of irreducibility, then, we can allow that the good of teams
transcends that of individuals.

However, taken in another sense it will not be reasonable to say that the good of a team transcends that of its members. It is certainly not part of the nature of teams that the good of the team transcends in the sense of *taking precedence over* the good of its members. Nor, therefore, will it be reasonable to say that the good of the team *determines* the good of individuals. Because you have aspirations and values as an individual, and because you may also be a member of more than one literal or metaphorical team, your own good can never simply be read off your membership of a team. Perhaps your good *qua* member of team A is less important than your good *qua* member of team B, and perhaps neither of these is as important as the good accruing from some choice you have made *qua* individual. Perhaps, too, your membership of a team gives you an overriding escape-interest of the kind discussed in chapter 4, section 3, in which case your own good would be determined by your membership of the team only in the most backhanded way. These possibilities must be evaluated in determining what is your good in any particular circumstances, in consequence of which judgement and decision, rather than determination by team membership, are unavoidable for a rational agent.

It thus emerges that elements from the two alternative conceptions of a team presented by Hollis can be combined into a hybrid third option. In the hybrid third option teams do transcend their members in the familiar sense that there is a range of predicates which are irreducibly applicable to the team but not to its members; and teams do have a good which transcends that of their members in the same sense of irreducibility. But their good does not transcend that of their members in the sense of taking precedence over, or determining, it. And the fact which explains why that is so – the need on the part of their members for decision and judgement – also explains why in the third option we can still insist that relations within a team are indeed constitutive relations between what are still separate people. That feature from Hollis's second conception can be combined with the features of transcendence in his first conception, at least on that acceptable interpretation of transcendence which has now been distinguished from the unacceptable interpretation. The possibility of decision and judgement, of *embracing* the good of a team after a process of reasoning, indicates how there can be solidaristic identification which is neither pure happenstance nor mere blind obedience, neither arbitrary nor mindless. But nor is the explanation for such identification confined to a story about the relation between different individual goods in the manner of Hollis's generalised reciprocity. It may arise out of a prior commitment to some abstract value which the collectivity itself functions to realise, for example, in the manner described in earlier arguments,[11] and that will amount to reasoned identification rather than blind or arbitrary identification.

But how does solidarity in this form relate to the idea of individual goods, and in particular to the idea of individual goods as conceptualised in the polarity between self-interest and altruism which is central to so many conceptions of morality? My suggestion is that it shares some features with altruism and some with self-interest but it is *sui generis* and distinct from both.

Consider the nature of self-interest. In chapter 5, section 2 I emphasised how agents have many different calls on their commitment from many different sources of reasons for acting. Even if we just take one source, such as self-interest, it will still be true that agents have many different calls on their commitment. Thus, someone may have an interest in living a comfortable existence, an interest in achieving certain important goals, and an interest in settling some old score. And it is standard, rather than exceptional, for the reasons stemming from such considerations to conflict: sometimes the merely contingent circumstances of the world and sometimes the nature of the interests themselves dictates that they cannot all be realised, that choices have to be made. In any event, if an agent is not to suffer from paralysis and inaction, decisions must be reached which privilege some reasons over others. Where that occurs, Susan Hurley usefully speaks of *pro tanto* reasons, to reflect the fact that the reasons not so privileged continue to have force, unlike *prima facie* reasons, which fall out of the picture altogether when not so privileged (Hurley 1989: 130).[12] I may, for example, have a reason for staying in bed and a reason for getting up, and decide that the reason for getting up is stronger. But then I suffer from weakness of will and stay in bed. In that case I fail to act on the reason which I have privileged; but I still act for a reason, and the continued influence of the non-privileged reason makes this intelligible.

This is a framework which is apposite for reasons of all types, including those associated with pure collective identification. Suppose that you

---

[11] See especially chapter 3, sections 6 and 7 and chapter 4, section 5.

[12] Hurley suggests that the relationships between different *pro tanto* reasons are in some ways like the relationships between individuals whose wills clash (134). Harry Frankfurt makes a similar point in suggesting that one person's making up their mind is like two people's making up their differences. This is compatible with a certain conflict or tension continuing, but a certain order has been introduced into it (Frankfurt 1988: 173).

privilege the reason you have for identifying with a collectivity but then act against your decision, and for some other reason which you had not so privileged. That is also a case in which you act for a reason which you had already decided was outweighed by other reasons. It is, to that extent, a manifestation of irrationality, and no special considerations would apply if the other reason in question happened to be one relating to your individual self-interest.

Now there is a tendency to suppose otherwise. There is a tendency to suppose that the privileging of a self-interested reason over other types is a kind of default position requiring no explanation. That is the thought which can underlie the uneasiness about the challenge to morality mentioned in section 1: it is felt that the force of moral considerations must be made intellectually compelling in the face of the fact that considerations pertaining to self-interest are much more obviously and unproblematically compelling. Correspondingly, there is a tendency to suppose that *sacrifice* is involved if a collectivity-related reason is privileged over a self-interested reason, because acting for the good of the collectivity is taken to be, or to be sufficiently similar to, acting altruistically. Taking that view does not depend on the thought that the collectivity itself is altruistic: on the contrary, it may be malign in the extreme. Rather, it may be thought that acting for some other entity than oneself involves self-abnegation and sacrifice in the same way that altruism on the part of an individual does, regardless of the nature of that other entity.

The language of sacrifice is apt to be invoked even in sympathetic discussions of collective identification. In arguing against the claim that all human behaviour is self-interested, for example, Amartya Sen says: 'Actions based on group loyalty may involve, in some respects, a sacrifice of purely personal interests, just as they can also facilitate, in other respects, a greater fulfilment of personal interests' (Sen 1987: 20). Offe and Wiesenthal say that no trade union could function 'in the absence of some rudimentary notions held by the members that being a member is of value in itself, that the individual organization costs must not be calculated in a utilitarian manner but have to be accepted as necessary sacrifices' (Offe and Wiesenthal 1985: 183). Susan Hurley does not speak of sacrifice but she describes an individual who identifies with a coordinated collective agent as becoming 'public-spirited' (Hurley 1989: 157). Even this may be misleading, however, in the light of the exact relation of this form of solidarity to altruism and self-interest.

The language of sacrifice assimilates pure collective identification too closely to altruism. There are two components to altruism: positively, a

concern for the interests of another person; negatively, a lack of concern
with one's own interests. I take it, that is, that if a concern for the interests
of another person is motivated by the thought that one's own interests will
be promoted through that concern, the case ceases to be one of genuine
altruism (as opposed to enlightened self-interest). Now it is true that pure
collective identification shares the negative characteristic. Recall the first
approximation to an account of collective identification in chapter 4,
section 2 which likened it to *treating the good of a collectivity as I would my own
individual good.* I argued in chapter 4, section 5 that this approximation was
inadequate in the case of pure collective identification: precisely because
the idea of non-individual good was indispensable to an understanding
of that case, it was inappropriate to invoke the idea of personal good
in clarifying it. In that negative respect the case is similar to that of
altruistic motivation. In pure collective identification I have reason to
promote the good of an entity distinct from myself, and a reason which
is unmediated by any consideration of self-interest as normally construed.
The motivation is not traceable back to some individual state of myself
which my behaviour or attitudes are designed to realise.

But in the positive respect pure collective identification is unlike
altruistic motivation. Altruistic motivation necessarily involves the good
of some other human being, whereas pure collective identification involves it only *per accidens.* It may consist in commitment to some joint
activity for its own sake, as in the orchestra example, so that properly
speaking the good of other human beings simply fails to enter the picture.
It may, alternatively, consist in commitment to some joint activity which I
believe will promote some abstract value that I endorse, and though this
will have beneficial effects on or for other human beings that is not the
reason for my commitment. For example, perhaps I belong to a regiment
which I regard as the embodiment of honour, and it is not that I value
honour because of its payoff for human beings, myself or others; rather, I
welcome the existence and appropriate relations between human beings
precisely as giving an opportunity for the actualisation of this abstract
value. Or, thirdly, it may consist in commitment to some joint activity for
the sake of its effects on *us considered as members of the collectivity,* as when we
are committed to attempting to secure success for the team. In none of
these cases, however, is there the necessary connection with the good of
other individuals which is the positive defining characteristic of altruism.

Now it might be objected at this point that, even if the positive similarity with altruism is absent, the negative similarity is sufficient to justify
talk of sacrifice in such cases. If solidarity here involves a neglect of

self-interest, how could it be otherwise? But matters are not quite so simple, and here we must attend to the complicated relation between pure collective identification and self-interest as normally construed. In pure collective identification my concern is indeed with an entity distinct from myself, but not an entity *entirely* distinct from myself. I am part of it and it is part of what I am, so my concern reaches outside my own skin yet at the same time is a concern for an entity which exists in part within my own skin. My concern is therefore in the most literal sense a concern with a part of my self, or a concern with something of which my self is a part. In pure collective identification I am committed to activities which necessarily touch my own existence.

But if that is a respect in which pure collective identification draws near to self-interested motivation, there is a respect in which it keeps its distance from it, as it does from altruism. For although my solidarity is with an entity of which I am part, in the pure case my identification is not dependent on the fact that the collective entity and I are mutually implicated in that way: it is not mediated by thoughts about my individual self. The commitment to undivided plurality precisely displaces such a preoccupation with self. It necessarily involves a broadening of horizons beyond the personal, even though as a matter of fact the person is not left behind.

This form of solidarity marks the point at which a framework consisting of a polarity between a concern with one's own self and a concern with other selves is simply inadequate. At the same time, once a concern with a collectivity of which one is a member is added to the framework, it is less plausible to talk in terms of a polarity between the self and the collectivity. To be sure, there can still be tensions between the self and the collectivity, but they will be tensions between me and us, so to speak, and that is a very different matter from tensions between me and you.[13] Accordingly, I believe that there are no *stronger* grounds for using the language of sacrifice in the case of pure collective identification than in the case where one self-interested reason is privileged over another. You have a reason for living a comfortable life but you may sacrifice this to the achievement of some cherished and worthwhile personal goal, or vice versa. In the same way, and no other way, you may sacrifice the comfortable life for the furthering of some collective goal which is similarly cherished and worthwhile.[14]

---

[13] For a compelling account of dramatic tensions between me and us in a fictional context, see McEwen 1997: 14–15.
[14] For a similar point, see Scanlon 1998: 127.

6.4 CONCLUSION

The challenge described at the beginning of this chapter was the challenge that any other form of practical reasoning might have to subordinate itself to moral reasoning. I suggested that, since the case for the paramountcy of moral reasons for acting is at best not made out, we should not arrange our thoughts or our language in a way which prejudices the question of whether it can in fact be made out. Moreover, far from other forms of reasoning having to accommodate to the demands of moral reasoning, the nature of the relations between individuals and the collectivities to which they belong suggests that, on the contrary, we may need to enlarge our conception of moral reasoning to take into account forms of reasoning from adjacent territory.

On the one hand, someone's acting for the good of the team (either literal or metaphorical) and for no extraneous reason is a perfectly familiar phenomenon. On the other hand, it is a phenomenon whose significance we may well be mistaken about. And indeed it may be the very prevalence of particular moral ways of thinking which helps to obscure the nature of this form of collective identification. If we think only in terms of individual selves and their goods and interests, it will be correspondingly more difficult to understand, and correspondingly more likely that we shall distort, its nature. By contrast, if we bring irreducible collectivities and irreducibly collective goods into the picture, it is easier to appreciate that there is a form of motivation available here which simply does not fit well into the polarity presupposed in dominant conceptions of morality. We may then understand that an individual member of a collectivity can choose to identify with it and embrace its well-being, unmediated by any thoughts of themself as an individual, but that their doing so is not by its nature more onerous or more demanding of sacrifice than any other form of identification. There is nothing especially problematic about this form of solidarity, nothing any more problematic than there is about commitment to courses of action in general.

Such solidarity is not of its nature moral, but it *may* occur for moral reasons; that is to say, an agent may invest their commitment to a collectivity with moral importance. Where that occurs, then a proper understanding of the nature of collectivities and our relation to them can itself flow back into, and enrich, the moral thinking which was lacking such understanding originally.

Conclusion

Samuel Scheffler has described, and challenged, 'a widespread though largely implicit conception of human social relations as consisting primarily in small-scale interactions, with clearly demarcated lines of causation, among independent individual agents' (Scheffler 1995: 227). Associated with that conception is a claim made by Hart and Honoré about the connection between responsibility and the distinctness of persons construed as separateness. They argue that

the idea that individuals are primarily responsible for the harm which their actions are sufficient to produce without the intervention of others or of extraordinary natural events is important, not merely to law and morality, but to the preservation of something else of great moment in human life. This is the individual's sense of himself as a separate person whose character is manifested in such actions. Individuals come to understand themselves as distinct persons, to whatever extent they do, and to acquire a sense of self-respect largely by reflection on those changes in the world about them which their actions are sufficient to bring about without the intervention of others and which are therefore attributable to them separately. (Hart and Honoré 1985: lxxx, cited in Scheffler 1995: 233)

It will be evident from my arguments in this book that I believe Scheffler is right to challenge this conception of social relations. Small-scale interactions with clearly demarcated lines of causation are merely the tip of an enormous iceberg. Even the simplest of such interactions take place against a background of immensely complicated networks of human interaction, and could not take place at all without that background. The fact of causal interconnection is an undeniable fact, but one which can easily go ignored in other parts of our thinking. Moreover, its exact reach may not be fully appreciated: if my arguments in chapter 2, section 2 were correct, then the iceberg is even more enormous than we normally take it to be, casting a shadow back into the past as well as forward into the future. In any event, the fact of causal interconnection ensures that our actions are never sufficient to bring about changes in the world without the intervention of others, and any conception of self or of responsibility which presupposes otherwise rests on a falsehood.

Just as the fact of causal interconnection, when consistently pursued, necessitates a re-evaluation of D2, the idea of the distinctness of persons construed as separateness, so the fact of collective agency, when similarly pursued, necessitates a re-evaluation of D1, the idea of the distinctness of persons construed qualitatively. Individual human beings are not the only entities to engage in reflection and decision-making or to be capable of ratiocinative action. These properties are also manifested in collective entities, and we spend a portion of our lives as members of such entities. That raises for us questions about whether and how far we wish to identify with, or dissociate from, what we do as members of collectivities.

Much more needs to be said about these questions of collective identification and dissociation than I have been able to say here. I have attempted to elaborate on the different forms which identification with collectivities can take, and in the case of pure collective identification I have attempted to show how such identification is not always reducible to a concern solely with states of individuals. But the question of what considerations ought to govern the actual collective identifications we make is a huge one, with huge political implications. The fact is that we live our lives in a multiplicity of collectivities, some of them overlapping, some of them in conflict with one another; and this situation presents major problems for any consistent and defensible stance of commitment and allegiance.[1] Even if we notice only the most obvious and familiar collective identifications which we are sometimes called on to make, such as those relating to class, gender, nationality and the like, the problems become apparent. In particular circumstances, acting in loyalty to one's class may preclude acting in loyalty to one's gender, and so on. External overlaps and conflicts between collectivities may in this way become reproduced internally within individuals. We need a much more systematic account of the considerations which would govern rational decisions to identify with or dissociate from particular collectivities.

It would, of course, be naïve in the extreme to suppose that for people to work through the tensions and conflicts involved in their membership

---

[1] That there are multiple calls on the loyalty of individuals should at the very least cause us to re-examine the basis of *political representation* in democratic contexts, which is most commonly tied to the single feature of geographical location. Why should the fact of living in a given locality be thought uniquely significant in establishing units of representation, to the exclusion of other, deeper features which electors possess and share with some, but not all, others?

of multiple collectivities all that is necessary is for them to recognise the validity of some abstractly stated considerations, after which they can be relied on to act in accordance with the dictates of reason. We cannot expect that any human agent just sits down and works out what it is rational for them to do or what collective agencies it is rational for them to identify with, or that all you have to do is give them a bunch of arguments and they will respond to them. No doubt there are many factors in our social circumstances and in our own make-up which militate against that. No doubt, too, the size of a collectivity may be one significant variable in aiding or hampering identification, as may the presence or absence of deep and long-standing traditions associated with it.[2]

But if it is important not to have any illusions about how much can be achieved by pure reasoning, it is equally important to recognise that rationality is one element in the process of formation of identity and plans for action, and it is an element to be encouraged.[3] Accordingly, it is worthwhile attempting to encourage an increased awareness of the inter-connected nature of human lives and of the extent to which individuals are themselves part of larger entities whose well-being does and should matter to them. In that way, the normative reasons we have for acting in particular ways may have an increased chance of actually becoming operative in our decision-making.

The emphasis on our social nature, on how we act together, and all the implications which follow from it, should lead us to see as far more problematic than we normally do the whole idea of acting out of self-interest. There is a whole series of difficult questions about who and what the self is which must be answered before the rationality of acting out of self-interest can be regarded as straightforward and unexceptionable. The time-honoured strategy for keeping the predations of self-interest in check is the appeal to a moral perspective, understood as an appeal to take more seriously the existence of other individuals besides oneself by tempering self-interest with altruism.[4] But, in a way, self-interest and morality survive by taking in each other's washing. A system of thought which simply pits them against each other fails to draw on resources, available in uncontentious facts about the life of human beings, which can themselves be used to the same end of reducing self-seeking behaviour

---

[2] For contrasting views on the constraints governing collective identification see, for example, Olson 1982 and Offe and Wiesenthal 1985. For the relevance of size and deep traditions see Sandel 1996: 338–51.

[3] As Bertrand Russell once put it, 'Some people would die sooner than think. In fact, they do.'

[4] For a book which follows that strategy, and in a way which might change lives, see Care 1987.

by calling attention to wider allegiances. An increased awareness of our collective existence encourages the realisation that we have reasons for acting which extend our horizons both beyond our own self and beyond other selves, but yet in a way which does not leave individual selves behind.

The view we have of ourselves is something which can change as we gain a clearer understanding of acknowledged facts about ourselves, and with that can come further changes. Our agency already gives us an enormous degree of control over our world, as compared with most if not all other creatures. Although, like all creatures, we must adjust to our environment, this is not a one-way process; and as a species we have in many respects changed our environment to suit our own purposes. The same potential is there in respect of our specifically social environment. While there is of course not infinite flexibility, we have the potential to *create* our social world in accordance with reason, rather than simply enduring it in accordance with fate. Unthinking immersion in social groups is not what we are condemned to; we have the option of rationally assessing the situation and opting for active dissociation from or identification with them.

This very possibility of dissociation or identification dictates that we should not go to the extravagant lengths of obliterating the individual self from our thinking altogether, in the manner of some contemporary social theory. Our having the power to choose between dissociation and identification already implies a distinction between the individual and the group. Indeed, we need to retain a lively sense *both* of the existence of individuals who have the power to embrace or distance themselves from groups *and* of the fact that a significant portion of any individual's life is bound up with collective existence and cannot be properly and fully described in purely individual terms. I have attempted to keep both of those thoughts in balance in this book.

Bibliography

Alexander, P. and Gill, R. (eds.) 1984, *Utopias*, London, Duckworth.

Altham, J. E. J. and Harrison, R. (eds.) 1995, *World Mind and Ethics: Essays on the Ethical Philosophy of Bernard Williams*, Cambridge, Cambridge University Press.

Anscombe, G. E. M. 1958, 'Modern moral philosophy', *Philosophy* 33, reprinted in Thomson, J. and Dworkin, G. (eds.) 1968, *Ethics*, New York, Harper and Row, pp. 186–210.

Archard, D. (ed.) 1996, *Philosophy and Pluralism*, Cambridge, Cambridge University Press.

Arendt, H. 1959, *The Human Condition*, New York, Doubleday Anchor.

Arrow, K. J. 1963, *Social Choice and Individual Values*, 2nd edn, New Haven and London, Yale University Press.

Arthur, J. (ed.) 1996, *Morality and Moral Controversies*, 4th edn, New Jersey, Prentice Hall.

Assiter, A. 1996, *Enlightened Women: Modernist Feminism in a Postmodernist Age*, London, Routledge.

Austin, J. L. 1962, *Sense and Sensibilia*, Oxford, Clarendon Press.

Barry, B. 1983, 'Self-government revisited', in Miller and Siedentop (eds.), pp. 121–54.

1986, 'Lady Chatterley's lover and Doctor Fischer's bomb party: liberalism, Pareto optimality, and the problem of objectionable preferences', in Elster and Hylland (eds.), pp. 11–43.

1990, *Political Argument*, revised edn, Hemel Hempstead, Harvester.

1995, *A Treatise on Social Justice; vol. 2: Justice as Impartiality*, Oxford, Clarendon Press.

Bell, D. 1993, *Communitarianism and its Critics*, Oxford, Clarendon Press.

Benhabib, S. 1992, *Situating the Self*, Cambridge, Polity.

Bentham, J. 1843, *The Works of Jeremy Bentham*, vol. 1, Edinburgh, William Tait.

Berger, S. (ed.) 1981, *Organizing Interests in Western Europe: Pluralism, Corporatism and the Transformation of Politics*, Cambridge, Cambridge University Press.

Berlin, I. 1991, *The Crooked Timber of Humanity*, New York, Knopf.

Beyleveld, D. 1991, *The Dialectical Necessity of Morality*, Chicago, University of Chicago Press.

Binkley, R., Bronaugh, R. and Marras, A. (eds.) 1971, *Agent, Action and Reason*, Oxford, Blackwell.

Blackburn, S. 1985, 'Supervenience revisited', in Hacking (ed.), pp. 47–67.

(ed.) 1996, *Oxford Dictionary of Philosophy*, Oxford, Oxford University Press.

Bradley, F. H. 1876, *Ethical Studies*, 2nd edn, ed. R. Wollheim, 1962, Oxford, Oxford University Press.

Bratman, M. 1992, 'Shared cooperative activity', *Philosophical Review* 101: 327–41.

Brecher, B., Halliday, J. and Kolinská, K. (eds.) 1998, *Nationalism and Racism in the Liberal Order*, Aldershot, Ashgate.

Brennan, G. and Lomasky, L. 1993, *Democracy and Decision: The Pure Theory of Electoral Preference*, Cambridge, Cambridge University Press.

Brink, D. 1993, 'The separateness of persons, distributive norms and moral theory', in Frey and Morris (eds.), pp. 252–89.

1997, 'Rational egoism and the separateness of persons', in Dancy (ed.), pp. 96–134.

Broad, C. D. 1930, *Five Types of Ethical Theory*, London, Kegan Paul.

Broome, J. 1991, *Weighing Goods*, Oxford, Blackwell.

Brown, S. C. (ed.) 1974, *Philosophy of Psychology*, London, Macmillan.

Calder, G. 1998, 'Liberalism without universalism?', in Brecher *et al.* (eds.), pp. 140–59.

Caney, S. 1999, 'Defending universalism', in Mackenzie and O'Neill (eds.), pp. 19–33.

Care, N. 1987, *On Sharing Fate*, Philadelphia, Temple University Press.

Carruthers, P. 1992, *The Animals Issue*, Cambridge, Cambridge University Press.

Christiano, T. 1993, 'Social choice and democracy', in Copp *et al.* (eds.), pp. 173–95.

Cohen, G. A. 1995, *Self-Ownership, Freedom and Equality*, Cambridge, Cambridge University Press.

1996, 'Reason, humanity and the moral law', in Korsgaard , pp. 167–88.

2000, *If You're an Egalitarian, How Come You're So Rich?*, Cambridge, Mass., Harvard University Press.

Cohen, J. 1997, 'Rethinking privacy: autonomy, identity and the abortion controversy', in Weintraub and Kumar (eds.), pp. 133–65.

Comte, A. 1851–4, *Système de Politique Positive*, reprinted in Lenzer, G. (ed.) 1983, *Auguste Comte and Positivism: The Essential Writings*, Chicago, University of Chicago Press.

Copp, D., Hampton, J. and Roemer, J. (eds.) 1993, *The Idea of Democracy*, Cambridge, Cambridge University Press.

Cornman, J. 1971, 'Comments' on Davidson, in Binkley *et al.* (eds.), pp. 26–37.

Cullity, G. and Gaut, B. (eds.) 1997, *Ethics and Practical Reason*, Oxford, Clarendon Press.

Dahl, R. 1970, *After the Revolution?*, New Haven, Yale University Press.

Dancy, J. (ed.) 1997, *Reading Parfit*, Oxford, Blackwell.

Daniels, N. (ed.) 1975, *Reading Rawls*, Oxford, Blackwell.

Davidson, D. 1971, 'Agency', in Binkley *et al.* (eds.), pp. 3–25.

1974, 'Psychology as philosophy', in Brown (ed.), pp. 41–52.

Doyal, L. and Gough, I. 1991, *A Theory of Human Need*, Basingstoke, Macmillan.

Dworkin, G. 1988, *The Theory and Practice of Autonomy*, Cambridge, Cambridge University Press.

Dworkin, R. 1978, *Taking Rights Seriously*, London, Duckworth.

1981, 'What is equality? Part one', *Philosophy and Public Affairs* 10: 185–246.

1986, *A Matter of Principle*, Oxford, Clarendon Press.

1989, 'Liberal community', *California Law Review* 77: 479–504.

1990a, 'Equality, democracy and the constitution', *Alberta Law Review* 28: 324–46.

1990b, 'Foundations of liberal equality', *Tanner Lectures on Human Values* 11: 1–119.

Elster, J. 1985, *Making Sense of Marx*, Cambridge, Cambridge University Press.

(ed.), 1986a, *Rational Choice*, Oxford, Blackwell.

1986b, 'Three challenges to class', in Roemer (ed.), pp 141–61.

Elster, J. and Hylland, A. (eds.) 1986, *Foundations of Social Choice Theory*, Cambridge, Cambridge University Press.

Evans, J. D. G. (ed.) 1988, *Moral Philosophy and Contemporary Problems*, Cambridge, Cambridge University Press.

Feinberg, J. 1986, *The Moral Limits of the Criminal Law, vol. 3: Harm to Self*, New York, Oxford University Press.

Frankfurt, H. 1988, *The Importance of What We Care About*, Cambridge, Cambridge University Press.

French, P. 1984, *Collective and Corporate Responsibility*, New York, Columbia University Press.

Frey, R. and Morris, C. (eds.) 1993, *Value, Welfare and Morality*, Cambridge, Cambridge University Press.

Galbraith, J. K. 1993, *The Culture of Contentment*, Harmondsworth, Penguin.

Galston, W. 1986, 'Equality of opportunity and liberal theory', in Lucash (ed.), pp. 89–107.

Gaus, G. 1990, *Value and Justification: The Foundations of Liberal Theory*, Cambridge, Cambridge University Press.

1996, *Justificatory Liberalism*, New York, Oxford University Press.

Gauthier, D. 1986, *Morals by Agreement*, Oxford, Clarendon Press.

Geras, N. 1995, *Solidarity in the Conversation of Humankind: The Ungroundable Liberalism of Richard Rorty*, London, Verso.

Gewirth, A. 1978, *Reason and Morality*, Chicago, University of Chicago Press.

1994, 'Is cultural pluralism relevant to moral knowledge?', *Social Philosophy and Policy* 11: 22–43.

Gilbert, M. 1996, *Living Together: Rationality, Sociality And Obligation*, New York, Rowman and Littlefield.

Goldman, A. 1970, *A Theory of Human Action*, Englewood Cliffs, Prentice Hall.

Goodin, R. 1986, 'Laundering preferences', in Elster and Hylland (eds.), pp. 75–102.

1992, 'Towards a minimally presumptuous social policy', in van Parijs (ed.), pp. 195–214.

Graham, K. 1975, 'Moral notions and moral misconceptions', *Analysis* 35: 65–78.

1984, 'Consensus in social decision-making: why is it Utopian?', in Alexander and Gill (eds.), pp. 49–60.

1986a, *The Battle of Democracy*, New Jersey, Barnes and Noble.

1986b, 'Morality and abstract individualism', *Proceedings of the Aristotelian Society* 87: 21–33.

1988, 'Morality, individuals and collectives', in Evans (ed.), pp. 1–18.

1989, 'Class – a simple view', *Inquiry* 32: 419–36.

1992, *Karl Marx, Our Contemporary*, Hemel Hempstead, Harvester Wheatsheaf.

1996a, 'Coping with the many-coloured dome', in Archard (ed.), pp. 135–46.

1996b, 'Voting and motivation', *Analysis* 56: 184–90.

1998, 'Being some body: choice and identity in a liberal pluralist world', in Brecher *et al.* (eds.), pp. 176–92.

1999a, 'Digging up Marx', in MacKenzie and O'Neill (eds.), pp. 35–50.

1999b, 'Normative argumentation in a pluralist world', *Proceedings of Fourth International Conference of the International Society for the Study of Argumentation*, Amsterdam, Sic Sat, pp. 266–70.

2000, 'Collective responsibility', in van den Beld (ed.), pp. 49–61.

Gray, J. 1996, *Mill on Liberty: A Defence*, 2nd edn, London, Routledge.

Gray, J. and Smith, G. W. (eds.) 1991, *J. S. Mill on Liberty*, London, Routledge.

Hacking, I. (ed.) 1985, *Exercises in Analysis: Essays by Students of Casimir Lewy*, Cambridge, Cambridge University Press.

Hampton, J. 1997, 'The wisdom of the egoist', *Social Philosophy and Policy* 14: 21–51.

1998, *The Authority of Reason*, Cambridge, Cambridge University Press.

Harrison, R. (ed.) 1980, *Rational Action*, Cambridge, Cambridge University Press.

Hart, H. L. A. and Honoré, A. M. 1985, *Causation in the Law*, 2nd edn, Oxford, Clarendon Press.

Hayek, F. 1960, *The Constitution of Liberty*, London, Routledge and Kegan Paul.

Held, D. (ed.) 1991, *Political Theory Today*, Cambridge, Polity.

Hollis, M. 1998, *Trust Within Reason*, Cambridge, Cambridge University Press.

Hurley, S. 1989, *Natural Reasons*, New York, Oxford University Press.

Kant, I. 1785, *Grundlegung zur Metaphysik der Sitten*, transl. L. W. Beck, 1959, *Foundations of the Metaphysics of Morals*, New York, Macmillan.

Keane, J. (ed.) 1985, *Disorganised Capitalism*, Cambridge, Mass., MIT Press.

Kekes, J. 1994, 'Pluralism and the value of life', *Social Philosophy and Policy* 11: 44–60.

Kim, J. 1984, 'Concepts of supervenience', *Philosophy and Phenomenological Research* 45: 153–74.

Korsgaard, C. 1996, with Cohen, G. A., Geuss, R., Nagel, T. and Williams, B., *The Sources of Normativity*, Cambridge, Cambridge University Press.

Kukathas, C. 1996, 'Liberalism, communitarianism and political community', *Social Philosophy and Policy* 13: 80–104.

Kymlicka, W. 1989, *Liberalism, Community and Culture*, Oxford, Clarendon Press.

1990, *Contemporary Political Philosophy*, Oxford, Clarendon Press.

Larmore, C. 1990, 'Political liberalism', *Political Theory* 18: 339–60.

1994, 'Pluralism and reasonable disagreement', *Social Philosophy and Policy* 11: 61–79.

Levine, A. 1987, *The End of the State*, London, Verso.

1993, *The General Will*, Cambridge, Cambridge University Press.

Lewis, H. D. 1948, 'Collective responsibility', *Philosophy* 23: 3–18.

Locke, J. 1690, *Second Treatise of Government*, ed. P. Laslett, 1988, Cambridge, Cambridge University Press.

Lomasky, L. 1987, *Persons, Rights and the Moral Community*, New York, Oxford University Press.

Lucash, F. (ed.) 1986, *Justice and Equality Here and Now*, New York, Cornell University Press.

MacIntyre, A. 1981, *After Virtue*, London, Duckworth.

1984, 'Is patriotism a virtue?', Lindley Lecture, University of Kansas, excerpted in Arthur (ed.), pp. 92–8.

Mackenzie, I. and O'Neill, S. (eds.) 1999, *Reconstituting Social Criticism*, London, Macmillan.

Mackie, J. L. 1977, *Ethics: Inventing Right and Wrong*, Harmondsworth, Penguin.

Malm, H. H. 1995, 'Liberalism and bad Samaritan law', *Ethics* 106: 4–31.

Marsh, R. C. (ed.) 1956, *Logic and Knowledge*, London, George Allen and Unwin.

Marx, K. 1867, *Capital*, vol. I, transl. B. Fowkes, 1976, Harmondsworth, Penguin.

May, L. 1987, *The Morality of Groups*, Notre Dame, University of Notre Dame Press.

1992, *Sharing Responsibility*, Chicago, University of Chicago Press.

McEwen, I. 1997, *Enduring Love*, London, Jonathan Cape.

McMahon, C. 1994, *Authority and Democracy*, Princeton, Princeton University Press.

Mellema, G. 1997, *Collective Responsibility*, Amsterdam, Rodopi.

Mill, J. S. 1859, *Essay on Liberty*, 1972, London, Dent.

Miller, D. 1995, *On Nationality*, Oxford, Clarendon Press.

Miller, D. and Siedentop, L. (eds.) 1983, *The Nature of Political Theory*, Oxford, Clarendon Press.

Montefiore, A. (ed.) 1973, *Philosophy and Personal Relations*, London, Routledge and Kegan Paul.

Morton, A. 1991, *Disasters and Dilemmas*, Oxford, Blackwell.

Murdoch, I. 1970, *The Sovereignty of Good*, London, Routledge and Kegan Paul.

Nagel, T. 1970, *The Possibility of Altruism*, Oxford, Clarendon Press.

1973, 'Rawls on Justice', *Philosophical Review* 82, reprinted in Daniels (ed.), pp. 1–15.

1986, *The View from Nowhere*, New York, Oxford University Press.

1987, 'Moral conflict and political legitimacy', *Philosophy and Public Affairs* 16: 215–40.

1996, 'Universality and the reflective self', in Korsgaard, pp. 200–9.

Nozick, R. 1974, *Anarchy, State, and Utopia*, New York, Basic Books.

1993, *The Nature of Rationality*, Princeton, Princeton University Press.

Offe, C. and Wiesenthal, H. 1985, 'Two logics of collective action', in Keane (ed.), pp. 170–220.

Okin, S. M. 1991, 'Gender, the public and the private', in Held (ed.), pp. 67–90.

Olson, M. Jr 1982, *The Rise and Decline of Nations*, New Haven, Yale University Press.

O'Neill, J. 1993, *Ecology, Policy And Politics*, London, Routledge.

1998, *The Market: Ethics, Knowledge and Politics*, London, Routledge.

O'Neill, O. 1996, *Towards Justice And Virtue*, Cambridge, Cambridge University Press.

Orwell, G. 1931, 'A hanging', *Adelphi*, reprinted in his *Collected Essays, Journalism and Letters*, vol. I, 1968, London, Secker and Warburg, pp. 44–8.

Parfit, D. 1973, 'Later selves and moral principles', in Montefiore (ed.), pp. 137–69.

1976, 'Lewis, Perry and what matters', in Rorty (ed.), pp. 91–107.

1984, *Reasons and Persons*, Oxford, Clarendon Press.

Pettit, P. 1993, *The Common Mind*, New York, Oxford University Press.

1997, *Republicanism: A Theory of Freedom and Government*, Oxford, Clarendon Press.

Pizzorno, A. 1981, 'Interests and parties in pluralism', in Berger (ed.), pp. 247–84.

Quine, W. v. O. 1961, 'On what there is', in his *From A Logical Point of View*, New York, Harper and Row, pp. 1–19.

Rawls, J. 1972, *A Theory of Justice*, Oxford, Oxford University Press.

1993, *Political Liberalism*, New York, Columbia University Press.

Raz, J. 1984, 'Right-based moralities', in Waldron (ed.), pp. 182–200.

1986, *The Morality of Freedom*, Oxford, Clarendon Press.

1995, *Ethics in the Public Domain*, Oxford, Clarendon Press.

Rees, J. C. 1960, 'A re-reading of Mill on liberty', *Political Studies* 8, reprinted in Gray and Smith (eds.), pp. 169–89.

Roemer, J. (ed.) 1986, *Analytical Marxism*, Cambridge, Cambridge University Press.

Rogers, K. 1997, 'Beyond self and others', *Social Philosophy and Policy* 14: 1–20.

Rorty, A. O. (ed.) 1976, *The Identities of Persons*, Berkeley, University of California Press.

1984, 'The hidden politics of cultural identification', *Political Theory* 22: 152–6.

Rorty, R. 1991, *Objectivity, Relativism and Truth: Philosophical Papers*, vol. I, Cambridge, Cambridge University Press.

Russell, B. 1956, 'The philosophy of logical atomism', in Marsh (ed.), pp. 175–282.

Sandel, M. 1982, *Liberalism and the Limits of Justice*, Cambridge, Cambridge University Press.

1996, *Democracy's Discontent*, Cambridge, Mass., Belknap Press of Harvard University Press.

Sartre, J.-P. 1960, *The Critique of Dialectical Reason*, London, Verso, 1976.

Scanlon, T. 1998, *What We Owe To Each Other*, Cambridge, Mass., Belknap Press of Harvard University Press.

Scheffler, S. 1982, *The Rejection of Consequentialism*, Oxford, Clarendon Press.

1992, *Human Morality*, Oxford, Clarendon Press.

1995, 'Individual responsibility in a global age', *Social Philosophy and Policy* 12: 219–36.

Searle, J. 1995, *The Construction of Social Reality*, London, Penguin.

Sen, A. 1970, *Collective Choice and Social Welfare*, San Francisco, Holden-Day, Inc.

1976, 'Liberty, unanimity and rights', *Economica* 43: 217–45.

1987, *On Ethics and Economics*, Oxford, Blackwell.

1992, *Inequality Reexamined*, Oxford, Clarendon Press.

Sidgwick, H. 1907, *Methods of Ethics*, 7th edn, 1963, London, Macmillan.

Simmel, G. 1908, *Soziologie, Untersuchungen über die Formen der Vergesellschaftungen*, in Wolff, K. H. (ed.) 1964, *The Sociology of Georg Simmel*, New York: Free Press of Glencoe, pp. 87–408.

Slote, M. 1995, *From Morality to Virtue*, Oxford, Oxford University Press.

Smart, J. J. C. and Williams, B. 1973, *Utilitarianism: For and Against*, Cambridge, Cambridge University Press.

Smith, A. 1776, *The Wealth of Nations*, Harmondsworth, Penguin, 1982.

Smith, M. 1994, *The Moral Problem*, Oxford, Blackwell.

Steiner, H. 1977, 'The natural right to the means of production', *Philosophical Quarterly* 27: 41–9.

Stephen, J. F. 1874, *Liberty, Equality, Fraternity*, 2nd edn, London, Smith and Elder.

Strawson, P. F. 1961, 'Social morality and individual ideal', *Philosophy* 36, reprinted in his *Freedom and Resentment*, 1974, London, Methuen, pp. 26–44.

Sugden, R. 1993, 'Thinking as a team', *Social Philosophy and Policy* 10: 69–89.

Sunnstein, C. 1993, 'Democracy and shifting preferences', in Copp *et al.* (eds.), pp. 196–230.

Taylor, C. 1985, *Philosophy and the Human Sciences: Philosophical Papers*, vol. II, Cambridge, Cambridge University Press.

1987–8, *Justice after Virtue*, Legal Theory workshop series, Faculty of Law, University of Toronto, WS no. 3.

1992, *Multiculturalism and 'The Politics of Recognition'*, Princeton, Princeton University Press.

1995a, 'A most peculiar institution', in Altham and Harrison (eds.), pp. 132–55.

1995b, 'Cross purposes: the liberal–communitarian debate', in his *Philosophical Arguments*, Cambridge, Mass., Harvard University Press, pp. 181–203.

1995c, 'Irreducibly social goods', in his *Philosophical Arguments*, Cambridge, Mass., Harvard University Press, pp. 127–45.

Taylor, M. 1982, *Community, Anarchy and Liberty*, Cambridge, Cambridge University Press.

Ten, C. L. 1980, *Mill on Liberty*, Oxford, Clarendon Press.

Tuomela, R. 1989, 'Collective action, supervenience and constitution', *Synthese* 80: 243–66.

1995, *The Importance of Us*, Stanford, Stanford University Press.

Valinas, B. Jr forthcoming, 'The logic of cliques and claques', in his *Sociality, Plurality and Ontogenesis: On Factions*.

Vallentyne, P. 1991, 'The problem of unauthorized welfare', *Nous* 25: 295–321.

van den Beld, T. (ed.) 2000, *Moral Responsibility and Ontology*, Dordrecht, Kluwer.

van Parijs, P. (ed.) 1992, *Arguing for Basic Income: Ethical Foundations for a Radical Reform*, London, Verso.

1995, *Real Freedom for All*, Oxford, Clarendon Press.

Waldron, J. (ed.) 1984, *Theories of Rights*, Oxford, Oxford University Press.

1993, 'Can communal goods be human rights?', *Archives européennes de sociologie* 27, reprinted in his *Liberal Rights*, Cambridge, Cambridge University Press, pp. 339–69.

Wallace, R. J. 1994, *Responsibility and the Moral Sentiments*, Cambridge, Mass., Harvard University Press.

Walzer, M. 1983, *Spheres of Justice*, Oxford, Martin Robertson.

Weintraub, J. and Kumar, K. (eds.) 1997, *Public and Private in Thought and Practice*, Chicago, University of Chicago Press.

Wiggins, D. 1967, *Identity and Spatio-temporal Continuity*, Oxford, Blackwell.

Williams, B. 1976, 'Persons, character and morality', in Rorty (ed.), reprinted in Williams 1981, pp. 1–19.

1980, 'Internal and external reasons', in Harrison (ed.), reprinted in Williams 1981, pp. 101–13.

1981, *Moral Luck*, Cambridge, Cambridge University Press.

1985, *Ethics and the Limits of Philosophy*, London, Fontana Press.

1993, *Shame and Necessity*, Berkeley, University of California Press.

1995a, *Making Sense of Humanity*, Cambridge, Cambridge University Press.

1995b, 'Replies to critics', in Altham and Harrison (eds.), pp. 185–224.

1998, 'The end of explanation?', *New York Review of Books*, 19 November, 1–12.

Wittgenstein, L. 1953, *Philosophical Investigations*, Oxford, Blackwell.

Wolf, S. 1997a, 'Happiness and meaning: two aspects of the good life', *Social Philosophy and Policy* 14: 207–25.

1997b, 'Meaning and morality', *Proceedings of the Aristotelian Society* 97: 299–315.

Wolff, R. P. 1976, *In Defense of Anarchism*, 2nd edn, New York, Harper and Row.

Index